I0475351

INNOVATION & ENTERPRISE

Secrets to Gain Sustainable Competitive Advantage in the 21st Century

Dr. R. Ray Gehani

The University of Akron, OH 44325
(rgehani@uakron.edu)

About the Author

Dr. Gehani has been teaching International Operations Management, Technology and Innovation Management, and Corporate Business Strategy at the executive, graduate, and undergraduate business programs at the University of Akron since 1997.

Education

Doctor of Philosophy
The City University of New York (Baruch), October 1996
Business-Strategic Management
Dissertation Topic: Relationships between a firm's performance and its allocation of resources to Technology Value-Chain: An exploratory study. Advisor: Professor S. P. Sethi (Baruch College). Nominated for admission to Beta Gamma Sigma society.

Master of Philosophy
The City University of New York (Baruch), October 1995

Graduate Business Diploma in International Management
International Management Institute (IMI), April 1987, N. Delhi (affiliated to IMI, Geneva)

Doctor of Engineering- Polymer Science & Technology
Tokyo Institute of Technology, Japan, March 1981
Dissertation Topic: Study of structure and performance characteristics of high-tech film products. Advisor: Professor Ichitaro Uematsu, Chairman Polymer Society of Japan (1980-81).

Diploma in Japanese Language
Osaka Univ. of Foreign Studies, Japan, August 1977

Master of Technology - Textile/Fibers
Indian Institute of Technology, N. Delhi, January 1977

Bachelor of Technology- Chemical Engineering
Indian Institute of Technology, Kanpur, February 1973

CONTENTS

WAL MART STORES:

SUSTAINING GROWTH MOMENTUM WITH SUPPLY-CHAIN INNOVATIONS

Dr. R. RAY GEHANI

Institute for Innovation and Technology Leadership (IITL)
Akron, Ohio

You can't just keep doing what works one time. Everything around you is always changing. To succeed stay out in front of the change.

- Sam Walton, Founder, Wal-Mart

ABSTRACT

Wal-Mart stores, starting in Arkansas, USA in 1962, have seen phenomenal global growth. Can this frugally managed company sustain its growth momentum and continue to help its value-conscious customers save money and live better?

GLOBAL RETAIL LEADERSHIP

For the past many years, Wal-Mart has grown phenomenally in the United States and world-wide. With this aggressive growth, however, also came an increase in expectations of Wal-Mart's customers. Wal-Mart was forced to catch-up. Wal-Mart's strategic leaders then decided in 2006 that to stay as retailing leader they had to get proactive, and stay ahead of such expectations. Wal-Mart had the opportunity to lead the industry in diversity, environmental sustainability, and ethical business practices. With recessionary slowdown, Wal-Mart changed its logo and slogan from "*We Sell for Less*" to "*Saving Money*" to help people "*Living Better*."

Wal-Mart Stores Inc. was founded in rural Arkansas. By 2006, Wal-Mart emerged as the world's largest retailer employing 1.3 million associates (or employees) in the United States and approximately 1.8 million worldwide. It had operations in all 50 states in the U.S., and in 15 countries, including Canada and Mexico in North America, Argentina, Brazil, Costa Rica, El Salvador, Guatemala, Honduras, Nicaragua, Puerto Rico in Latin America, and the United Kingdom in the Western Europe. Wal-Mart had a stake in a major Japanese chain, and a joint venture agreement with a Chinese partner.

TRANSFORMATIONAL NEW CHANGES

In 2008, Wal-Mart's **CEO H. Lee Scott** presented a grand success story to more than 16,000 shareholders attending the annual meeting at the **Bud Walton Arena** on the campus of the **University of Arkansas**. Throughout **The Annual Day,** the company's successes were celebrated with entertainment and customer appreciation activities. In 2006, Wal-Mart started a transformational change refocusing management attention on employee appreciating its 2.1 million associates and improving its customers' experiences. In addition to changing logo, and slogan including "Live Better," a number of other initiatives listed below were launched.

1. More Affordable Pharmaceuticals

A flat $4 price was charged for generic versions of 200 prescription drugs. In first 20 months this program saved est. $1,100 million. This was extended in 2008 to include 90-day supply of certain prescription medicines for a flat $10 price. Wal-Mart also reduced the prices of approx. 100,000 OTC (over-the-counter) pharmaceuticals.

2. More-Affordable Employee Health-care

Every full-time and part-time Wal-Mart associate, and their children, are now eligible to receive health insurance. After working and being eligible for one year, for most expenses there was no lifetime maximum. Some health insurance increased from 90.4% employees in 2006, to 92.7% in 2008.

Full-time Wal-Mart associates earned on average $10.83 per hour. Majority of Wal-Mart employees were full time, with 34-40 hours per week.

Most Wal-Mart jobs are entry-level retailing jobs requiring minimum skills. A new store in Chicago area with 325 jobs in January 2006, received more than 25,00 applications. A new store in Maryland with 300 jobs in March 2007 received 11,000 applications. More than 75% of Wal-Mart managers started as hourly workers.

3. Higher Renewable and Efficient Energy Use

New store designs were developed to reduce pollutants, energy use and use of natural resources. In 2007, recycled building materials were used to build 3 high energy-efficient stores, using 20% less energy than a typical Wal-Mart Supercenter. These "greener" buildings used motion-sensing LED lighting, reflective white roofs, and low-flow bathroom faucets. Additional 22 stores in California and Hawaii were being pilot-tested for solar-power.

4. Promoting "Green" Stewardship of Planet

In Nov. 2006, Wal-Mart started promoting the use of environmentally friendly compact fluorescent light bulbs. By early, Wal-Mart sold 192 million bulbs, saving customers $6 billion in electricity costs, eliminating the need for 3 power plants (producing carbon dioxide and other emissions causing global emissions).

Wal-Mart stores have stocked increasingly more organic foods grown with more sustainable agriculture. They decrease use of chemical fertilizers and pesticides.

Wal-Mart's sale of 5 key eco-friendly products increased in 2007-2008 by 66%.

5.   Zero Waste Campaign

Wal-Mart partnered with elementary schools in 12 states to start plastic bag recycling. For collection of each 60 gallon bag that young students brought to local Wal-Mart store, they received $5. Reusable shopping bags were introduced in October 2007, with "*Paper or Plastic? Neither?*" printed on each bag. Each such bag was expected to save use of 100 plastic bags. During the Earth Month of April 2008, Wal-Mart donated 1 million reusable plastic bags. Overall, these efforts may have saved the use of 400 million plastic bags.

Keeping in mind that Wal-Mart sells approx. 25% of all laundry detergents sold in the U.S. and Canada, Wal-Mart introduced concentrated laundry detergent, in partnership with laundry detergent manufacturers. In 3 years, this was expected to save 95 million pounds polymer resin, 125 million pounds of cardboard, and 400 million gallons of water.

Wal-Mart demanded its 66,000 suppliers to develop and use more bio-degradable packaging. Wal-Mart promoted 20% increase in fuel-efficiency of its fleet of 72,000 trucks. These logged estimated more than 1 billion miles in 2007.

Broadening Customer Appeal

Wal-Mart upgraded its apparel lines to attract new upscale customers. Redecorated stores and widened aisles to reduce cluttering. Lighting and shelving were improved for better customer reach. Store managers were given more powers to store local merchandise, such as local professional and university sports teams' apparel. Wal-Mart Superstores stock local produce.

Contributing to Local Quality of Life

Wal-Mart started 9 disaster distribution centers across the United States stocked with relief supplies after the Katrina disaster. By 2010, Wal-Mart stores would establish 400 Clinics, to be leased and operated by local health professionals.

In 2007, Wal-Mart donated $ 296 million to more than 4,000 communities. To well-established charities like the United Negro College Fund, the Special Olympics, the Boys and Girls Scouts of America, the Muscular Dystrophy Association, Wal-Mart donated more than $1 million each.

SUSTAINING GROWTH

The annual sales of **Wal-Mart** had reached a record high of **US$ 312.4 billion in 2006**, jumping from US$ 285.2 billion in 2005 (See Exhibit – 1). This had come with aggressive cost cutting out of its enterprise-wide supply-chain and aggressive opening of new Wal-Mart stores. Wal-Mart's closest global rival was **Carrefour SA of France**, with annual sales of US$ 88.2 billion (See Exhibit – 2). Sales of **Target Corporation** were US$ 52.6 billion ranked at distant global rank of 8. Costco, with global operations like Wal-Mart had annual sales of US$ 53.0 billion.

SUPPLY CHAIN BASED SOURCES OF COMPETITIVE ADVANTAGE

In the past, **Wal-Mart** streamlined its global supply chain to gain and sustain its competitive advantages and phenomenal growth. The strategic leaders at Wal-Mart struggled in identifying how such a mammoth sized Wal-Mart would sustain its momentum, and retain its world leadership in the years to come?

Wal-Mart's distribution costs in 1986 were far lower than its rivals, K-Mart and **Sears**. The distribution costs at Wal-Mart were approximately 1.7% of its cost of sales, compared to 5.0% of total sales for **Sears** and 3.5% of totals sales for **K-Mart** (Discount Store News, 1989, x-ref#2). Wal-Mart also strived hard to keep its inventory growth at 50% of its sales growth. In the recent years, it was hard to achieve this target.

Many of Wal-Mart's rivals were increasingly imitating its leader's best practices. They (a) adopted bar codes, (b) collected real-time point-of-sales data, (c) nurtured its key suppliers, and (d) used in-house distribution fleets.

RIVALRY IN U.S. RETAIL INDUSTRY

The U.S. retail industry consisted of a large number of independent owner operated single-store retailers, including discount stores, department stores, convenient stores, specialty stores, and super-centers. In addition, there were catalog retailers and internet retailers. Collectively, they competed for the retail customers.

In 2005, the U.S. retail sales (excluding auto and parts dealers) exceeded US$ 2.8 trillion (US Census, accessed 06Hbc, Xref#3).

SAMUEL WALTON (1918 - 1992)
FOUNDING A DISCOUNT RETAILING GIANT

SAM'S FAMILY BACKGROUND

Samuel Moore Walton was born on **Friday, March 29, 1918** in a farmhouse near Kingfisher, Oklahoma.

His father Thomas named his son Sam after his grandfather, whom Sam never knew. Grandpa Sam died within one year of grandson's birth. Samuel's dad Thomas was brought up by relatives, and he grew up to join farm loan business which he did not like. He returned to farming in 1917, just one year prior to the birth of Samuel. The 1920s were hard to be in farming, and father Thomas gave up after a few years joining Walton Mortgage Company of his half brother.

Samuel later described his father as waking early to put in long hours, and working awfully hard. He was also known to be completely honest with high integrity. He also loved to trade, negotiating with an instinct to know the lowest limit. Samuel was embarrassed by his father's low offers he made to repossess hundreds of farms from 1929 to 1931. Samuel traveled with his father, and saw the hardships framers felt – vowing never to be ever poor in his life (Tedlow, 2003: 320, *Giants of Enterprise xref#16*). During the Great Depression, many American farmers in the hard-hit region lost the farming lands their families had farmed for multiple generations.

Samuel Walton also admitted that his father and mother were mismatched, except for their consensus not to spend money. The parents did not get on well, but they stayed together for 33 years (till death separated them) primarily because of Samuel and his brother Bud. When the sons grew up, their parents even separated for some time. Their parents' differences motivated Samuel "to stay busy all the time" (Tedlow (2003: 320, *Giants of Enterprise*, xref#20). Samuel's mother died of cancer at the young age of 52 in 1950, never seeing his son's rise. Samuel's father, however, witnessed the great transformation of his son, until the age of 92 when he died in 1984.

EARLY CHILDHOOD

Samuel, from his early life, became quite ambitious. In 1931, at the age of 13, he became the youngest ever Eagle Scout in the state of Missouri. He enjoyed running his basketball team, and learned the value of teamwork. He was only 5 feet nine inches but he was drafted in high school basketball team because of his swiftness. His team remained undefeated for the season and won the state championship. Samuel also played football, with undefeated season and a state championship. He admits that he was not a gifted athlete, not a great passer nor a great runner, but he was very competitive and a winner.

Sam also admitted that he was not a great student, but he worked very hard and made the honor roll. Samuel was elected as the president of the student body, and joined many clubs. His peers voted him the "Most Versatile Boy" (Tedlow, 2003: 322, *Giants of Enterprise*, xref#27).

When he entered the University of Missouri, Samuel aspired to emerge as the president of the student body. Even though sometimes Samuel was perceived as shy, he figured out that proactively speaking to many people would help him get elected. Samuel also became the president and captain of the elite military organization of ROTC (Tedlow, 2003: 323, *Giants of Enterprise*, xref#28). He financed his tuition, as well as fraternity and other miscellaneous dues, by running paper routes, earning US$ 4,000 to US$ 5,000, a handsome amount in 1939 and 1940 (Tedlow, 2003: 323, *Giants of Enterprise*, xref#29).

Samuel Walton graduated with a degree in economics from the University of Missouri in May 1941 with job offers from J.C. Penny and Sears. He chose J.C. Penny, and joined as management trainee at Des Moines, Iowa, for US$ 75 a month (Tedlow, 2003: 324, *Giants of Enterprise*, xref#31). He instantly took to liking retail selling. He enjoyed speaking to customers, benchmarking rival retailers, and got an opportunity to meet his founder James Cash Penny (Tedlow, 2003: 324, *Giants of Enterprise*, xref#32).

RECOVERING FROM SETBACKS

As the United States entered World War II, Samuel Walton as a graduate of ROTC was already designated as a second lieutenant in the U.S. Army Reserve in its artillery unit. His physical check up discovered irregular heartbeat, and he was shocked to learn that h was cleared only for "limited duty" (Tedlow, 2003: 324, *Giants of Enterprise*, xref#33). He was not going to be assigned to any military action.

Sam's brother was drafted as a torpedo bomber pilot and was involved in the US invasion of Okinawa. As he left, the parents separated and both moved away. In anticipation for joining military service, Samuel Walton left **J. C. Penny** after 18 months and took a job at **Pryor ammunition plant, near Tulsa**.

In 1942, when Samuel was 24 he was attracted by his future wife Helen at a bowling alley. He was impressed by his future father-in law, who was a highly persuasive salesman, with in-depth knowledge of finance and law. Samuel was inspired to emulate and be like his father-in-law one day (Tedlow, 2003: 321, *Giants of Enterprise*, xref#22).

When the World War II ended, Samuel had worked as a lieutenant and a captain supervising security at aircraft plants and POW plants (Tedlow, 2003: 327, *Giants of Enterprise*, xref#42). In 1944, Samuel and Helen had their first son, Samuel Robson Walton. Together they decided to not live in the shadow of Helen's father. Helen also insisted that they live in a small town of not more than 10,000. In the fall of 1945, Sam and Helen chose to settle in Newport, Arkansas on the White River, with a population of approximately 4,300. This town was less than 100 miles northwest of Memphis and Northeast of Little Rock.

Sam returned from the military service with entrepreneurial spirit and did not plan to return to J. C. Penny. He started looking for something challenging, and decided to franchise a Ben Franklin retail store in Newport, Arkansas.

On September 1, 1945, Samuel Walton, with no experience of running a business opened a 5,000 square foot **Ben Franklin variety store**, overlooking the railroad tracks. The previous owner of the store had lost money on revenues of $72,000 in the previous year, only half compared to a comparable variety store across the street making close to US$ 150,000 **(**Tedlow, 2003: 331, *Giants of Enterprise*, xref#64**).** Samuel, who loved setting and achieving goals for himself, decided to set the goal of becoming the most profitable five-and-dime variety store in Arkansas in five years (Tedlow, 2003: 328, *Giants of Enterprise*, Xref# 49,**).**

The franchise fee set by **Butler Brothers** headquartered in St. Louis, was US$ 25,000. The franchisee had to buy goods supplied by Butler Brothers, to be marked up substantially, and never to be discounted.

In 1945, the United States had 1.7 million retail stores, with many failing every day. With no prior experience in running a business, Samuel had agreed to pay the high rent of 5% of sales, the highest in the variety business.

Samuel turned all these odds against him, and turned this poor investment into a spectacular success (Tedlow, 2003: 320, *Giants of Enterprise*).

Sam lost his lease on his store building five years later. He chose to take risk by buying a building in Bentonville, Arkansas. There he opened Walton's 5 & 10 – affiliated to Ben Franklin. He steadily expanded to 9 Ben Franklin franchises by 1960.

FOUNDING WAL-MART

Sam Walton founded Wal-Mart in Bentonville, Arkansas in 1962.

VISION OF DISCOUNT RETAILING

Sam Walton saw discount retail stores and giant supermarkets emerging on the competitive horizon of retailing. He confirmed this by piloting his plane, to study from up in the air how retail stores were expanding geographically. Sam contacted the senior executives at **Ben Franklin headquarters in Chicago** recommending diversification into discount retailing. The senior executives did not see the future growth potential in discount retailing the way Sam Walton envisioned.

Sam Walton decided to implement his vision. On July 2, 1962, he opened his first **Wal-Mart Discount City in Rogers, Arkansas**. His business model of discount retailing strategy was a commercial success. Sam wanted to replicate his success formula, and he started looking for other small tows to open more Wal-Mart Discount City stores. He was intuitive in listening to his employees and developing his good management practices.

In **1969, Sam Walton incorporated Wal-Mart Stores**, and chose to establish **its headquarters in Bentonville, Arkansas**. In 1970, Wal-Mart Stores went public with annual sales of US$ 44.2 million from 38 stores. By the end of the 1970s, Wal-Mart Stores expanded its operations to 276 stores in 11 states, with 21,000 employees and exceeding sales of US$ 1 billion. This was the fastest time a US company had grown to a billion dollar company.

Sam Walton achieved his phenomenal growth primarily by working closely with his employees and inspiring them. He referred to them as his associates, looking to them as source of continuous innovation. He was genuinely concerned about the welfare of his employees, their families, and their communities. His and his company's reputation steadily improved in the 1980s. Large number of people inside and outside this firm liked their founder leader.

Sam Walton passed away in 1992, before accomplishing his ambitious vision to make Wal-Mart a US$ 125 billion company by 2000.

STRATEGIC LEADERSHIP SUCCESSION AT WAL-MART

LEADERSHIP OF DAVID GLASS

Sam's handpicked successor David Glass worked hard, and achieved Sam Walton's target by 1998 – two years before his founder's dream vision.

David Glass took over as the second leader of Wal-Mart in 1988, when the annual sales were US$ 20.6 billion. He retired in January 2000, increasing the sales to US 156 billion, with an annual compound growth of 19%.

LEADERSHIP OF LEE SCOTT

David Glass was followed by **Lee Scott** as the third leader of Wal-Mart. Within 5 years, Wal-Mart added another US$ 145 billion under the leadership of Lee Scott.

RETAIL INNOVATION STRATEGY

Wal-Mart's retail strategy was to provide a wide variety of quality (and often branded) goods and services. Wal-Mart's stores, in the 1960s, attracted customers by selling merchandise purchased by Sam Walton in bulk. He believed that discounting merchandise off the suggested retail prices would boost his growth. Its discount stores sold textile apparel, house wares, small appliances, electronics and hardware.

In the 1970s and 1980s, Wal-Mart innovated and intensely promoted its *"Everyday Low Prices" (EDLP) retail strategy*. This meant that goods were always discounted and not just at the occasional sales. In the traditional "sale" discounting, different goods were discounted at different times. This required stockpiling large inventories of certain products in anticipation of the upcoming "sale." This caused a significant "bullwhip" effect. The innovative EDLP strategy smoothed out the demand, and significantly reduced the bullwhip effect.

With innovative EDLP retailing strategy, Wal-Mart saved on advertising expenses relative to its rival retailers. The savings it accrued, were shared with the customers. This boosted their demand volumes further, and it allowed the Wal-Mart buyers to exercise higher bargaining power with its selected suppliers. The Wal-Mart buyers, thus negotiated price rollbacks for 90 days with the suppliers, to boost sales volumes by 2-5 times.

Beaver (2005 xref#13) confirmed from his research studies that Wal-Mart's prices were on average 8 - 27% lower than those of its rivals.

WAL-MART's WINNING INNOVATION STRATEGY

From its inception, Wal-Mart asserted its low-cost leadership strategy. None of its rivals could come close. Wal-Mart implemented this low-cost strategy by eliminating waste and negotiating lower costs in each element of its enterprise-wide supply-chain. Suppliers were aggressively urged to cut their costs. High volumes help Wal-Mart gain economies of scale. Logistics operations were made more efficient. And inventories were kept at the minimum needed level. Wal-Mart is great at implementing its low-cost leadership strategy.

Multiple Store Formats

There were 4 different store formats in 2008. These are as described below:

1. **Wal-Mart discount stores** on average have approx. 100,000 sq. feet (ranging between 30,000 to 224,000 square feet). These stock approx. 80,000 items, and are manned by 150 people. Their annual sales range between $40 to 80 million. These were being gradually expanded into Supercenters.

1. Wal-Mart Supercenters, started in 1988, are approx. 200,000 square feet (ranging between 98,000 to 246,000 square feet). These stock approx. 150,000 different items, including 30,000 grocery items, for 1-stop shopping experience for families. These bring in between $70 to $100 million revenue annually.

2. **Sam's Clubs were launched in 1983**, as member's only warehouses with 4,000 commonly used branded items. These on average have 130,000 square feet (ranging between 71,000 to 10,000 square feet). Their prices are 10-15% lower than Wal-Mart's discount stores and Supercenters. Annual membership fees were $35 for businesses, $40 for individuals. These employed approx 125 people, and generated approx $75 million annually.

3. **Wal-Mart Neighborhood Markets** were launched most recently in 1998, for the most essential items. These had on average 40,000 square feet (ranging between 35,000 to 55,000 square feet), and on average employed 100 people.

State-of-the Art Information Technology

Wal-Mart was often an early adopter of the latest innovations in informational technology that helped its managers make better decisions. Wal-Mart was the first store to adopt computers in early 1980s to control its inventories. In mid-1980s, Wal-Mart installed its dedicated satellite network to facilitate its electronic commerce with its vendors. IN mid-1990s, Wal-Mart pioneered automated reordering system with the help of its key supplier Procter and Gamble. In 2003, Wal-Mart pioneered the initiative to introduce Radio Frequency Identification (RFID) systems in place of manually scanned barcodes.

Wal-Mart used more than 7,500 company-owned trucks, and more than 8,000 drivers to transport goods between its stores and over 120 distribution centers scattered throughout the United States.

Limited Advertising

For its huge size, Wal-Mart invests very limited resources on advertisement and promotions. For many years, its overall advertising budget was barely 0.3% of its sales, compared to 2.3% for rival Target and 1.5% for the failing K-Mart. Most print advertisements were targeted to local customers.

Fine Tuning Merchandise

Wal-Mart was very good at carefully selecting the merchandise that moved the fastest. Wal-Mart store managers were able to adapt quickly with the slightest shifts in their target customers' shifts in preferences. Suggestions were sought, screened, and implemented rapidly.

Hard Negotiations with Suppliers

Wal-Mart was well-known for bargaining strongly for rock-bottom prices from its carefully selected 66,000 suppliers; 61,000 in the US and 5,000 worldwide in 40 countries. Usually, Wal-Mart bought such large quantities from each supplier, so that Wal-Mart could easily make or break a supplier of almost any size. Invariably, Wal-Mart was the biggest buyer for each of its suppliers. Many of the biggest 200 suppliers maintained offices in Bentonville, in an area dubbed as "Vendorville." In 2005, for example, **Hewlett-Packard** dedicated 3 of its 10 plants to exclusively produce computers for Wal-Mart. Wal-Mart looked for suppliers who could scale up easily depending on demand fluctuations, and were still very dependable in meeting their commitments for deliveries. In 2005, Wal-Mart purchases exceeded $200 billion, and accounted for 3 million jobs.

ENVIRONMENTAL SUSTAINABILITY

Considering its size, and its impact on various economies, Wal-Mart started taking a leadership role in environmental sustainability. Their goal is to minimize waste, improve flexibility, trim down unnecessary packaging, and make optimum use of energy. These goals, would in turn contribute hundreds of millions of dollars of new profits. In 2005, former CEO H. Lee Scott offered his vision for the "Twenty-First Century Leadership" with 3 measurable goals: (1) Use 100% renewable energy, (2) minimize zero waste, and (3) offer products that sustain environment's natural resources. He then demanded the following:

1. Improve 25% Truck fleet efficiency n 3 years, and 100% in 10 years;
2. Reduce 25% solid waste in US stores in 3 years;
3. Reduce 30% energy usage.

There was some resistance, but CEO Scott persisted with his commitments. He also started collaborating with its suppliers to follow Wal-Mart's sustainable strategy. General Electric helped innovate superefficient LED lighting bulb. Kimberly-Clark compressed its paper towels and toilet paper. PepsiCo introduced recycled plastic bottles. Procter & Gamble and Unilever innovated more concentrated laundry detergents. Significant milestones were achieved by 2008.

FUTURE CHALLENGES

Wal-Mart's founder CEO Sam Walton started the discount store wave. His successor CEO David Glass diversified into Supercenters including grocery goods. CEO H. Lee Scott aggressively expanded Wal-Mart globally. As Wal-Mart grew in prominence, it also attracted increasing criticism. But, the company has stayed true to its core-mission and core-passion for providing low-cost leadership. Wal-Mart provided valuable service to alleviate pain and suffering caused by the Katarina hurricane. In a slow economy, each announcement for opening a new store is attracting thousands of new applications.

Does Wal-Mart help build the United States, or does Wal-Mart subtract value? Do they add jobs or reduce jobs?

ADDITIONAL RESOURCES AND REFERENCES: WAL-MART

Beaver, William. 2005. Battling Wal-Mart: How Communities Can Respond. *Business and Society Review*, 110(2, summer): 159. xref#13.

Berner, Robert. 2005. Can Wal-Mart Fit Into a White Hat? *Business Week*, Oct. 3: 94.

Bianco, Anthony and Zellner, Wendy. 2003. Is Wal-Mart Too Powerful? *Business Week*, Oct. 6: 103.

Discount Store News, 1989. Low distribution costs buttress chain's profits. December 18. xref#2

Gunter, Marc. 2006. The Green Machine. *Fortune*, Aug. 7: 48.

Johnson, Fraser. 2006. Supply Chain Management at Wal-Mart, Case #9B07D001, Richard Ivey School of Business, The University of Western Ontario, Canada.

Lynn, Barry C. 2006. Breaking the Chain. Harper's Magazine, July: 33. (xre#14)

Tedlow, Richard S. 2003. *Giants of Enterprise Seven Business Innovators and the Empires They Built*. New York: Harper Business. Ch. 6: 315-. Sam Walton: All-American.

Useem, Jerry. 2003. One Nation Under Wal-Mart. *Fortune*, March 3: 66.

www.walmart.com   See various pages.

www.walmart-stores.com   See for Wal-Mart culture.

www.walmartwatch.com   See for various issues.

Schlender, Brent. 2005. Wal-Mart's $288 Billion Meeting. *Fortune*, April 18: 102.

Walton, Sam and Huey, John. 1992. *Sam Walton: Made in America*. New York: Doubleday.

Wysocki, Bernard and Zimmerman, Ann. 2003. Wal-Mart Cost-Cutting Finds Big Target in Health Benefits. *The Wall-Street Journal*, Sep. 30: A1, A16.

LIST OF EXHIBITS: WAL-MART

Exhibit – 1.   **GLOBAL TOP 10 RETAILERS (2006)**

Exhibit – 2.   **WAL-MART'S EXPONENTIAL GROWTH**

Exhibit – 3.   **SAM WALTON'S 10 GOLDEN RULES FOR GROWTH OF BUSINESS**

Exhibit – 4.   **ETHNIC DIVERSITY AT WAL-MART (2008)**

Exhibit – 5A.   **WAL-MART OPERATIONS FINANCES (US$ millions)**

Exhibit – 5B.   **WAL-MART FINANCES FROM CONTINUING OPERATIONS**

Exhibit – 6.   **WAL MART AND KEY RIVALS' FINANCIALS (US$ Million) IN 2005**

Exhibit – 7.   **STORE SALES GROWTH FOR RIVAL RETAILERS**

Exhibit – 8.   **US RETAIL INDUSTRY (IN US$ Billions)**

Exhibit – 9.   **GROWTH OF NUMBER OF WAL-MART STORES**

Exhibit – 10.   **REGIONAL DISTRIBUTION OF US WAL-MART STORE COUNTS (JAN 2005)**

Exhibit – 11.   **INTERNATIONAL DISTRIBUTION OF WAL-MART STORE COUNTS (IN JAN 2005)**

Exhibit – 12.   **WAL-MART AS A BUYER OF SELECTED KEY SUPPLIERS**

Exhibit – 13.   **U.S. MARKET SHARE OF WAL-MART**

Exhibit – 1.   **GLOBAL TOP 10 RETAILERS (2006)**

Global Rank	Retailer	Home Country	Sales (2006) US$ Million
#G1	Wal-Mart	USA	312.4
#G2	Carrefour SA	France	88.2
#G3	Home Depot	USA	81.5
#G4	Metro AG	Germany	66.0
#G5	Tesco	UK	63.7
#G6	Kroger Co.	USA	60.6
#G7	Costco	USA	53.0
#G8	Target Corp.	USA	52.6
#G9	Royal Ahold	Netherlands	52.2
#G10	Aldi Group	Germany	37.0[1]
	TOP 10 RETAILERS		**867.2**

[1]Estimated
Source: Adapted from www.hoovers.com and Company Annual Reports.

Exhibit – 2.   **WAL-MART'S EXPONENTIAL GROWTH**

Year	Stores	Sales US$ million	Profits US$ million
1962	9	1.4	0.1
1970	32	31.0	1.2
1980	276	1,200.0	41.0
1990	1,528	26,000.0	1,000.0
2000	4,188	191,000.0	6,300.0
2005	5,289	285,000.0	10,300.0
2008	7,262	375,000.0	12,700.0

Source: Adapted from various Wal-Mart Annual Reports.

Exhibit – 3. **SAM WALTON'S 10 GOLDEN RULES FOR GROWTH OF BUSINESS**

RULE #   KEY RECOMMENDATIONS

---

1   Commit to your business

2   Share profits with associates; and treat them as partners

3.   **Motivate Your Partners**

4.   **Communicate Everything You Can to Your Partners**

5.   **Appreciate Everything Your Associates Do for the Business**

6.   **Celebrate Your Successes**

7.   **Listen to Everyone in Your Company**

8.   **Exceed Your Customers' Expectations**

9.   **Control Your Expenses Better Than Your Competitors**

10.   **Swim Upstream**

Exhibit – 4. **Ethnic Diversity at Wal-Mart (2008)**

Total Global Employees 2,100,000
Total US Employees

Hispanics	154,000
African-Americans	237,000
Asian-Americans	41,000
Native-Americans	15,000
Women 826,000	
People $\geq$ 55 Years	256,000

Exhibit – 5A.   **WAL-MART OPERATIONS FINANCES (US$ $ million)**
Fiscal Year ends Jan 31

Year	Net Sales	Cost of Sales Expenses	Operating & SGA Expense	Net Interest	Income	Net Income from Contg. Ops.	Income
1993	55,500	44,200	8,300	300			2,000
2000	156,249	121,825	26,025	840		5,394	5,324
2001	180,787	140,720	30,822	1,196		6,087	6,235
2002	204,011	159,097	35,147	1,183		6,448	6,592
2003	229,616	178,299	39,983	927		7,818	7,955
2004	256,329	198,747	44,909	832		8,861	9,054
2005	285,222	219,793	51,248	986		10,267	10,267
2006	312,427	240,391	56,733	1,172		11,231	11,231

Sauce: Adapted from Wal-Mart Annual Reports.

Exhibit – 5B. **WAL-MART FINANCES FROM CONTINUING OPERATIONS**
(All US$ Values in $ million)

Year	Current Assets	Inven-tories	Prop., Eq. & Cap. Assets, Net[1]	Total Assets	Current Liabilities	L.T. Debt[2]	Share-holders' Equity
1993	10,200		9,800	20,600	6,800	1,800	8,600
2000	23,478	19,296	35,533	68,983	25,525	13,653	25,878
2001	25,344	20,987	40,461	76,231	28,366	12,489	31,407
2002	26,615	22,053	45,248	81,549	26,795	15,676	35,192
2003	29,543	24,401	51,374	92,900	32,225	16,597	39,461
2004	34,421	26,612	59,023	105,405	37,840	17,102	43,623
2005	38,854	29,762	68,118	120,154	43,182	20,087	49,396
2006	43,824	32,191	79,290	138,187	48,826	26.429	53,171

Sauce: Adapted from Wal-Mart Annual Reports.
[1]Property, equipment and capital lease assets, net
[2]Long-term debt

Exhibit – 6. **WAL MART AND KEY RIVALS' FINANCIALS (US$ Million) IN 2005**

	Wal-Mart	Target	Sears Holdings	Costco Wholesale	Federated[1] Dept. Stores
Sales	312,427	52,620	49,124	52,935	22,390
COGS	240,391	34,927	35,505	46,347	13,272
SG&A	56,733	11,185	10,759	5,044	6,980
Net Income	11,231	2,408	858	1,063	1,406
Inventories	32,191	5,838	9,068	4,015	5,459
Assets	138,187	34,995	30,573	16,514	33,168

[1]Federated Department Stores data for 2004
Sauce: Adapted from various Company Annual Reports.

Exhibit – 7.   **STORE SALES GROWTH FOR RIVAL RETAILERS**

	Wal-Mart[1] Stores	Sam's	Target	Sears	Costco Holdings	Federated[2] Wholesale Dept. Stores
%	3.0%	5.0%	5.6%	- 5.3%	7.0%	2.6%

[1] **U.S. stores accounted for 67.2% of total Wal-Mart sales. SAM's Club accounts for 12.7% and International accounted for 20.1%.**

[2]**Federated Department Stores data prior to merger**

Exhibit – 8.   **US RETAIL INDUSTRY (IN US$ Billions)**

RETAIL CATEGORY	2005 Sales	Per Capita
1. General Merchandise	525.7	
2. Food and Beverage	519.3	
3. Food Services and Drinking Places	396.6	
4. Gasoline	388.3	
5. Building Materials, Gardening Equipment & Supplies	327.0	
6. Furniture, Home Furnishings, electronics & appliances	211.7	
7. Health and Personal Care	208.4	
8. Clothing and Clothing Accessories	201.7	
9. Sporting Goods, Hobbies, Books, Music	81.9	

Exhibit – 9. **GROWTH OF NUMBER OF WAL-MART STORES**

Year	US Discount Stores	US Supercenters	US Sam's Clubs	US Neighborhood Markets	International Stores
1993	1,848	34	256	None	10
2000 2001	1,801	721	463	7	991
2002	1,647	1,066	500	31	1,154
2003	1,568	1,258	525	49	1,272
2004	1,478	1,471	538	64	1,355
2005	1,353	1,713	551	85	1,587

Source: Adapted from Company Annual Reports; Thompson, 2006: C-413. Case#25.

Exhibit – 10. **REGIONAL DISTRIBUTION OF US WAL-MART STORE COUNTS**

(JAN 2005)

State In USA	Discount Stores	Supercenters	Sam's Clubs	Neighborhood Markets
SOUTH				
Alabama	18	71	11	2
Arizona	18	33	11	5
Arkansas	26	54	5	6
Oklahoma	33	49	8	14
PACIFIC COAST				
California	149	3	33	0
Colorado	15	40	15	0
EAST COAST				
Connecticut	28	4	3	0
MID-WEST				
Illinois	78	45	28	0
Indiana	31	56	15	4
Ohio	69	45	27	0
Alaska	7	0	3	0
Hawaii	7	0	2	0

Exhibit – 11. **INTERNATIONAL DISTRIBUTION OF WAL-MART STORE COUNTS (IN JAN 2005)**

	Discount Supercenters Stores		Sam's Clubs	Neighborhood Markets
NORTH AMERICA				
Canada	256	0	6	0
Mexico	529	89	61	0
LATIN AMERICA				
Argentina	0	11	0	0
Brazil	118	17	12	2
Puerto Rico	9	4	9	32
EUROPE				
United Kingdom	263	19	0	0
Germany	0	91	0	0
ASIA				
China	0	38	3	2
South Korea	0	16	0	0

Source: Estimated from Corporate Annual Report, 2005.

Exhibit – 12. **WAL-MART AS A BUYER OF SELECTED KEY SUPPLIERS**

Supplier Name	Goods	% Total Sales as Wal-Mart Sales
Tandy	Accessories	39
Dial		28
Del Monte	Foods	24
Clorox	Cleaners	23
Revlon	Cosmetics	22
RJR	Tobacco	20
Procter & Gamble	Personal Goods	17
Disney		
Campbell	Soup	
Kraft	Food	
Gillette		

Exhibit – 13. **U.S. MARKET SHARE OF WAL-MART**

Product Group		% Market Share
PET SUPPLIES	Dog Food	36%
PERSONAL GOODS	Paper Towels	30
	Disposable diapers	32
	Shampoo	30
	Toothpaste	26
DRUGS	Pain Medicines	21
ENTERTAINMENT	Photographic Film	30
	CDs, DVDs, Videos	15
	Magazine singles	15

Wal-Mart biggest seller of	toys
	Guns
	Diamonds
	Detergent
	Games
	Socks
	Bedding

Apple Inc.

Serial Innovating in 2010

Dr. R. RAY GEHANI

Institute for Innovation and Technology Leadership (IITL)
Akron, Ohio.

Disclaimer:

> *This draft case-in-progress is meant strictly for classroom discussion and learning. It must not be considered as a comment on this firm's strategic management decisions or actions.*

REPOLISHING APPLE IN THE 21st CENTURY

In March 2010, the *Fortune* magazine announced that for the third consecutive year, Apple was ranked as the Number 1 Most Admired Company in 2009. The survey was conducted by *Fortune* in collaboration with Hay Group (Bernasek, 2010: 123 Fortune Mar. 22). They surveyed 4,170 executives about the companies they admired most out of about 1400 largest companies selected from around the world. Apple was a leader by the highest margin in 2009. More than 51%, an unprecedented majority, of strategic business leaders surveyed shared that they admired Apple for single-handedly changing the way we do many things from listening to music to accessing information and engaging with others around the world. Business leaders and consumers trusted Apple's innovations, and its dynamic capability to develop innovative new products. Apple was admired for showing the next great thing. The CEO of BMW, Norbert Reithofer admired that Apple's customers tend to become more than consumers – as Apple's fans. When Apple announced iPad, the whole world held its breath (Bernasek, 2010: 124 Fortune Mar. 22).

Lately, **Apple CEO Steve Jobs** was excited about his life. In early 2009 he successfully received a liver transplant. He had decided that he could slow down, and work only part time.

In January 2010, Steve Jobs announced Apple's intent to launch a much awaited tablet computer iPad in April 2010, something in between a netbook and Apple's iPhone, closer to a netbook. This shook up the eBook industry, and mega-rivals like **Microsoft, Sony, Dell, Acer, Lenovo, Asus, and Amazon**. Though many Chinese knockoffs are also expected to intensify the rivalry, Apple was expected to sell more than 6 million iPads in 2010.

Not much earlier, on June 19 in 2009, Steve Jobs launched the **innovative iPhone 3GS** with much fanfare and hype. Within three days it sold more than 1 million units. **The App Store** was launched, and within one year more than 1.5 billion iPhone applications were downloaded. By year-end 2008, iPhone accounted for 12.9% market share, and it ranked third in a fast growing worldwide smart phone industry. Many of Apple's rivals in telephony, however, were rapidly imitating some of iPhone's innovative features.

Steve Jobs' transformational leadership of Apple, headquartered at **1 Infinite Loop, Cupertino, California**, with the recent launches of iPod and iTunes catapulted Apple as a leader in music player industry.

This also revitalized Apple's position in the personal computer industry. Then Apple's iPhone redefined the customers' expectations. Steve Jobs has proven to be a serial innovator, transforming Apple with one disruptive innovation after another. Many years ago, in 1982, *Time* magazine put Steve Jobs on its cover as one of *America's Risk Takers*. He has been repeatedly taking risks for the past quarter century. He has also pruned Apple of some of its under-performing divisions. The mature Steve Jobs had the discipline that the young Steve Jobs had lacked earlier.

Apple's biggest market in the United States, however, was facing one of its longest recessions in 2008 and 2009 since the Great Depression. This was based on persistent decline in Gross Domestic Product. During this period, consumer technology sales such as PC shipments had declined by 4-5%.

LEGENDARY START-UP OF APPLE IN 1976

Steve Jobs, with the help of hardware designed by Steve Wozniak, received a marketing order in 1976 for a highly innovative personal computer Apple I targeted to computer programming hobby enthusiasts in the Silicon Valley. This led to the start-up of Apple Computer in 1976. In 1978, the two Steves improved their fast-selling product and developed Apple II, for reaching out to mass-market consumers. Thus personal computer rapidly evolved from a hobby pastime tool to a functionally indispensible tool for business and personal productivity.

Firing of Steve Jobs

With the release of Windows 95 by Microsoft, the Win-Tel personal computers with Windows software and Intel microprocessor, imitated a Mac-like graphical user interface (GUI), and dominated the personal computer industry. By 1997, Apple was in deep crisis. Just one year after the release of Mac, Apple's co-founder Steve Jobs was fired by his board of directors, under the guidance of John Sculley, an outsider handpicked from Pepsi by Steve Jobs to market Apple better.

Homecoming of Steve Jobs

When away from Apple, Steve Jobs try to create the NeXT computer and Pixar Animation Studios. With the block-buster success of animated movie Toy Story produced by Pixar, Steve Jobs' star was back flying high among Corporate America. When Walt Disney acquired the animated film studio Pixar for more than $7 billion (Watson, Albert. 2006. Nov. 27. Fortune, Portraits of Power. 105-138), Steve Jobs became the largest share holder of Disney. With iTunes, Jobs took network TV online.

In 1997, as Apple acquired NeXT, Steve Jobs came back home to Apple. He started searching for ways to prove his innovative Midas touch to the world.

Steve Jobs noticed a particularly promising young designer **Jonathan Ive,** buried deep in the design department. Steve left a message for Jonathan to come and see him. Jonathan knew about Steve's tendency to throw tantrums and be mean to other Apple employees. He carefully drafted a resignation letter, and brought it with him, in case his interaction with Steve Jobs got too ugly (Fry, 2010: 42). Instead, Jonathan received from Steve all the freedom Jonathan needed to unleash his creative designing talent.

This miracle gave birth to the eye-popping iMac in radical new housing, and all-in-one functionality. This was followed soon with game-changing iPod and iPhone.

DAWN OF THE 21st CENTURY FOR APPLE

Steve Jobs declared in early 2000 that he intended to be the permanent CEO of Apple. The computer industry, after the Y2K threat passed, was in a bust. Apple slowed down too, reported its quarterly loss in 3 years, and cut prices of most of its products.

In 2001, Apple released new PowerMacs with many additional features. These had optical drives which enabled owners to burn CDs while listening, and read as well as write on DVDs. Apple also announced in May 2001 that it would open many retail stores which will sell Apple products as well as third-party digital cameras, MP3 players, and digital video cameras.

LAUNCH OF iPod

Apple launched its iPod digital music player for hefty $399 in October 2001. This emerged as a fashion statement and radically transformed the music player industry, the way Sony's Walkman did earlier in 1980. By June 2005, Apple acquired more than 70% market share for digital music players, and over 40% market share for flash memory players.

LAUNCH OF iTunes

In 2003, Apple launched the online retail store iTunes, enabling customers to legally download one song at a time, at an affordable price such as $0.99. The demand for legally downloading single songs skyrocketed. Initially, this facility was available only on Apple's Macs. But, later this was also available on rival PCs.

By 2004, Apple had sold more than 100 million downloaded songs. iTunes gained 70% market share of legal online music download business.

Collaborating with Timothy Cook

Steve Jobs benefitted significantly from collaborating with the highly professional **Timothy D. Cook**. Cook was Apple's executive vice president responsible for worldwide sales and operations. Earlier Cook had gained valuable experience at **IBM and Compaq**. At Apple, Cook managed supply chain, sales, service and support, and reported directly to the CEO.

Apple, under Cook's leadership, became agile and was able to meet the needs of its more demanding customers. Cook could put in practice the innovative vision provided by Jobs. When Steve Jobs took leave of absence to diagnose his falling health, Timothy Cook successfully took over as the acting CEO. Especially in Fall 2008, when the health of Steve Jobs could not be hidden anymore from outsiders.

APPLE 'S SUCCESS IN 2008

In 2008, under the leadership of Acting **CEO Timothy Cook**, Apple had record sales of $32,479 million, increasing from $24,006 million in 2007, and it was still growing robustly in the sales of iPods, iTunes downloads, iPhones, and Mac computers (see Apple's summary of financial performance in Exhibit 3).

Apple managed its global business by geographic regions: Americas (including North America and South America); Europe, Africa, and the Middle East; and Japan. Its retail division opened and ran the Apple-owned stores in the U.S., Canada, U.K., Italy, and Japan.

Apple's net sales by its product line, and geographic segments are shown in Exhibit –1, 2. Apple's primary product lines are: Macintosh desktop and portable products; iPhones; iPods; iTunes and other music-related products; peripherals including other hardware products; and software, service, and other sales.

APPLE AND PERSONAL COMPUTER INDUSTRY

In the early part of 2009, the global as well as the U.S. personal computer (PC) industry declined by 5% and 1.2% respectively. The U.S. PC industry was dominated by 5 major PC producers: Dell, Hewlett-Packard, Acer, Apple, and Toshiba. Together, these 5 major PC makers accounted for 81.4% of the U.S. PC market, and 60.1% of the international market. Apple accounted for only 2% of the international PC market. The PC industry was earlier expected to grow at about 5% per year, to more than $350 billion by 2012, but the economic slowdown of 2008 and 2009 reduced these further.

In the past few years, Apple's net sales were increasingly coming from non-PC sector, such as iPod and iPhone. But, Apple still looked at itself as a differentiated personal computer maker, and charged approx. 20% premium prices for its computers. MACs were differentiated from PCs by Apple's stronger graphical handling capabilities, and proprietary operating system.

Large number of consumers owning PCs was unwilling to switch to Macs because of the different operating system and the premium pricing of Macs. If they were provided PC at work, they owned PC at home as well. Apple was expecting to get a similar network externality effect with the large number of new owners of iPod and iPhone – and hoping that some of them would own Macs for better compatibility.

Apple offered a family of computers in many different configurations. Power branded products were targeted to for higher end consumers who were willing to pay premium prices for higher computing power. Apple's other computers has relatively less computing power but still charged premiums over PC computers based on Windows software – Intel chip configurations.

Mac Pro computers were targeted on professional business users, iMac computers were targeted on common consumers in educational and business environments. Mac Mini computer was customized by consumers.

Apple also had 3 notebook offerings. MacBook Pro was targeted to professional and advanced users, and MacBook was targeted to common consumers in education and business environments. MacBook Air, introduced most recently, was 3 pounds light weight and 0.76 inch thin. It was targeted to professional and consumers most concerned with light-weight portability but needed power. It had 13.3 inch screen, built-in video camera, wireless connectivity, and full-size keyboard. This was well received by the market and critics, and was helping Apple recover some of its lost ground in computer industry.

In June 2009, Apple reduced the price of all its premium-priced products by 10% or more. Price of MacBook Air was reduced by $300 to $1,499, and MacBook was priced down to $1,199.

Apple's greatest growth was projected to come from the synergistic sales effects of iPhone and iPod. Apple's family of computer products was expected to grow faster, with the new owners of other new Apple products

APPLE'S RIVALS IN THE PC INDUSTRY

1. Dell

Dell, the leader in PC computer sales, recorded net revenues of $61.1 billion for 2009. Dell also suffered from decline in PC computer sales because of the U.S. economic recession. There was a significant shift from desktop computer users to mobility computers such as laptops, notebooks, tablets, netbooks, and handheld devices. Dell also offered its desktop computers and laptops in a variety of configurations for different prices. Dell also diversified into computer related peripherals such as monitors, printers, projectors, and some Wi-Fi products. See Exhibit – 5A.

2. HEWLETT-PACKARD

Hewlett-Packard is a large enterprise with $118 billion revenues in 2008. Of this, only 35.7% revenues came from its Personal Systems Group (PSG). From 2007 to 2008, PSG had an annual growth of 16.2% revenue and 22% increase in unit sales. The desktop sales grew by only 5% whereas the laptop sales jumped by 28%. The next biggest division was Imaging and Services, with 24.8% of HP's revenue in 2008. See Exhibit – 5B.

3. ACER

Acer was founded in 1976 in Taiwan with 11 employees as a multi- technology enterprise. It started exporting computers in 1979, and founded Taiwan's franchised retail stores in 1985. It was renamed as in 1987, and in 1997 plunged deeper into the U.S. market with the purchase of the mobile PC division from Texas Instruments.

In 2008, Acer was the world's 3rd largest computer manufacturer with $16.6 billion consolidated revenues and $429 million operating income from PC computers, desktops, notebooks, servers, LCD monitors, high definition TVs and projectors. These represented 18% annual growth in revenue and 38% annual boost in operating income between 2007 and 2008. Acer also emerged in 2008 as the fastest growing PC computer manufacturer, exporter, and seller of PCs in the United States.

More than 54.3% Acer's sales came from Europe, Middle East, and Africa region. Acer was planning to sustain its growth in the US market with low-priced notebook computers distributed through discount consumer electronic stores.

PERSONAL MEDIA PLAYER (MP) INDUSTRY

Whereas there were 4 major players in this industry (Apple, Microsoft, Creative, and SanDisk), there were more than 100 manufacturers of media players. See the Exhibit for market shares of major rivals. Apple dominates, with premium pricing of its differentiated product offerings. The growth in this industry comes from converting new customers. Flash-based players, touch-screens, and Bluetooth connectivity helped extend the life cycle of this product. Prices slip as the market matures.

Apple iPod

Apple launched its digital music player iPod in October 2001 for $399, and changed the rules of the competitive game. The first portable digital player was not introduced by Sony, the inventor of Walkman, but by EigerLabs (in 1998). Apple's iPod was considered too expensive. By June 1005, iPod dominated with 70% market share, and a great lead ahead of its nearest rivals. By 2009, Apple maintained its market leadership by offering 4 different models: **iPod Shuffle, iPod Nano (2005), iPod Classic, and iPod Touch**. Each new product introduced the latest technological innovations. Early iPods had short battery lives or limited digital storage capacity. These were remedied in subsequent product generations.

Apple iTunes

Apple's innovation of legally downloadable iTunes digital music at affordable prices catapulted the popularity of Apple's iPod. Launch of iPod in 2001 helped music lovers make their favorite music easily transferable and portable. The fourth edition of iTunes was launched in 2003, with the announcement of collaboration with 5 major music labels willing to sell their large library of popular songs in an easy-to-use legally copy-protected form. Apple compressed the iTunes music using proprietary file compression software. In October 2003, iTunes Music Store was also released for Microsoft Windows users.

In October 2005, Apple was selling not only music audio files but also videos, and TV shows using its video iPod. This time Apple collaborated with all the major broadcasters.

Apple iPhone

On June 29, 2007, Apple revolutionized the phone industry by launching its first generation 4 Giga Byte iPhone with a multitouch screen, and a variety of easy to use applications. It included iPod like media player, voice mail, internet connectivity, a digital keyboard for text-messaging, and a digital camera.

This was developed in collaboration with AT&T Mobility, formerly Cingular Wireless. Code-named Purple 2 during the development phase, the new product was developed at the estimated cost of $150 million. Within months of the initial launch, on September 5, 2007, a more powerful **8 Giga Byte iPhone** was launched by Apple with a much lower $399 price tag. Buyers of previous model of iPhone were permitted to switch within 14 days. The Time magazine awarded iPhone the **Invention of the Year 2007**.

On June 19, 2009, **iPhone 3GS** was launched with 32 Giga Byte flash memory, and access to more than 800 new applications. The base 16 Giga Byte model was repositioned at $199 with 2 year AT&T service contract. By July 2009, Apple's application store offered 65,000 applications. These were developed so fast through open innovation with the help of 100,000 developers scattered all over the world.

In 2008, the 27% growth in smart phone exceeded far more than 4% growth in mobile phones. **Nokia** and other mobile phone makers were following closely behind the success of Apple.

When Apple launched iPhone, only rival **Research In Motion (RIM)** had a competing multimedia phone, primarily targeted to business use (Copeland, 2010: 153). The birth of iPhone boosted the birth of many other smartphones, such as MyTouch, Droid and others. Apple's iPhone controlled only 14.4% of the total smart-phone market, shared by many other players.

LAUNCHING APPLE'S iPAD
IN A RECOVERING ECONOMY

Apple offered iPad when customers had heard and passed the announcement of tablet computers by rival innovators, like **Microsoft's Bill Gates**. At COMDEX 2000, the Computer industry's main exposition and trade exhibition held every year in Las Vegas, Bill Gates held up a flat computer without a keyboard, a Tablet PC. He suggested that this would become the most popular computer in 5 years **(Grossman, 2010: 37. Launch Pad, *Time*). It did not excite computer users.** Bill Gates reintroduced Tablet PC at Comdex 2001. Still no takers for the underpowered netbook without a keyboard. The Tablet PC was like a piece of paper – much heavier, more expensive, and if you dropped it broke and lost all its value.

Steve's Hype and Feature Fanfare

Apple and Steve Jobs, unlike **Microsoft and Bill Gates**, launch their new products with a lot of fanfare and hype. Sometimes, Steve's hype is justified. Apple's iPad is ½ inch thin (1.2 cm), 1.5 pound (or 680 gm) light, with a 9.7 inch (or 25 cm diagonally) super-crisp and super-bright touch-screen, with no keyboard or mouse. It was priced at $499 for 16 gigabytes of memory, and $829 for 64 gigabytes of memory and 3G. This price is in the ballpark of netbooks. This compact device is powered by a new home-made **1 gigahertz A4 Apple processor**. Apple recommends iPad users to subscribe to 3G service, which adds $130 to the cost of the device, and $15-30 per month for AT&T data plans (Jeroslovsky, 2010 Apr 12: 18).

The iPad does many things for many customers. Loaded with Wi-Fi and Bluetooth, iPad was pitched as a device that can help a consumer consume media in many different forms. You can use it with one hand to browse web, e-mail, synchronize calendars, share photos, enjoy your favorite music, watch movies, play games, word process documents, prepare presentations, crunch numbers in spreadsheets, and read eBooks and magazines. Many other devices, unfortunately, can also do all these things.

Apple, however, has also enriched iPad with some of its proprietary technologies, such as patented multi-touch technology that runs iPhones. Many rival companies have tried to imitate, but failed to match Apple's multi-touch genius. The iPad is also loaded with Apple's sparkling displays, and low-power computing engineering: one charge gives iPad enough juice to go one for 10 hours. And, iPad looks as pretty as Apple's other legendry and envy-evoking appliances.

The iPad tablet comes filled with a whole colony full of Apple applications. In under 2 years, Apple's App Store has amassed more than 150,000 applications. This has turned iPad into a great mobile-gaming platform, right into the market territory of Nintendo's DS. Founder of GameLoft, Michel Guillermot, was excited that iPad was ushering in the fourth wave of evolution of gaming, after the use of minicomputer, the dedicated console, and the smart phone. In addition, iPad came ready loaded with **iBook application** to butt heads with **Amazon's Kindle** for eBook market. Many newspaper and magazine publishers were being enticed to revive their slipping sales by offering digital versions of their publications on iPad.

Many publishers were not happy with Amazon's unilateral pricing decisions. Apple's iPad gives much more control back to publishers like **Penguin** to price their books as they please. University education could also be radically transformed by iPad with its conduit to converge a variety of course materials such as in text, video, audio, including student input.

Apple had an enormous competitive advantage over its rivals, based on Apple's innovative ecosystem of a variety of innovative new products. The App Store, iPhone, iTunes, iBooks all provided iPad consumers to access, buy, and consume content seamlessly. Apple offers an entire experience, including the full food-chain including hardware, software, and content distribution (Copeland, 2010: 153. Fortune, Mar. 22).

iPad Blemishes

But, there are some blemishes too. First, iPad falls right between a mobile phone and a laptop. It is not big enough to be treated a proper computer, and it is not small enough to be called a portable mobile device. Some saw iPad as a scaled-up iPhone or a souped up iPod Touch.

Apple also selectively decided to hold back on jamming certain features into iPad. First, there is no camera in iPad. It only runs on **Safari browser**, and it does not have **Adobe flash** memory. It doesn't have great file handling system, and as in the case of iPhone, iPad is not very good at multi-tasking. It has only 16-64 giga-bytes of solid-state memory, much less than the typical 160 giga-byte storage on many netbooks (Jeroslovsky, 2010. Apr 12: 18). In other words, iPad is a great conduit to tap into the knowledge universe on the Internet, but it is not a great technological tool for creating your knowledge and contributing your knowledge back into the universe. Would consumers mainly use iPad for accessing and passively absorbing pre-existing knowledge and other people's master creations such as music and movies?

Rivalry

The launch of iPad in April 2010 has made many of Apple's rivals, such as **Microsoft and Google**, to rethink their competitive market position. This is similar to the tech-war that started when Apple launched its iPhone by selling a variety of its own and others' Apps. **Rival Google**, on the other hand, offered its **Chrome operating software** free for customers to connect to Google services (Jeroslovsky, 2010 Apr.12: 18). Google also developed an app-friendly mobile operating system, Android. Google may also launch a netbook powered by its Chrome operating system (Copeland, 2010: 153).

Global computer leaders, such as **Toshiba and Panasonic**, have been producing similar tablet/slate computers for their large industrial clients. Toshiba's U.S. Notebook Division saw this as a creation of new computer category, and started planning to launch a new line of consumer tablets/slates by early 2011.

Hardware makers, such as **Hewlett-Packard (HP) and Dell**, were also anxiously watching if large number of consumers would switch over to iPad (Copeland, 2010: 151). A few weeks prior to the launch of iPad, Microsoft's Steve Balmer had also re-launched **HP's Slate**, with a tentative birthday sometime in 2010. HP had been a 5-year roadmap to develop their slate computer. **Intel** also worried that iPad runs on Apple's proprietary processor A4. Apple designed A4, and gets it custom-manufactured.

Asus, the innovator of netbooks and creator of its market segment, also planned to launch their own slate computer before the end of 2010 (Copeland, 2010: 153 *Fortune*). Its founder Johnny Shih was planning to offer the features Apple left out, such as including (1) a camera for video-conferencing, (2) an operating system that runs on Adobe's Flash, and (3) multitasking capability.

Amazon had to reconsider whether it wants to stay and compete in the hardware market with its Kindle eBook reader, or to altogether get out of the hardware eReader market (Copeland, 2010: 152).

Studying Apple App Programming

The computer science students in the past primarily learned how to program mainframe computers. Then they learned about programming personal computers. And now, they are naturally progressing to the smartphones and tablet computers. At the University of Maryland, a visiting Apple engineer teaches an advanced computer course completely dedicated to iPhone programming (Kaplan, 2010 May 24: 22). Apple does not disclose the terms of their partnership with the various universities. The programming language students learn will also apply to iPad, and other smartphones, such as Google's Android devices. Stanford, not far from Apple headquarters, has offered similar courses since 2009. The University of Washington continuing education also help students program apps for Apple's iPhone, smartphones, and iPad – with dreams of making a lot of wealth. If an App becomes successful, Apple gets its 30% commission on sales.

Perfecting the Game of Developing Product Innovation

Apple has come a long way in perfecting its game and style of developing radically innovative new products. When Steve Jobs launched iPhone in June 2007, Apple was a lagging underdog in smart phone industry, trying to catch-up from way behind. The smart-phone industry was dominated by well-established giants like **Nokia, Palm, Sony Ericsson, Blackberry, and Windows Mobile**. But, this time, for launching its iPad innovation, Apple and Steve Jobs are strutting like top dogs. This has some advantages as well as some disadvantages. Whereas Apple and Steve Jobs got more visibility, the critics and watchdogs were also ready to attack the front-runners. Who cares for this ill-defined computing device? Will iPad be a block-buster success like the sale of 6 million iPhones in its first year, or will iPad flop like Apple's Newton?

Under Steve's leadership, Apple's product developers have learned to focus on customers' experience rather than be obsessed with features and technical numbers. Steve does not want customers to view iPad as a tool, but as a dependable friend, or a loving pet animal. Focus on emotional feelings rather than material specifications. If customers are going to carry around iPad for many hours every day, then it must make its owner smile, as users touch and be tickled, strike and be stimulated (Fry, 2010: 42).

Apple designer Jonathan Ive, shares that designers at Apple do not try to predict what others, either competitors or customers, would do. Instead they focus on what they think is right, and offer that to the customers and market. Apple does not believe in inviting and relying on asking focus groups of customers and asking them what they want. Instead, Apple tells its potential customers what they are going to be delighted with, and would want next. Whereas rival giant Microsoft prefers to enter well-established markets, and dominate these with brute financial power, Apple prefers to focus on creating innovative new niches. They rule these from the start.

To achieve this, Apple designers work for long hours on perfecting the smallest detail. They know that many consumers would not notice thousands of such details and innovations embedded into Apple's revolutionary products. These products are not only built beautifully, but they are also robust and work reliably. They can be thrown in the backseat of a car or on top of a cargo luggage, and yet boot up when clicked at the other end of their heavy wear and tear.

MATURING OF AILING STEVE JOBS

Much of Apple's style and spirit is attributed to its legendary leader and chief innovator Steve Jobs. Over the past quarter century, he has emerged as an undisputed king of multiple radical innovations that have dramatically impacted the world. He is a visionary and an opportunist, a cheerleader enthusiast as well as a perfectionist task-master. He is extremely confident, and very glad at selling almost anything to the most toughest buyers. His personal magnetism is almost hypnotic.

Steve Jobs usually wears a black turtleneck with a Levi's jeans. When he announced iPad in January 2010, he stood between two street signs, and told the audience that he has always seen Apple as located at the inter-section of the Liberal Arts and Technology. He agrees that it is also at the intersection of commerce, as what Apple does must also make commercial sense. But, they often start with the product innovation and the immersive user experience it promises - and delivers delightfully and repeatedly. He shows how every iPad was loaded with the **_Winnie the Pooh_** iBook. The iPad case was designed carefully so that it can also be reused as a stand or a lectern.

At the iPad launch, Steve Jobs promised the potential consumers that iPad would change everything, and the customers' immersive experience will be magical (Fry, 2010:43). Whereas, he did not clearly know how large number of consumers would eventually use iPad, he was hoping that iPad would become the first true home-wide computer. Most conventional personal computers are primarily used in studies, and laptops may occasionally end up in the living rooms. Steve hoped that iPad would be used by the entire family, going from one family member to another, traveling through living room for entertainment, kitchen for a cooking book, and bedroom for reflective journaling. With enough power and wireless connectivity, iPad would move freely without getting tethered to any restrictive thing.

Since the disclosure of his struggle with two critical health scares, is Steve Jobs getting ready to leave Apple with the launch of iPad as a high note of his innovative career? He shares that, he does not see his many years full of making innovative fun stuff as a career, but as a way of living his life.

FUTURE CHALLENGES AT APPLE

Under the strategic leadership of Steve Jobs, Apple has repeatedly launched game-rule changing disruptive innovations. Marketed by the expert salesman Steve, these radical innovations have been highly successfully. His health, however, has made many Apple watchers worry about the future of Apple. Will Steve Jobs be able to launch a game-changing successor leader with the same ease with which he introduces innovative new products? Or, is **Time Cook** the real innovator at Apple, and Steve Jobs merely a front for Apple's serial innovative successes?

LIST OF EXHIBITS: APPLE'S INNOVATIONS

Exhibit – 1:   APPLE'S NET SALES BY GEOGRAPHIC SEGMENTS (in $ million)

	Americas	Europe	Japan	Retail	Others	Total
2004	4,019	1,799	677	1,185	599	8,279
2005	6,950	3,073	920	2,350	998	13,931
2006	9,415	4,096	1,211	3,246	1,347	19,315
2007	11,596	5,460	1,082	4,115	1,753	24,006
2008	14,573	7,622	1,509	6,315	2,460	32,479

Exhibit – 2:   APPLE'S NET SALES BY PRODUCT SEGMENTS (in $ million, and units)

	Deskt-tops	Portables Mac 1	Total	iPod	Other Musical2	iPhone +related	Peri-pherals3	Software + serv. 4	Total Net Sales
IN $ NET SALES									
2004	2,373	2,550	4,923	1,306	278	-- 951	821		8,279
2005	3,436	2,839	6,275	4,540	899	--1,126	1,091		13,931
2006	3,319	4,056	7,375	7,375	1,885	--1,100	1,279		19,315
2007	4,020	6,294	10,314	8,305	2,496	123 1,260	1,508		24,006
2008	5,603	8,673	14,276	9,153	3,340	1,844 1,659	2,207		32,479

Year	Desktops	Portables	Total Macs	iPod	iPhone	Net Sales/ Mac	Net Sales/ iPod
IN UNIT SALES							
2004	1,625	1,665	3,290	4,416	---	$1,496	$ 296
2005	2,520	2,014	4,534	22,497	---	$1,384	$ 202
2006	2,434	2,869	5,303	39,409	---	$1,391	$ 195
2007	2,714	4,337	7,051	51,630	---	$1,463	$ 161
2008	3,712	6,003	9,715	54,828	11,627	$1,469	$ 167

Exhibit – 3.   APPLE'S FINANCIAL PERFORMANCE

| | NET SALES | | | COSTS AND EXPENSES | | | | Operating | Net |
	USA	Intnl.	Total Sales	Cost of	R&D	SG&A	Total Op. Expenses	Income	Income
2005	8,334	5,597	13,931	9,889	535	1,864	2,399	1,643	1,328
2006	11,486	7,829	19,315	13,717	712	2,433	3,145	2,453	1,989
2007	14,128	9,878	24,006	15,852	782	2,963	3,745	4,409	3,496
2008	18,469	14,010	32,479	21,334	1,109	3,761	4,870	6,275	4,834

Exhibit – 4.   APPLE'S MISCELLANEOUS GENERAL INFORMATION

| | Earnings/ Share Diluted | Diluted Shares million | EMPLOYEES | | Intnl. Net Sales/ Total Net Sales% | Gross Margin/ Net Sales | R&D/ N.Sales |
			Regular	Temp.			
2005	$1.55	856.9	14,806	2,020	40.0%	29.0%	4.0%
2006	$2.27	877.5	17,787	2,399	41.0%	29.0%	4.0%
2007	$3.93	889.3	21,550	2,116	41.0%	34.0%	3.0%
2008	$5.36	902.1	32,010	3,066	43.0%	34.3%	3.0%

Exhibit – 5.   PRODUCTS OFFERED BY APPLE'S RIVALS

A.   DELL PRODUCT MIX

	Mobility-Notebooks+	Desktop PCs	Software & Peripherals	Servers & Networking	Support Services	Storage Products
Around Feb 1						
2007	27%	34%	16%	10%	9%	4%
2008	28%	32%	16%	11%	9%	4%
2009	31%	29%	17%	10%	9%	4%

B.   HEWLETT-PACKARD REVENUES ($ millions)

	Notebooks	Desktops	Handhelds	Workstations	Others	Total
2005	$9,763	14,406	836	1,195	541	26,741
2006	12,005	14,641	650	1,368	502	29,166
2007	17,650	15,889	531	1,721	618	36,409
2008	22,657	16,626	360	1,902	750	42,295

Exhibit – 6. MP3 CUSTOMER SATISFACTION, PC MAGAZINE READER SURVEY

MP3 Players	Sound Quality	Ease of Use	Reliability	Overall
Apple	8.7	8.6	8.3	8.3
Microsoft	8.7	8.3	8.2	8.1
Creative	8.4	7.5	8.1	7.8
Archos	8.1	7.6	8.0	7.6
iRiver	8.4	7.2	8.1	7.6
Toshiba	8.5	8.1	8.0	7.6
SanDisk	8.0	7.5	7.9	7.5
Samsung	8.0	7.5	7.9	7.4
Sony	8.0	7.4	7.8	7.3
INDUSTRY AVERAGE	8.1	7.6	7.8	7.4

Industry Average includes others such as Panasonic, Philips, RCA, Dell, and Rio.
Source: Adapted from *PC Magazine Customer Survey*, 2007, Oct. 31. www.pcmag.com.

Exhibit – 7.   DIGITAL MUSIC PLAYER MARKET SHARES

	Apple	SanDisk	Creative	Microsoft	Others	Total
2007*	72%	10%	4%	3%	11%	100%
2008*	71%	11%	2%	4%	12%	100%

Notes: *: Numbers in First Quarter.
Source: Adapted from NPD Group, May 12, 2008. In Case on Apple, by Marino, Lou, Hattaway, John and Jackson, Katy Beth. Apple Inc. in 2009.

Exhibit – 8.　　　THE 50 ALL STARS. MOST ADMIRED COMPANIES

2009 Overall Rank		Industry	2009 Indy. Rank	2008 Indy. Rank
1.	Apple	2. Computers	1	2
2.	Google	4. Internet Services	1	1
3.	Berkshire Hathaway	22.Insurance Property	1	1
4.	Johnson & Johnson	31.Pharmaceuticals	2	1
5.	Amazon.Com	4. internet services	2	2
6.	Proctor & Gamble	12.Soaps & cosmetics	1	1
7.	Toyota Motor	54. motor vehicles	3	2
8.	Goldman Sachs Gr.	23. megabanks	1	1
9.	Wal-Mart Stores	43.Genl.Merchandise	1	1
10.	Coca-Cola	8. Beverages	1	3
11.	Microsoft	1. Computer software	5	5
12.	Southwest Airlines	50. airlines	4	3
13.	Fedex	51. delivery	2	1
14.	McDonald's	42. Food services	1	1
15.	IBM	3. Info Tech Services	1	1
16.	General Electric	36. electronics	1	1
17.	3M			
18.	JP Morgan Chase	23. megabanks	2	2
19.	Walt Disney	25. Entertainment	1	1
20	Cisco	5.Network Comm. Eq.	1	1
21.	Costco Wholesale	44.specl. retailers	1	1
22.	BMW	54. motor vehicles	1	1
23.	Target	43. gen. merchandise	2	2
24.	Nike	7. Apparel	1	1
25.	PepsiCo	9. Consumer Foods	2	2
26.	Starbucks	42. food services	3	2

REFERENCES AND ADDITIONAL READINGS: APPLE

Bernasek, Anna. 2010. Who Does Business Trust? The 50-All Star Most Admired Companies. Fortune Mar. 22. 122-136.

Copeland, Michael. 2010. The iPad Changes Everything. Fortune, March 22: 150-153.

Fry, Stephen. 2010. On the Mothership. A Confessed Apple fanboy gets finger time with the iPad – and face time with Steve Jobs. *Time*, April 12: 40-43.

Grossman, Lev. 2010. Launch Pad. It's here. It's hot. But what on earth is the iPad for? *Time*, April 12: 37-40.

Jeroslovsky, Rich. 2010. The iPad isn't just fun and games. Bloomberg Businessweek, April 12: 18-20.

Kaplan, David. 2010. Apps: Hot Course on Campus. Fortune, May 24: 22.

Eastman Kodak's Strategy for Innovating Business Model:
From Leadership in Photo-Film Technology Leadership to Implementing Digital Imaging Innovations

Dr. R. RAY GEHANI

Institute for Innovation and Technology Leadership (IITL)
Akron, Ohio.

Disclaimer:

This draft case-in-progress is meant strictly for classroom discussion and learning. It must not be considered as a comment on the company's strategic decisions or actions.

In the late Fall of 2010, **CEO Antonio Perez** looked at the changing colors of tree tops from his office in the Kodak Tower adjoining downtown Rochester in Upstate New York. He was thinking about Kodak's performance under his leadership for the past five years. He was happy about the positive cash flow generated from operations during the Third Quarter of 2009[1]. Losing less money than expected pleased Wall Street and boosted Kodak stock price up nearly 15% to $4.58. But, Kodak had reported loss in 10 out of its last 18 quarters under his leadership. He was worried about the low return on equity for the past five years as per Kodak's 2009 Annual Report (Exhibit – 1). In December 2009, Kodak's 5-Year Cumulative returns, for a $100 investment in December 2004, had fallen down to $14.5. Kodak's stock price for the second half of 2010 was still languishing between $3 and $5 (Exhibit – 2). What gifts would Santa Claus bring to him and Eastman Kodak for the upcoming 2010 Holiday season?

Perez vividly remembered that Spring day, less than 5 years ago, when Kodak's shareholders assembling for their 2005 Annual Meeting in Rochester on May 11 got the shocking news that their **Chief Executive Officer Daniel Crap,** championing digital technology strategy, was suddenly stepping down by the end of May, less than 20 days later. Carp would no more stay as the Chairman after the end of 2005 [2]. Perez, who was President then, was hurriedly promoted and installed in place of Carp. Carp had been with the company for more than 35 years. He had led Kodak's digital imaging strategy since January 2000. Carp was departing far before he was expected to leave. The Kodak Board of Directors and shareholders were not satisfied with the financial performance outcomes under his leadership.

SHOCKING STRATEGIC LEADERSHIP SHIFT

This change in strategic leadership at Kodak was rather abrupt for any major company. But it was particularly shocking for Kodak that made changes more calmly and gradually. In late April 2005, Kodak was humiliated by its bond rating drastically downgraded to junk by **Standard and Poor and Moody's Investor Service**. Kodak had missed its earnings for 2005Q1, and announced a quarterly loss of $142 million[3]. In addition, Carp had borrowed additional $1.4 billion debt to pay for new digital acquisitions. By early May in 2005, Kodak stock crashed 30% to $25-26, below its 52-week high of $34 (See Exhibit – 3, Kodak Stock Price During CEO Carp Era). Kodak's stock price was nowhere in the vicinity of $94 just a few years earlier in 1997 (See Exhibit – 4, Kodak Stock Price During CEO George Fisher).

In 2003, Carp had forecasted that the film industry in the U.S. would decline by 10% a year, and decline by 6% worldwide[4]. He then formulated the digital strategy to let the declining photographic film business die, while diverting the company's financial and manpower resources to develop, commercialize and grow the fast emerging digital imaging innovations. To please the angry shareholders, Carp had recently laid off 11,000 workers, and he had formulated new plans to fire another 15,000 Kodak workers by 2007. He had also tried to cut costs on dividend (See Exhibit – 5 for Dividend History).

Kodak shareholders were not happy because Carp had moved too slowly to transition the 110+ year old pioneer of photography to digital imaging technology.   Since 2005, the film industry's revenues were disappearing three times faster than anticipated - by 30% a year in the United States, and by 20% globally. Kodak's $8.2 billion revenues from traditional businesses, including photographic film, were estimated to drop by 17% for the year. Kodak's $5.3 billion digital business earned meager $46 million in operating profits for the preceding year.

Kodak needed a new digital leader to guide Kodak's transformation. And, Perez seemed to be the chosen answer.

CEO ANTONIO M. PEREZ ERA (2005 – TO DATE)

On June 1, 2005, Carp was replaced swiftly with Antonio Perez, 59, who had joined Kodak in April 2003 as president and Chief Operating Officer. Perez was often considered by most Kodak insiders and outsiders as the heir apparent of Carp. At the computer and printer giant **Hewlett-Packard (HP),** first in Europe and then in the United States, Perez spent 25 years managing the rapid growth of printer business to cross $10 billion mark. Perhaps he left HP due to differences with then **CEO Carleton S. Fiorina**. The stock market cheered the new appointment of Perez at Kodak, and Kodak stock rallied back 4% to $27 [5].

When Perez took over as CEO, he assembled his top 7 executives to the spacious well-paneled 2nd Floor Conference room in Kodak Tower. He told them, "*You have to burn the boats*" – just like the famous **Spanish conquistador Herman Cortez** when he discovered Latin America[6]. In other words, there was no going back to Kodak's old slow ways *of* changing after extensive protracted analysis. Perez also stressed that product innovation was not sufficient, and Kodak would not try to do internally all the innovating necessary from manufacturing to selling and servicing. Perez was committed to transforming Kodak by innovating its business model – just like Steve Jobs did at Apple. Perez wanted to lead Kodak away from relying on fast commoditizing low profit-margin products to higher value-added innovative services. Within 5 years, Perez replaced all but 3 of the 20 original senior-level executives. He replaced most of the former chemical-based executives with executives having digital imaging experience (See Exhibit - 6).

Antonio M. Perez was born in the coastal town of Vigo, Spain[7]. There his father owned a wholesale fish business. Antonio helped his father's business, but he refused to take over the fish business. He studied electrical engineering at Madrid University, and then joined HP in Madrid.

Over the years at HP, Perez developed a management style of spotting new market opportunities, taking risks, and developing a strong focus on operations. He was often intense about getting the job done quickly as well as doing it right. At HP, Perez was obsessed with relentlessly innovating a new product category every 2 years. He motivated his troops to innovate new creative uses for inkjet heads. First they innovated color inkjets, followed by large format printers, all-in-one printers, and photo printers.

When Perez joined Kodak he formulated a 4-year strategic plan for transforming the company's digital business. He quickly speeded up launches of Kodak's digital new-products. As he took over as Kodak's CEO in May 2005 he promised that he would increase digital operating earnings by 4 times to more than $275 million in 2005-06 – growing it faster than the falling profits from film. He based this phenomenal growth on a shift from low margin digital cameras to printing of digital images. When taking over as CEO, Perez realized that Eastman Kodak was still heavily dependent on revenues and profits from the traditional film businesses. He noted that Kodak had $3 billion in film-related assets that could not be dis-assembled easily.

Perez also noted in 2003 that Kodak was desperately seeking a new vision. It was already investing in digital technology, and it had a strong brand image and substantial intellectual property[8]. Perez helped Kodak eliminate businesses that were not likely to be number 1 or 2. After much blood-bath on the cutting floor and much strategy searching, Kodak decided to keep analog film business, as long as there were consumers willing to buy film. In addition, Kodak kept consumer digital imaging, commercial printing and health care.

Perez knew that he had to implement his digital technology strategy faster and more productively than his predecessor Daniel Crap.

CEO CARP'S STRATEGIC RESPONSE TO
DISRUPTIVE DIGITAL TECHNOLOGY INNOVATIONS

In 2003, Daniel Carp, Chairman and CEO of **Eastman Kodak** since January 2000, was getting highly concerned about the sharp erosion of the pioneering photo company's U.S. and world-wide silver halide photographic film business. Photographic films had been the company's core business since 1880. Many experts had projected a double-digit fall in photographic film sales in the next three-year period. There was a rapid rise in the adoption of digital imaging technology based cameras by many photographers in the U.S. and in most other parts of the world.

Carp set himself, *"...a goal of becoming a $20 billion company by 2010, reflecting a healthy mix of businesses that are commercial and consumer, traditional and digital, new and established – and all of them taking advantage of the opportunities available in the $385 billion info-imaging market."*

In September 2003, Carp announced a strategic investment of $3 billion in Kodak's various consumer, health, and commercial digital-related businesses. He projected this would increase Kodak's annual sales revenue by $3 billion in 3 years, from $13 billion in 2003 to $16 billion in 2006. To save this amount he proposed to drastically cut Kodak's 2002 dividend of $1.80 per share down to $0.50 a share for the next year (See Exhibit – 5).

To focus on the digital imaging consumers, Carp also restructured one more time Kodak's all consumer-related businesses into a new "Digital and Film Imaging Systems" group. This was one of the five Strategic Product and Service Groups. Other four groups were: Health Imaging Group, Commercial Imaging Group, Commercial Printing Group, and Display Group.

Stakeholders' Outrage

Many Kodak employees and external stakeholders considered Carp's new plan as just another temporary "Slogan of the Month." Since the 1980s, and under the leadership of **previous CEO George Fisher**, the company had gone through frequent restructurings. But, the sales kept declining from the high of $19 billion in 1991 down to $13 billion in 2004.

Carp's 2003 announcement had a sharp downward impact on the U.S. stock market's perception of making equity investments in Kodak. The Kodak stock price, with lower expected dividend, crashed by 14% See Exhibit – 5, for Dividend History. Investors and the external analysts seriously doubted the CEO's promised results.

Top management executives from rival companies acknowledged that Eastman Kodak had great photography technology and consumer marketing capabilities. But they doubted that Kodak management had the ability to focus and commercialize these capabilities into tangible market performance. Eastman Kodak also had to reconsider and rely less on its entrenched position in silver-halide chemical technology, and acquire newer capabilities in consumer electronics and digital imaging. Kodak must reconsider breaking the very foundation stones on which it was built more than a century ago by founder George Eastman.

INNOVATIVE LEGACY OF
FOUNDER GEORGE EASTMAN (1884 -1924)

George Eastman (1854-1932), while growing up in Rochester, Upstate New York, got interested in photography as a hobby. He, however, hated carrying around bulky photo equipment and fragile photosensitive glass plates needed to take outdoor pictures, or to sit still for hours to take portraits indoors.

In 1880, while still working as an accountant, George Eastman, tinkered in his free time and innovated a more efficient and faster process for coating photosensitive silver halide on dry photographic plates. The glass plates were still heavy and bulky, and too fragile to carry around freely. George Eastman was not completely satisfied, and he was not yet done innovating photographic equipment. With W. H. Walker, Eastman pioneered the application of a flexible roll of photographic film. Together they founded **Eastman Dry Plate and Film Company in 1884**. Eastman chose the brand name Kodak, because it had the initials of his mother's name and it sounded like the click of a camera.

INNOVATIVE BIRTH OF BROWNIE

In 1888, Eastman introduced the first portable Kodak camera loaded with a roll of sensitized paper on a holder. After a few market trials, George Eastman launched a Kodak camera loaded with a flexible celluloid film enough to take 100 snapshots encased in a box. This portable box had a lens and a film-forwarding mechanism. This camera was priced affordably at $25.

The consumer who bought the camera, shot all the pictures, and then brought it back to a Kodak licensed store to process the exposed photographic film and to develop the positive prints. Eastman's marketing slogan was, "*You press the button, we do the rest.*" For another $10, Kodak loaded the camera with another roll of film.

In 1900, George Eastman simplified the cameras and launched it as Brownie Camera.

George Eastman's skillful business and marketing practices turned Kodak cameras and photographic picture taking into common household activity. He also shifted the world's center of photography from France, where photography was invented, to the United States. Eastman continually innovated his photographic film technology and launched a series of new user-friendly cameras in the market. He shifted the focus of photography from the professional photographers to the amateur family men and women, easily capturing their memorable "*Kodak Moments.*"

George Eastman retired from day-to-day management in 1925. In March 1932, George Eastman shot himself. In his suicide note, he simply said: "*My work is done. Why wait?*"

Kodak continued the tradition of innovation laid firmly by George Eastman. See Exhibit – 8 for the list of strategic leaders since Kodak's inception. The sales of Eastman Kodak crossed $1 billion in 1962 under CEO and President William S. Vaughn. In the mid-1970s, Eastman Kodak dominated the photography market in the U.S. with 90% of the film sales and 85% of the camera sales under CEO Colby Chandler. The sales crossed $10 billion by the early 1980s, with annual income of $923 million. Kodak's sales growth, however, started declining as its Japanese rival; Fuji Photo Film Company started catching up technologically.

MERGERS, TAKEOVERS AND NEGLECTING A COMPANY'S CORE TECHNOLOGY

During the roaring growth of the 1980s, a merger mania and multiple serious takeover threats for Kodak came from **T. Boone Pickens Jr. of GAF, Ivan Boesky** and others. The senior executives at Kodak under **CEO and Chairman Colby Chandler** became very busy in leveraged external acquisitions of unrelated businesses. The core photography technology took a back seat.

Kodak's strategic leaders tried to diversify and grow with external acquisitions. Notable among these were the expensive acquisitions of

Sterling Pharmaceuticals in 1988, and **Atex**, a newspaper software supplier. With these acquisitions, Kodak's long-term debt skyrocketed to $7 billion, with a high annual debt-servicing burden. The projected growth in sales, however, did not materialize, as Eastman Kodak did not possess the core-capabilities needed in these unrelated technological areas. The acquired unrelated businesses proved highly unprofitable over time.

TECHNOLOGICAL DISRUPTIONS IN IMAGING

DISRUPTIVE ENTRY OF SONY'S DIGITAL IMAGING TECHNOLOGY

While Kodak's top management was busy getting excited about unrelated businesses such as pharmaceuticals and newspapers, the photography industry saw a fast emerging threat of substitute from silicon based digital imaging technology. This substitute technology innovation would threaten the hefty profits of Kodak in the dominant silver halide photographic film business. On **August 24, 1981 Sony** launched its **digital camera Mavica**, that captured and stored images in a computer chip. This shook Kodak's highly profitable world based on selling and processing photographic film.

This digital innovation eliminated the need for the photographing consumer to go to a photo studio to develop the exposed negative photo film and print photographs. The digital image had the advantage that it could be stored, manipulated (enlarged and shrunk), and transmitted over distance, more conveniently than the photographs.

Initially, the available digital camera was very expensive, and **Mavica digital camera** was *not* highly successful in consumer market. The quality resolution of the digital images was much worse than the quality resolution of a chemical film-based photograph. But the potential of digital camera seemed enormous.

Under intense pressure from the Wall Street, Kodak rushed to please investors and downsize, rather than invest needed resources to innovate in the emerging digital technology.

KODAK'S INADEQUATE DISK-FILM TEHNOLOGY RESPONSE

To show to the consumers that the photographic giant was a leader in its photographic field, in 1982, Kodak launched a disk-film camera. The miniaturized photographic film was loaded on a "View

© 2010 Dr. R. RAY GEHANI

Master" like disc. Emerging electronics technology was applied to make the manufacturing process more automatic. Kodak hoped that by reducing the size of the negative film, the company would increase its productivity and profit margins for films.

Due to the smaller size of the negative disk film, the printed photographs came out grainy. Eastman Kodak invested large amounts of funds to single-handedly do the needed research and then develop the new photographic product standard alone. But, Kodak customers were not satisfied or delighted by the disk-film camera. Industry experts felt that Kodak's disk-camera was launched before the disk film technology was fully developed[9]. Customers complained that it produced grainy pictures, and the new disc camera technology failed to get anyone excited. In the meantime optimistic Kodak leaders kept hiring thousands of workers for this new disk-camera program.

In 1988, after investing enormous resources, Kodak reluctantly decided to discontinue the manufacture, marketing, and processing of the disk-film cameras and films. Disk-film camera was an inadequate response offered at the wrong time in the shifting photography market.

FUJI PHOTO'S RIVALRY

While the strategic leaders at Eastman Kodak were investing most of their time and efforts at managing the unrelated diversification acquisitions and making profit in these new technological and market areas, Kodak's primary photographic rival, Fuji Photo Film of Japan steadily increased its film market share in the United States from nothing to 12%.

Single-Use Camera Innovation

The strategic leaders at **Fuji Photo** focused their efforts on improving and innovating in their core photographic film and camera business. **Fuji Photo** saw a large market potential for tourists and travelers not carrying their expensive cameras, for the fear of losing them, and yet wanting to capture the photographs of their sights or events. For example, when the potential photo consumers were at festivals and at weddings. Fuji Photo developed and launched a single-use disposable camera for such consumers.

The 24- or 36-exposure film was encased in a cardboard camera with an economical optical engine. The consumers shot their pictures and then brought back the camera to their photographic studio for processing and developing of photo prints. The core "optical engine" in the single-use camera was reconditioned and reused approximately 10 times, until damaged. Without incurring much additional costs, and priced at 2-3 times the price of a roll of film, Fuji Photo innovated new customers, new applications of photo cameras, and significantly increased its profit margin per roll of film. The single-use cameras also increased the visibility of Fuji Photo in the United States and world markets.

Gradually, many other generic store brands of films and cameras also emerged. These captured 15% of the U.S. market by 1992. This pushed the market share of Eastman Kodak down to about 70%. At this time, Kodak commanded annual revenues of US$20 billion, with $994 million income.

KODAK'S FLING SINGLE-USE CAMERA

Kodak's bureaucratic structure was somewhat late in responding to the auto-focus camera technology coming from Japan. Kodak thought of launching its single-use 35 mm camera, **Fling**, in 1987. The product concept was an easy-to-use camera to take pictures in daylight, as good as common auto-focus and point-and-shoot cameras. In 1989, Kodak launched **Stretch 35** to take panoramic pictures of landscapes, 3.5 inches by 10 inches. **Weekend 35** was a waterproof camera for taking pictures while scuba diving, or at beach, or snow skiing. This required developing only a few additional parts. Within 8 months, these 3 camera products went from concept to production. The new cameras were shipped to distribution centers and targeted retail outlets. To achieve this, Kodak used advanced manufacturing technologies such as computer-aided design, design for assembly, just-in-time inventory, statistical process control, and more.

The name *Fling* infuriated environmentalists who called it disposable camera. Initially the camera casing was welded tight so that consumers could not reload their cameras with Kodak's competing film. This posed difficulty for Kodak contractors trying to recycle the core photo engine of this camera.

The sales of this camera grew at 50% a year, and continued at this rate for the next 5 years. This also implied that a large number of the "welded" cameras found their way into landfills. Cameras had to be redesigned so that these cameras could be recycled more easily. A recycling process was developed for the single-use camera and suggested to Kodak's top management. The management did not approve it. As the public outcry against Kodak's "disposable" camera built up, the management relented. The parts were redesigned so that these could be dropped and snap-fitted for easy unloading and reloading at a Kodak facility, using some specific tools and fixtures. Designers and injection mold makers were networked and integrated together.

Next product launched was **FunSaver Flash** camera. It required some electronics components and an alkaline battery. A counter was included to keep track of the number of times the electronic components were reused. Soon thereafter, **Telephoto 35** was developed with a zoom 2.4 times the magnitude of the lens in other cameras, for use in sports arenas. The camera could take pictures in sunlight and floodlight.

After a customer took all the pictures with a single-use camera, it was taken to a photo finisher. Photo finisher extracted the exposed film and produced the prints for the customer. Kodak bought the empty single use camera cases from the photo finisher, who shipped these to Kodak's recycling center in Rochester, New York. There physically- and mentally-disabled workers removed and sorted the color coded electronic and optical parts. Some parts were tested and reused. Rejected parts were screened for metal, and then ground and remolded for reuse 10 times in single-use cameras. Approximately 86% of camera's material was reused in single-use cameras. In the remanufactured cameras a fresh unexposed film was loaded, to be resold to Kodak customers.

In 1990, more than one million cameras were recycled. This jumped to 2.9 million cameras in 1991. Each million recycled cameras represented recycling of 140,000 pounds of materials. Kodak introduced similar recycling programs in Canada, Europe, and Japan.

POLAROID LAW SUIT

In the midst of this radical transformation in the industry, another ongoing crisis came to an unfavorable conclusion. Kodak got into a conflict with instant Polaroid technology. The courts fined Kodak $900 million for violating Polaroid's instant photography patents.

KODAK'S DIGITAL WHITE KNIGHT: ARRIVAL OF OUTSIDER DR. GEORGE FISHER (1993 – 1999)

Late in 1993, Kodak's Board of Directors hurriedly edged out **CEO Kay Whitmore** for not laying off enough workers fast. In place of the chemical engineer, the Board ushered in the **Motorola Chief Executive George M. C. Fisher**, a mathematician, with a $5 million signing bonus and a multi-million dollar compensation package. Fisher brought with him experience in the consumer electronics businesses at Motorola to the primarily chemical company Kodak.

The Wall Street loved Fisher's announcement, and the Kodak stock price jumped overnight by $3 a share (See Exhibit – 4 for Share Price History in Fisher Era). Many Kodak employees, afraid of being included in the next 10,000-job cut, were appalled. Others cheered, hopeful that George Fisher, like Kodak Founder George Eastman 100 years earlier, would return Kodak to its former profit-rich glory.

DIVESTING UNRELATED BUSINESSES AT BARGAIN

Kodak was still bleeding heavily from servicing its staggering high long-term debt of $7.8 billion. To improve the debt and save the interest payout, Fisher quickly divested Kodak's non-core unrelated businesses such as **Sterling Winthrop pharmaceutical business, L&F household product business** etc. at bargain prices. This reduced the company's multi-billion dollar long-term debt substantially by $1.6 billion.

OPENING GLOBAL MARKETS

Dr. Fisher, however, also brought with him his animosity with the Japanese rivals from his Motorola years. He launched a major campaign for filing cases in the **World Trade Organization,** accusing the Japanese government for protecting the Japanese markets from Kodak's penetration. Most of these cases were rejected after many years of deliberations.

In addition, Fisher saw great market opportunities in the emerging markets of India and China (a Fuji photo stronghold). Kodak signed a deal with a Chinese distributor to increase its foothold there. Kodak had been historically active in selling its film stock to India's booming Bollywood industry.

HYBRID ADVANTIX CAMERA TECHNOLOGY:
A PIONEER LEADER TURNS INTO A FOLLOWER

In the traditional photographic film markets, Kodak followed Fuji Photo by launching its own single-use cameras (first named disposable cameras, causing some public criticism). Seeing a rapid growth in this business segment, Kodak too launched more differentiated single-use cameras, such as its panoramic, underwater, and telephoto versions.

Kodak also launched a low-end Funtime photo film, after much internal resistance for years.

COLLABORATIVELY INNOVATING
HYBRID PHOTO-DIGITAL PHOTOGRAPHY

In the 1990s, instead of developing a full-fledged large product line of digital cameras, Kodak allocated more resources for developing "Advanced Photo System (APS)," and Advantix cameras. **In 1995, Advantix used a new smaller 25 mm silver-halide photographic film format. The smarter camera also used some electronics to expose/define photographs in 3 formats: standard, high definition format, and panoramic.**

Recalling its past mishap of single-handedly developing disk-film camera technology, to develop the **Advantix photographic standard**, Kodak used an unprecedented business strategy – collaboratively innovating with its rival, **Fuji Photo** and other Japanese camera makers, **Canon, Nikon, and Minolta**. To promote a new joint photographic technology standard, Kodak and the co-developers of new technology also licensed their APS innovations to 40 other companies to develop APS related products and services[10].

Why did Kodak collaborate its technological innovations with its potential rivals to develop APS? Kodak, Fuji Photo, and the leading photographic camera makers, relying heavily on their revenues from their photographic film based businesses quickly realized that they faced a far bigger threat from digital imaging technology than they did from one another. They had to revitalize the photo-taking habit of their customers. Some of their customers were still having difficulty loading photographic films in their cameras. Most customers wanted easier film loading, and multiple photo formats. They also wanted more compact, user-friendly, and better picture-taking cameras. Kodak and its collaborators knew that one company alone could not afford to develop a new photography format to revitalize the world-wide photography market.

In April 1991, the Kodak management instructed the general manager of its new Advanced Photo System business to form a cross-functional technology development team by drawing multi-skilled members from different functional disciplines. These included camera design groups, film manufacturing, market research, and other departments. Few months later, Kodak signed a joint technology development agreement with **Fuji, Canon, Minolta, and Nikon**, a group called G-5[11].

The goal of the G-5 group was to develop a new photographic technology platform standard, from film making, to photo capturing, and photo-finishing. The patents already obtained by G-5 collaborators were pooled and swapped with one another. For the next 5 years, the G-5 collaborators organized alternate meetings with their lawyers in Japan and US, to jointly develop the needed new product and process innovations for the new photographic standard.

The **Advanced Photo System (APS)** was rolled out globally in February 1996. Kodak promoted its APS products under the Advantix brand, and launched "**Take Pictures Further**" slogan. Kodak's researchers and technicians who co-owned the patents for the digital magnetic components incorporated in the APS cameras received the "Inventor of the Year" award from the Intellectual Property Owners Association[12].

By 1997, Kodak had invested $500 million in developing Advantix film and camera technology. But, it did not have enough photo finishers to help customers switch to processing Advantix photo prints, and did not have enough cameras to supply to its dealers. In addition, with increasing availability of digital imaging cameras, only a few camera users adopted the film-based Advantix cameras.

STALLING DIGITAL IMAGING TECHNOLOGY

By the end of 1994, Kodak's 45% revenue and 75% profit still came from its photographic film business. Dr. Fisher seemed afraid to disturb that cash cow.

For the digital imaging technology, Dr. Fisher formed the **Digital and Applied Imaging division**, to consolidate the different efforts in this area scattered around the different parts of Kodak. He noted that digital imaging involved five value-adding links: (1) image capturing, (2) image processing, (3) image manipulation, (4) delivery output, and (5) storage and communication (over long distances). Whereas consumers looked for a full service provider, Kodak had technological capabilities only in some of these five areas. To develop Kodak's complete digital imaging portfolio, Dr. Fisher tried to fill in the gaps by making alliances with others, such as **Hewlett Packard, IBM, Kinko, Microsoft, Sprint** and more.

Dr. Fisher also announced that he was going to end management-by-Wall Street, and he independently decided to stress both the photographic film business as well as the digital imaging business. Kodak's stock price steadily rose under Dr. Fisher to **over $94 in February 1997** (See Exhibit - 4 for Stock Price History in CEO Fisher Era).

But then Kodak's slide started again. Within a month of the peak, the Kodak stock price slid to $79 on March 21, 1997.

In May 1997, Dr. Fisher admitted that the US companies had become too callous to their workforce. The drastic downsizing had frightened and disheartened to many employees. He noted, *"what we've done in our workplace to our employees deserves very special attention -- otherwise I think we've got an Achilles' heel."*

HUMAN COSTS FOR UNDERMINING CORE TECHNOLOGY

But, the CEO George Fisher's opinion and actions changed rapidly thereafter.

The summer of 1997 brought a stiff competition from rival Fuji. Kodak decided to overlook the competitive threat. Soon thereafter, Kodak lost its profitable **Wal-Mart** account, and the **Advanced Photo System**, the radical new photo system, did not help in reviving the sliding film revenues. Fuji gained its market share in the U.S. to a significantly higher level of 20%.

In October 1997, George Fisher announced that he planned to prune middle and senior management ranks by getting rid of **one out of every five managerial positions**, or 200 managers. The **Financial Times** reported that the company's return to downsizing on massive scale indicated its difficulty of breaking away from relying on constant job cuts to fix its bottom line.

On November 11, 1997, the Kodak stock opened at only $66, and it was falling by noon to $61 when Dr. George Fisher announced that he would shed about 10,000 jobs worldwide to reduce $1 billion in expenses. Kodak stock price recovered a little but remained in low $60s. One week before Christmas on December 18, when Kodak stock price opened at $56 ½, Dr. Fisher increased his job cuts at Kodak to 19,900 (See Exhibit – 4 for Stock Price History in Fisher Era). This managed to spike up the Kodak's stock price to $59 ½. But, it slid down to $58 before the stock market closed for the day.

Many Kodak workers, who were still in shock from the November announcement of 10,000 job-cuts, were dazed by the additional 6,600 job cuts informed to them in an electronic memo for town meetings. When an employee asked when this (job-cutting program) was going to stop, the management response was that "it's not going to stop...It depends on business needs." Some workers felt that the new job cuts were motivated and calculated to play to Wall Street expectations because the stock price did not react favorably enough the first time. Dr. Fisher added, **"Maybe Wall Street is finally appeased. There's enough blood in the water from all the sharks."** Some felt that the workers felt kind of resigned, and that there was nothing they could do to help the company or secure their jobs.

THE WILD FRONTIER OF DIGITAL CAMERA TECHNOLOGY

In 1995, Kodak introduced its first digital camera (**DC-40**) in market for $1,000. This along with its successor **DC-25 digital camera** failed to impress Kodak's picture-taking customers. Kodak's losses continued. Kodak promoted digital camera technology in kiosk market segments, installing 13,000 kiosks. Kodak's rivals focused on the digital home consumers, which Kodak tried to avoid for the fear of cannibalizing Kodak's highly lucrative silver halide film market. Kodak kept installing more kiosks, which incurred millions more in investments.

On August 1, 1997, Eastman Kodak launched **DC-20 digital camera kit** into the cyber-market, making it available over the Internet. This was targeted for computer savvy customers who wanted to include their pictures in their emails and web pages. The DC20 Web Camera promotion kit was priced at US$ 219, which included a US$ 199 DC20 camera with 200,000 pixels bundled with a $49 flash, special software, a camera bag, and a copy of *Fun With Digital Photography*.

In the meantime, **Fuji Photo** launched a price war for photographic films, so that in 1997 Kodak's sales fell to US $14.7 billion, Kodak's earnings were meager US$5 million. Dr. Fisher's magic touch was wearing out.

Dr. Fisher's solution to Kodak's poor performance was to save $1 billion by 1999 by cutting another 20,000 jobs including 200 executives.

To enter faster in digital imaging technology, Kodak invested in buying 51% of online photo-finishing film, **Picture Vision**, and merged its **PhotoNet** with its own **Kodak Picture Network**. Kodak's market share in digital imaging increased to 20%, though digital business still made losses. However, on the total sales of $13 billion in 1999, Kodak's earnings had increased to US$1.4 billion.

The year 1999, and the march towards a new millennium marked the sale of 2 million digital cameras and the launch of 2 mega-pixel digital cameras. Some analysts predicted that the sales growth of photo films would level to 1% till 2003, and negative thereafter. Kodak disagreed and predicted that the photographic film sales would continue to increase annually by 5%, and Kodak would continue to rely heavily on this film business producing 80% of its revenue. Actual film sales grew by 2% a year. Kodak's sales in 1999 grew slightly over 1998 to $14 billion, while the earnings remained level at US$1.4 billion.

To everyone's surprise, Chairman and **CEO George Fisher retired in January 2000, one year before his contracted time**. Insider **Daniel** carp was promoted to be the next CEO to help enhance Kodak's digital imaging businesses. By 1999, Kodak had invested more than $5 billion in digital imaging technology, with revenues of only $20 million in 1999.

THE DIGITAL STRATEGY LEADERSHIP
OF CEO DANIEL CARP (2000 – 2005)

CEO Carp expected the digital imaging business in consumer, professional, and health care areas to grow rapidly. He focused Kodak's resources on cameras (image capture), online photo manipulation services, and image output devices such as inkjet printers, kiosks, inks, and paper. He took the charge for turning Kodak into a leader in digital cameras.

The U.S. economy slowed down in 2001, After the 9/11 terrorist attack. Kodak saw 5% decline in sales of photographic film business. Kodak leaders attributed the declining film sales to the September 11 attacks. The overall sales were US$ 13,234 million with a meager net income of only US$ 76 million. To save face, Kodak announced 7,500 job cuts and some more organizational restructuring to make some strategic product groups more autonomous and more accountable for their performance.

Premium high-end film, **MaxHQ**, with maximum versatility, was introduced. **Perfect Touch Processing** service technology applied special software to scan film negatives, for better quality picture. This increased Kodak's photo-finishing volumes by greater than 20%.

Whereas, Kodak's annual sales for 2001 declined, the sales of digital cameras increased to 9 million cameras, the price of digital camera steadily came down from $460 in 2000 to $300 in 2002. Kodak extended its digital imaging product offerings to entertainment imaging and professional imaging segments as well.

Kodak's digital cameras sales of $400 million resulted in a loss of $75 million. But Carp continued to invest on digital cameras. Kodak spent enormous amounts of time, energy and money on studying customers' behavior with the new digital imaging. The market researchers discovered that many women consumers loved taking digital pictures. But, they were highly frustrated in moving their digital pictures to their personal computers.[13] Doing so seemed too hard and cumbersome to do. Kodak's market researchers had identified a huge unmet market need. Kodak's product innovation team took over and launched a series of cameras that easily allowed exchanging photos with friends and family members.

Thus, in 2001, **EasyShare** digital camera was launched. This camera had a docking station that recharged the cameras and with one click transferred it's images to a personal computer. Customer loved this user-friendly camera and docking station, and Kodak dreamed of selling a lot of photographic paper.

In the case of online photo-finishing business, Carp invested resources to increase online repository images in **PhotoNet** for retailers and consumers. Print@Kodak website was launched selling services to **Ememories, MyFamily.com, PhotoPoint, Snapfish** and other web retailers. Kodak had 15% share of $ 425 million web-based printing market. Kodak led with 40% share of inkjet photo-quality paper. **Ofoto Inc.**, offering image storage, processing online, and private sharing/editing images, was acquired. Kiosks were increased to 24,000 in US and 35,000 worldwide.

EMERGING GLOBAL DIGITAL MARKETS

Expecting sluggish growth in the U.S. (See Exhibit – 7 for Geographic Distribution of Kodak's sales during CEO Carp Era), CEO Carp focused Kodak's investments in the emerging markets of China, India, and Russia. These emerging economies reported 25%, 8%, and 20% growth respectively. In China, Kodak invested $100 million to acquire 20% of China's largest color film maker **Lucky Film Corp**. They signed a 20-year agreement, with Kodak providing equipment upgrades, technical and training assistance. Kodak hoped this would keep **Fuji**

Photo from penetrating deeper into Chinese market, and projected that the low-end **Lucky film** consumers would migrate to higher end **Kodak MAX** versatility film, single-use cameras, and other Kodak film and digital products. Lucky, however, had 36% decline in its profits for 2003 due to decrease in tourism to China due to SARS scare and increase in the use of digital cameras.

In 2003, Kodak's revenue inched up slightly to US$13,317 million with US$ 238 million net income after taxes. Digital camera sales doubled, exceeding film sales, replacing reloadable cameras (excluding single-use cameras), and became profitable for the first time. The Digital imaging business contributed US$ 4 billion revenue.

CEO CARP'S DIGITAL TECHNOLOGY STRATEGY

The future seemed brighter for Kodak's digital camera sales, expecting to grow annually by 15%. The film sales, on the other hand, were expected to decline annually by 12%.

This is what prompted **CEO Daniel Carp** to invest $3 billion in digital imaging. He also announced more 8,000 job cuts, reducing Kodak's manpower to 62,000 by the end of 2003.

Kodak expanded its **EasyShare digital cameras** with 6 new models, costing from US$100 to US$500, all compatible with Kodak **EasyShare printer dock**.

Mobile Telephone Imaging Service

Kodak, in collaboration with **AT&T wireless, Cingular Wireless, and Nokia** launched www.kmobile.com service to help customers view, store, share, and organize their digital pictures by cameras or by mobile phones, for a $2.99 fee per month. By 2004, more than 97 million mobile phones with cameras were expected to be in use.

In collaboration with **Microsoft, Ofoto** members could use **Windows Media Center Edition 2004** to view and share their online photos on a TV set.

Photo-finishing

Kodak strengthened its leadership in photo-finishing paper for high speed digital mini-labs. Kodak expanded its kiosk family, and enabled digitization of 35 mm film. Mini-labs around the world were expanded.

CARP'S DIGITAL IMAGING RIVALS IN 2003

Unfortunately, between 1999 and 2003, due to a variety of external and internal contingencies, Kodak's sales of analog cameras kept falling steeply in Japan and Europe, and fell somewhat in the U.S. and other parts of the world (See Exhibit – 7 for geographic sales). Whereas the unit sales of digital cameras increased rapidly in the Americas, Europe, Japan, and the rest of the world, the profit margins were small due to intense competitive rivalry.

In 2003, digital camera sales crossed 50 million units worldwide, increasing annually by 15%. Digital imaging market in Europe, migrating from film, was increasing faster than the market in the US and Japan. Worldwide, **Sony** led the market with 18% share, followed by **Canon, Olympus, and Kodak** with 16%, 13% and 12% shares respectively.

1. FUJI FILM, JAPAN

Kodak's traditional rival in photographic films, and a rival in emerging digital imaging, **Fuji Film** had sales of US$20 billion and operating income of US$1.3 billion in 2003. These numbers represented, an annual increase of 4.4% in sales and a decrease of 5% in operating income. The company pursued a **"Hybrid Imaging" strategy**, integrating its traditional imaging technologies with the emerging electronics technology.

Fuji Film was organized into three business segments: (a) the Imaging Solutions, (b) the Information Solutions, and (c) the Document Solutions segment. In 2003, these contributed 28.9%, 33.2%, and 37.9% of total revenue, respectively.

The Imaging Solutions business segment included film, film cameras, digital cameras, lab equipment, color paper as well as chemicals and services for photo-finishing. Fuji Film boosted its sales of Imaging Solutions by innovating new digital camera models compatible with **PictBridge** standard for printing from home using **Fuji's Premium Plus Inkjet Photo Printer**. The users could upload and store their pictures online.

Fuji Film led the digital minilab market with its **Digital Minilab Frontier** series. Fuji Film was chasing Kodak in kiosk market, with its **Aladdin** and **PrintPix kiosks**.

Fuji Film's other business segments included the **Information Solutions Segment**, with medical imaging products, graphic arts systems products, LCD materials and recording media.

The third business segment, **Document Solutions segment**, operating **Fuji Xerox Co.** Ltd., as a consolidated subsidiary of Fuji and Xerox. It sold printers, copying machines, fax machines, and consumable supplies for office document service.

2. SONY CORPORATION, JAPAN

Sony, based in Tokyo, with sales of $22 billion in 2003, was the new leader in digital camera technology. Its electronics segment, sold US$14 billion worth digital cameras and Charge Coupled Devices (CCDs), **with $493 million operating income. Digital camera prices were declining, and yen was getting stronger against dollar. Sony focused for growth in** Audio and Video goods, **part of electronic business, especially in the high growth markets of digital camera, Plasma and Liquid Crystal displays.**

Mavica and Cyber-Shot digital cameras, with prices from $200-$1,000, were targeted to amateur and professional photographers. **Sony in collaboration with Fuji Photo, Canon, Olympus, Seiko Epson, and HP, innovated PictBridge** that directly connected digital camera to a printer using USB port. To facilitate photo printing without a personal computer, Sony innovated **Digital Photo Printer** with built-in photo editing.

3. CANON, JAPAN

Canon, also headquartered in Tokyo, had US$ 29 billion sales in 2003, with US$ 2.5 billion earnings. Sales had increased by 8.8% and the earnings had increased by 44%.

Canon leveraged its core technological capability in optical and image processing by innovating 6 new digital cameras in 2003-04. The company had gained 17% market share in worldwide digital camera market. Canon's camera business segment, including film cameras, digital still cameras, and video cameras, contributed $6 billion sales with 34.5% growth, and $1 billion operating profit with 79.7% annual growth. Canon cameras were compatible with **PictBridge technology standard**. Canon was leading in inkjet printer market with 25% worldwide share.

4. OLYMPUS, JAPAN

Olympus Optical Co., headquartered in Tokyo, Japan, had 2003 sales of $4.7 billion, with $520 million operating income. The sales had increased annually by 47.4% and the operating income increased annually by 6.8%. Olympus was organized into four businesses. In addition to medical systems group, the industrial systems group, and the life sciences group, its imaging systems group consisted of film cameras, digital cameras, recorders, and magneto-optical disk drives.

The imaging group sales had increased to $2 billion, with $152 million operating income. This was boosted by $1.4 billion from sales of 4.4 million digital cameras, representing an increase of 26.8%. Until the year before, digital cameras contributed losses. The situation changed when Olympus moved its manufacturing plants from Japan to China.

Olympus collaborated with **Ofoto**, Kodak's wholly owned subsidiary, to help digital camera users share, edit, and print their images. Olympus also offered **Pictorico Paper, and PicBridge** standard to allow users to print directly from their cameras.

5. NIKON, JAPAN

Nikon was organized into three business companies: **(a) the Imaging Company, (b) Precision Equipment Company, and (c) Instruments Company**. The Imaging Company was concerned with digital cameras and digital imaging equipment business. Nikon accounted for 24.6 million digital cameras or 11% share of the digital cameras originating in and from Japan. Integrated Circuit steppers and Liquid Crystal Device steppers were part of Precision Equipment Company. Nikon's Instruments Company developed, produced, and sold microscopes, inspection instruments, and measuring equipments.

Nikon's technology strategy included sustaining and growing its dominance in the digital **single lens reflex (SLR) cameras**. In the medium and popular-class consumer digital camera segments, Nikon hoped to boost its market share. Nikon also endeavored to expand its manufacturing in China to cut their costs.

6. HEWLETT- PACKARD (HP), USA

In Hewlett-Packard, headquartered in the Silicon Valley in California, the imaging and printing group contributed $21.2 billion in 2003, selling its digital cameras, printer hardware, scanners, all-in-one, and related supplies and accessories. Other business groups included the **Enterprise Systems Group**, providing IT infrastructure technologies, and the **Personal Systems Group**, including the desktop personal computers, notebooks, workstations, smart handheld devices, personal devices, and related services.

HP's technology strategy was for low cost leadership for its high-tech products executed by leveraging its large economies of scale, and economies of scope. Unlike Kodak's focus on kiosks, HP focused on products and services that facilitated home digital printing. **HP's Photosmart digital cameras** had memory card slots and printer docks for direct printing. HP continued to lead market in inkjet printers and supplies, laser printers and supplies, with significant profit margins.

CEO CARP'S SHRINKING STRATEGIC CHOICES

For most of its historical existence, Eastman Kodak relied on photographic film products for a majority of its revenues. In the early years of the 21st century, the global photography industry saw significant shifts because of disruptive innovations in digital imaging technology. Though Kodak's 2003 sales of digital cameras were meager US$ 75 million, these were increasing annually at a significant rate.

In 2004, worldwide sales of digital cameras were expected to be 54 million units, with 15% growth rate. Sales of photographic films, however, were expected to decrease by 2006 by 10%.

To speed up Kodak's development of digital camera technology, **CEO Carp** increased Kodak's investment in Japan's **Chinon Industries** from 59% to 89%. To please demanding shareholders, **CEO Carp** also announced a further 15,000-20,000 reduction in workforce, and one-third reduction in its manufacturing square footage. He projected that these efforts would save about $1 billion by 2007. Few industry experts were impressed. Kodak top management had often failed to focus, and deliver acceptable performance. Where was the pioneering spirit of Kodak's founder-innovator George Eastman? Finally, Kodak's impatient shareholders got frustrated with CEO Carp's promises but lack-luster financial performance. They wanted to handover the strategic responsibility to a seasoned outsider – such as HP veteran Antonio Perez.

CEO PEREZ RE-INNOVATING DIGITAL ECOSPHERE

As mentioned before, Antonio Perez, who had joined Eastman Kodak in 1993 as President, stepped into the digital shoes of Daniel Carp without much notice in June 2005.

DECLINING PHOTOGRAPHIC FILM USAGE

In 2008, the number of U.S. households owning film cameras declined to 46% from 55% in 2007, and 66% in 2006 (See Exhibit - 9). The households purchasing films dropped down to estimated 38%. Approximately 27% U.S. households processed photographic film, with an average of 3.4 rolls of film or one-time-use cameras. Typically, the households not owning a digital camera purchased and processed more photographic films.[14]

COMPETING AND SUPPORTING IMAGING TECHNOLOGIES

In November 2005 Kodak launched the first wireless **EasyShareOne digital camera ($599)**. This allowed uploading photos, getting high quality prints, and sending e-mails without any wires or cables. The high-resolution rotating LCD touch screen permitted editing 1500 images and e-mailing these using a public hotspot or a home network, without any computer. In addition, the camera allowed shooting 80 minutes of TVH quality video with built-in sound recording (www.kodak.com). The accompanying **EasyShare printer dock plus series 3** ($179) helped print multiple images in a variety of sizes. The **EasyShare Picture Viewer** ($99) stored 150 images on its 2.5" screen, and allowed 2x magnification for closer viewing.

RADICAL PRODUCT INNOVATIONS

In January 2006, at the Consumer Electronics Show in Las Vegas, Perez unveiled dual-lens digital **Kodak EasyShare v570**, a radical product innovation first of its kind[15]. He noted that most of the available digital cameras were like non-adapting dinosaurs. The product design of most digital cameras was same as that of silver halide photographic cameras, with the small exception of using a small piece of silicon in place of silver halide coating. These cameras did not evolve as fast as the rapidly changing ecosystem around these. They still used one light path with flash. Digital cameras could easily use more than one digital light sensors which could see in much darker light without any flash. Kodak EasyShare v570 did that.

Perez noted that Kodak was the pioneering film camera company announcing to the global digital industry that the traditional film camera design was wrong and unsuitable for digital imaging technology.

He also noted that the digital camera industry was growing at the phenomenal rate of 600-700 percent during the first five years of the 21st century. But, it was also highly fragmented with large number of rivals. Many of these rivals barely invested in research & development, and were likely to fall by the wayside as soon as the annual growth matures to single digits.

COLLABORATIVE DIGITAL INNOVATIONS

According to Perez, one way to speed up innovations in digital technology, and shift the prevailing rigid paradigm, was to innovate collaboratively with complimentary technological partners. The goal was to create a seamless value-adding image chain of image capture, transmission, storage and archiving, organization, and sharing across multiple consumer electronics devices.[16]

Unlike some of his early impressions, Perez believed that seemingly substituting camera phones can also be converted into great opportunities for Kodak. He entered into a 10-year strategic cross-licensing and marketing relationship with Motorola to integrate Kodak CMOS photo sensors into **Motorola** cellular phones, printer docks, online services, and retail kiosks. Together they would collaborate to develop other innovative mobile imaging products.

Kodak also announced its collaborative partnership with **PC-VoIP service Skype**, to integrate it with Kodak's EasyShare Gallery web site.[17]

INNOVATING IN DIGITAL IMAGING ECOSPHERE

In 2005, approximately 6 billion people scattered around the world snapped approx. 48 billion digital photos. But, most of these digital images languished in different crevices of our computers.

A. PEREZ'S RULES FOR NEW PRODUCT INNOVATIONS

Perez proposed the following 5 rules for developing new products in the digital ecosphere.

1. Consumers MUST have the full ownership of their digital images. They should be able to freely access their digital images anytime from anywhere.

2. "You push the button, we do the rest" must generate high quality images.

3. Easy sharing of images.

4. Easy and permanent archiving of images.

5. Provide truly portable images.

To promote this new digital image ecosphere, Perez proposed Kodak to leverage its century old brand, use large portfolio of intellectual property, and fill the needed gaps with cross-industry technological licenses.

He planned to focus on the following 3 game-changing rules to drive the digital market forward at a brisk pace.

A. Flawless imaging enabled by **Kodak's Perfect Touch** software,

B. Intelligent Content searching and auto-archiving using **Kodak's E-Finder technology**,

C. Semantic understanding achieved with **Kodak's E-Moment** that learns a consumer's preferences with every use. This helps simplify future tasks.

Perez conceded that Kodak was going through hard times, as many employees were losing their jobs. He believed in listening, and communicating a lot, while acting with honesty and generosity. People in hardships understood and appreciated Kodak's generosity and honesty.

B. INNOVATING BUSINESS MODEL

Gradually, CEO Perez became clearer in wanting to reinvent Kodak's core business model.[18] He wanted to make Kodak to do for the photo ecosphere what Steve Jobs at Apple did for music ecosphere: help millions of people to make their personal libraries of thousands of images. Perez hoped to commercialize new digital photo scanning and sharing services to target consumers, while raking in high returns.

Migrating from relying on product innovations to relying on service innovations required reinventing the architecture and the cultural DNA of Kodak. Kodak was always considered a global icon for product innovations. But, it became reluctant to accept disruptive digital imaging innovations. It was late to recognize emerging signs, slow to react, and it preferred to pursue less risky which proved to be wrong innovation trajectories.

CEO Perez dreamt and drove his executive leaders to replicate Apple's success of transforming from its dwindling Mac computer business to fast growing iPod and iTunes downloading services compatible with rival Windows PCs. Thus, Steve Jobs helped Apple switch from being a great innovator of computer products into a greater innovator of consumer experiences via its well-designed devices and user-friendly services. Downloading music accounted for more than 40% of Apple's revenues, and even higher percentage of its profits.

One of the critical challenges CEO Perez faced at bringing about such a transformation at Kodak was that he could not get many Kodak employees to come forward and openly disagree with him. Most Kodak employees were conditioned to look up to their domineering leaders.

IMPLEMENTING BUSINESS MODEL INNOVATION STRATEGY AT KODAK

C. INNOVATING DIGITAL SUPPLY-CHAIN

Kodak's business transformation from traditional photography to digital imaging
demanded a matching transformation of Kodak's supply-chain management. Innovating digital supply-chain management at Kodak was guided by increasing pressures for providing high value-adding, high

visibility, and high velocity. Digital product margins tend to be low, while the customer expectations are steadily increasing.[19]

Digital imaging business demanded very different inputs and outputs than those required by silver halide photography business. In general, the digital supply chain must be faster and it was expanding global.

Kodak offered a variety of digital products. These ranged from technology-intensive computer radiography equipment for trauma centers in hospitals to user-friendly Photo Maker kiosks installed in retail stores like Walgreen and CVS. These required digital parts such as optical sensors and lenses, circuit boards, central processing units (CPUs), LED monitors. Many of these digital parts had high prices AND short life cycles. These high-tech digital parts became obsolete fast.

DIGITAL PRODUCT LIFE CYCLE AND SUPPLY-CHAIN

Kodak's digital supply-chain added new paradoxical challenges in addition to the pressures faced by the company's traditional supply-chain. Whereas the inventory levels of digital parts must be minimized to reduce the working capital requirements and parts obsolescence, high customer service levels must be maintained which demand more digital parts in stock. This paradox demanded careful optimization of **value, visibility, and velocity** over the life cycle of each digital product. In the introductory stage of a new digital product, demand tends to be uncertain, and the digital components may vary. In this stage, high supply-chain velocity is achieved by using few parts. On the other hand, the maturity stage of a digital product demands high efficiency and low distribution costs. In the decline stage of a digital product, supply-chain visibility helps economize product support costs.

Addressing these paradoxical challenges demanded radically increasing the levels of engagement by Kodak field engineers as well as the supply-chain and logistics planners. In the past, 50% inventory of digital parts was maintained by the central warehouse in Rochester, New York, and 50% inventory was maintained by the different field engineers. Repairable digital parts had to be returned to the central Rochester warehouse. Innovating digital supply-chain required classifying the different digital parts using A-B-C analysis based on the total annual value of different parts. This analysis helped discover that expensive parts costing over $700 accounted for only 5% of usage.[20] Instead of maintaining inventories of expensive parts with the field engineers, these higher priced parts were supplied as needed from the central warehouse. The ratio of the inventory of digital parts held at central warehouse was increased from 50% to 70%. Some parts of managing the innovated digital supply-chain were outsourced to third-party logistics (3PL) providers such as **UPS Supply Chain Solutions** and **Baxter Planning Systems**. These service providers helped position more than **60 Forward Stock Locations (FSLs)**, and develop the supply-chain metrics shown in Exhibit - 10).

A highly competent supply-chain manager was selected with good technical and communication skills. Most field engineers recognized the potential benefits of transforming a stationary inventory model into a dynamic inventory model, and they welcomed the changes in their digital supply-chains. Promising results were achieved with the use of FSL. Some highlights are listed in Exhibit – 10.

MANAGING COMPETING AND SUPPORTING IMAGING TECHNOLOGIES

D. DIFFUSION OF DIGITAL PHOTO-FRAME OWNERSHIP

As the majority of U.S. households owned a digital camera in 2009, they looked for digital photo-frames to creatively display their digital pictures. Digital photo-frames helped consumers view many digital images without making prints, and without having a handy access to a computer.

In 2009, 26% of households owning digital cameras also owned digital photo frames. Overall, 20% of U.S. households owned digital photo frames.[21] In 2009, 8% of U.S. households purchased a digital photo-frame, and 8% U.S. households received a digital photo-frame as gift. The ownership of digital photo frames increases with household income. Approx. 29% of households earning annual income of $75,000 or more in 2009 owned digital photo-frames (18% in 2008). This number dropped to approximately 11% for the households with annual income less than $30,000 (8% in 2008). The household spending on a new camera increased with the household earning.

Interestingly, in 2009, 58% digital photo-frame purchasers were females. This was significantly higher than 42% of male purchasers. The most popular screen size was 7-inch frames, accounting for 29% digital photo-frames purchased.[22]

E. ONLINE PHOTO STORAGE AND FINISHING

CEO Perez was seriously considering emulating Steve Jobs at Apple to transform Eastman Kodak from a product innovation driven company to a service innovation driven company. Developing a profitable business model with sustainable competitive advantage was expected to be a big challenge.

Many digital camera owners tend to print some of their pictures at home. Photographers could also take their digital images to print online using a variety of photo-finishing services from home, instead of going to a retailer. These sites allowed free storage and sharing of photos online, charging only for the prints made.

Using a photofinisher, however, can save on ink cartridges, paper jams, and other irritations. With online services, customers upload their photos to a web site that make them available for viewing and ordering at a store kiosk or terminal near you. These kiosks can also take pictures from a camera memory card, and allow the customers to edit their digital pictures.[23] Multiple retail chains, like **Walgreens** and **CVS**, offered speedy services. **HP**, a dominant player in home printers, announced plans to enter retail photofinishing by installing **PhotoSmart Express** kiosks at **Albertson's** and other retailers. Field surveys and tests have shown that kiosks connected to a minilab offered better quality. Minilab prints were also more water resistant.   Stand-alone kiosks, on the other hand, provided faster speed. These kiosks deliver prints like ATMs dispense money.

Kodak provided the online photo-finishing services through **Ofoto** and the **Kodak Picture Center**. In collaboration with **Snapfish**, customers could print on Kodak paper.

The shares of digital prints, either at home or at a retailer have steadily increased relative to declining traditional photo prints.

FLICKR.COM ONLINE IMAGE SHARING SITE

Kodak's Flickr.com is a popular and more sophisticated photo sharing site than many other photofinishers. In June 2010, Flickr updated its photo gallery with 30% larger 640 pixels wide (from 500 pixels).[24] It also offered a new light box that allowed a customer to photos against a dark background. The site became 50% faster to navigate. It leverages the information at the moment of the capture of a digital photo – such as when and geographically where a picture was taken, with what camera, and under what conditions. In 2010, Apple iPhones emerged as the most popular camera phone models, followed by Nokia and Blackberry.[25]

F. DIFFUSION OF MOBILE PHONE CAMERA

Another emerging competing imaging technology on the horizon was mobile phones with embedded cameras. By the end of 2003, there were 81 million such phones with cameras worldwide, expected to grow to about 97 million units for 2004.[26] Mobile phones for 2004 were expected to be about 500 million. The mobile phone's memories, picture resolution, and battery lives were expected to increase steadily. These posed a significant risk of reducing sales revenues of digital camera manufacturers.

In 2004, the sales of digital cameras overtook the sales of film cameras. At that time, the majority of digital cameras had 4 megapixel resolution or higher.

Over the next few years, the adoption of camera phones was fast catching up and surpassing the adoption and penetration of digital cameras. The number of U.S. households owning camera phones exceeded the number of households owning digital cameras. In 2009, 62% of U.S. households owned digital cameras, and 78% of U.S. households owned camera phones.[27] The increase in households owning camera phones is shown in Exhibit - 9. Whereas the percent of households owning camera phones was barely 2.5% in 2003, and 10.2% in 2004, this percent has been steadily rising in the subsequent years. The percent of households owning at least one camera phone steadily increased from 25.9% in 2005 to 57.6% in 2008. In 2009, this percentage penetration increased only marginally to 61.0%. Almost one in eight households owned three or more camera phones.[28]

However, in 2009 digital cameras were used far more than phone cameras to take digital pictures. The number of digital pictures taken by digital cameras was approx. 12 times more than the number of digital pictures taken using phone cameras. Phone cameras were used to take pictures primarily for spontaneous occasions when consumers did not have access to a digital camera. Particularly, customers owning photo cameras with less than 3 megapixel resolution units were not highly satisfied with their phone pictures.

According to the PMA Marketing Research mentioned before, 87% of the camera phone users said that their use of phone cameras **did not** have any adverse effect on the number of pictures they took with their digital cameras. Only 7% said that they took fewer pictures with their digital cameras because of using their phone cameras. And, 6% said that the use of phone camera has made them take more pictures with their digital cameras.

MANAGEMENT'S DISCUSSION AND ANALYSIS OF KODAK'S FINANCIAL PERFORMANCE AND RESULTS OF OPERATIONS

Kodak continues to claim to be the world's foremost imaging innovator. It has a broad portfolio of products and services that includes image capture and output devices, consumables, systems and solutions for many consumer, business, and commercial printing applications. Kodak reports its financial performance in three major reportable business segments. These are: Consumer Digital Imaging Group (CDG), Film, Photofinishing and Entertainment Group (FPEG), and Graphic Communications Group (GCG).

Exhibits – 11 to 15 show Kodak's financial performance from fiscal years 2005 to 2009.[29-32] During this period, Kodak's financial performance, and particularly its revenue, has been severely affected by the global economic recession that started in 2008. Furthermore, the demand, sales, and earnings for Kodak's consumer products largely tend to be finicky and discretionary. Decline in consumer demand has adversely affected sales of Kodak digital camera and digital picture frame businesses. The earnings from this segment, however, significantly improved from a loss of $131 million in 2005, to a gain of $35 million (See Exhibit – 11).

For the Graphics Communication Group (GCG), a weak economy and lack of availability of credit significantly reduced capital spending by businesses. The earnings from this segment improved from a loss of $ 41 million in 2005, to a gain of $104 million in 2007, but then it fell back to a loss of $42 million in 2009 (See Exhibit – 11).

Whereas the entertainment imaging business saw some improvement in 2009Q4, the Film Capture business, also included in FPEG saw a steady decline in earnings from a significant gain of $ 540 million in 2005, to a smaller gain of $ 159 million in 2009 (Exhibit -11).

In order to mitigate the continued slowdown in the U.S. and European economies, Kodak intensely focused its efforts on cash generation and conservation in 2009. On April 30, 2009, the Kodak Board of Directors announced suspension of future cash dividends on its common stock. During 2009, the U.S. based Kodak employees were required to take one week unpaid leave. Compensations were reduced for the CEO, other executive officers, and the Directors on the Board.[33]

MARKET FOOTPRINT AND COMPETITIVENESS OF SELECTED KODAK PRODUCTS

As mentioned before, Eastman Kodak competes in a diverse variety of market segments listed below.

Consumer Digital Imaging Group Segment (CDG) includes digital still and video cameras, digital image-related devices such as photo frames, kiosks and other related media, APEX drylab systems, consumer inkjet printing systems, Kodak Gallery products and services, and imaging sensors. This Group also encompasses licensing of Kodak's extensive intellectual property in digital imaging products and processes.

Film, Photofinishing and Entertainment Group Segment (FPEG) includes consumer and professional film, one-time-use cameras, graphic arts film, aerial and industrial film, and entertainment imaging products and services to a wide variety of loyal and potential customers.

Graphics Communication Group Segment offers a wide range of media, software, and hardware products such as commercial inkjet printers to customers in data center, commercial printing, packaging, newspaper and other related market segments. Kodak offers many solutions for prepress equipment, workflow software, analog and digital printing, and document scanning related services.

In addition to these, Kodak serves and supports other market segments such as display businesses and other miscellaneous services.

Exhibits 16 to 20 illustrate Kodak's competitive market position in 2010 in its two key business segments: digital cameras and digital picture frames. This was evaluated by the independent and highly trustworthy *Consumer Reports*.[34] Annually, they compare prices of different available digital cameras against their overall quality scores, including image quality, versatility, mega-pixel resolution, weight, life as measured in number of shots, and other functions such as zooming power.

For compact point and shoot digital cameras, the quality of Kodak EasyShare digital cameras ranked at #6, #20, and #30 in 2010 (Exhibit – 16). The top 5 positions in this category of digital cameras in 2010 were held by two Canon PowerShot cameras, two Panasonic Lumix cameras, and a Nikon CoolPix camera. For subcompact point and shoot digital cameras, all the top 10 positions in 2010 were held by Kodak's Japanese rivals (Exhibit – 17). Sony CyberShot ranked at the top position, and four Canon Powershot digital cameras dominated this category. In the case of Superzoom Point and Shoot cameras, a Canon PowerShot camera ranked at the top, but three Kodak's EasyShare cameras dominated the top 10 list in 2010 by taking #2, #6, and #8 positions (Exhibit – 18). In the twin-category of the most expensive ($700 - $ 1,600) and high-performing single lens reflex (SLR) basic and advanced cameras, Canon and Nikon shared four of the top six cameras in 2010 (Exhibit – 19).

Rival digital picture frames were compared for their price and overall quality score, including picture quality, ease of use, and memory capacity (Exhibit – 20). The top rank in 2010 was held by HP df800, priced at $170 and with an overall quality score of 75. It was scored excellent for ease of use, but not so good on picture quality. Kodak's SV811 model, priced at $150, ranked #7 with an overall quality score of 56. It was also evaluated to have excellent ease of use and a good picture quality with comparable memory capacity. Other top 10 rivals included Samsung, SmartParts, Digital, and Mustek.

Exhibit – 21 gives a comparison for the key rival online photofinishing processors. Kodak's EasyShare Gallery dominates, with Shutterfly.com, Target, Yahoo, and Webshots in the top 5 positions. Kodak's service was tested to be excellent in print quality and editing, and it was scored very good for managing albums. Walgreens Photo Center, Sam's Club, and Wal-Mart Digital Photo Center are also included in the top 12 online processing service provider.

These comparisons indicate that Kodak faces stiff competition from its Japanese, U.S., and Korean rival electronics companies. This is unlike the dominating position Kodak held for more than 100 years in silver halide photography film markets. Gaining a similar leadership position in digital imaging is likely to be a tough challenge for CEO Perez and his team of other strategic leaders.

STRATEGIC TECHNOLOGICAL PARADOX
FOR CEO ANTONIO PEREZ

2010 KODAK PERFORMANCE: A MIXED BAG

On October 15, 2010, the U.S. White House named ten recipients of the National Medal of Science. This list included retired Kodak research scientist Steven J. Sasson for the National Medal of Technology and Innovation for his ground-breaking invention of the first digital camera in 1975.[35] Kodak was somewhat reluctant to phase out its dominating photographic film business. Digital imaging efforts at Kodak were often disconnected. Kodak did not start selling mass-market digital cameras until 2001. Kodak, however, gathered more than 1,000 digital imaging related patents during this period.

Less than two weeks later, on October 28, 2010, Eastman Kodak also reported their third-quarter results, with $1,758 billion in sales, and a loss of 43 million (or $0.16 per share) from its continuing operations. The sales declined 1% from the year-ago third quarter, with 2% unfavorable foreign exchange impact.

The revenue from the company's digital businesses grew 10%, the revenue from the commercial printing business grew 13%, whereas the revenue from the company's Film, Photofinishing and Entertainment Group declined by 25%. In the corresponding period in 2009, the overall loss from continuing operations was $111 million, or $0.41 per share.

Kodak Chairman and CEO Antonio Perez remarked that their 2010Q3 performance was marked by "continuing acceleration in our strategic digital growth businesses, positive cash generation, improved profit margins, and continued operational improvements across the company." He also noted that he was particularly pleased with the performance of their core growth businesses – consumer inkjet, commercial inkjet, packaging solutions, and workflow software and services. Revenue grew in these businesses by 23%. This gave him increased confidence that Kodak was "on track for a strong fourth-quarter performance, and continued improvement as we move forward."

For the remainder of 2010, Kodak was focused on three key financial goals announced in its February 2010 investor meeting. These were (a) digital revenue growth, (b) earnings from operations, and cash generation. For entire 2010, Kodak was targeting company revenue of

$7.5 to $ 7.8 billion, but continued to forecast 2010 loss of $ 50 million to $150 million from continuing operations, on the basis of U.S. Generally Accepted Accounting Practices (GAAP).

SUMMARY

In summary, Eastman Kodak is a Rochester, New York based U.S. enterprise that pioneered the silver-halide based photographic film technology in 1884. In 1981, the pioneer Kodak came under severe market attack from its U.S. and Japanese competitors developing disruptive digital imaging technology. Two decades later, in 2003, Kodak **CEO Daniel Carp** was still confronting the duel dilemma of defending its entrenched photographic film market, and innovating in the emerging digital imaging market. Over the two decades, Kodak developed a number of reactive technological strategies. These strategies have produced mixed results. How can the new strategic leadership of Eastman Kodak, under CEO Antonio M. Perez stop Kodak's decade-long slippery slide? How can they reacquire their historical leadership in the emerging digital imaging technology based industry?

REFERENCES: EASTMAN KODAK TRANSFORMING BUSINESS MODEL INNOVATION

[1]www.kodak.com. News.

[2]*Economist*, 2005. Another Kodak Moment. May 14.

[3]Stone, Brad. 2006. What's Kodak's Strategy? *Newsweek*, Jan. 16.

[4]*Economist*, 2005.

[5]Symonds, William C. and Burrows, Peter. 2005. A Digital Warrior for Kodak. *Business Week*, May 23.

[6]Stone. 2006.

[7]Symonds and Burrows. 2005.

[8]Stone. 2006.

[9]Swasy, Alecia. 1997. *Changing Focus: Kodak and Its Battle to Save a Great American Company*. New York: Times Business/Random House.

[10]Gehani, R. Ray. 1998. *Management of Technology and Operations.* New York: John Wiley & Sons.

[11]Gehani, R. Ray. 1998.

[12]Gehani, R. Ray. 1998.

[13]Hamm, Steve and Symmonds, William C. 2007. Kodak: Mistakes Made on the Road to Innovation. *Business Week Online*, Sep. 17. Accessed October 30, 2010.

[14]Clairmont, Kristy. 2010. A Look at Film Usage and Digital Camera Users. *PMA Data Watch,* Jan 4.

[15]Scoblete, 2006. Kodak's Perez Pitches Partners, Paradigm Shift. *This Week in Consumer Electronics Week.*

[16]ibid Scoblete, 2006.

[17]ibid Scoblete, 2006.

[18]Hamm and Symmonds. 2007.

[19]Brienzi, Mark and Kekre, Sham. 2005. How Kodak Transformed its Service Parts Supply Chain. *Supply Chain Management* Review, October: 25-27.

[20]ibid.

[21]Clairmont, Kristy. 2010. A Look at Digital Photo Frame Ownership and Purchasing. *PMA Data Watch,* March 8.

[22]Clairmont, Kristy. 2010. Camera Phone Penetration continues to rise. *PMA Data Watch,* March 15.

[23]*Consumer Reports*, 2006. Photofinishing Online vs. In-store. July: 35-36. www.ConsumerReports.org.

[24]Worthington, Paul. 2010. Your Photos Happier – Flickr Expands Images. PMA Data Watch, June 24.

[25]Clairmont, Kristy. 2010. Uploading Activity in the Flickr Community. *PMA Data Watch*, May 3.

[26]*Photo Industry 2010 Report*.

[27] *ibid Photo Industry 2010 Report*.

[28]Clairmont, Kristy. 2010. Camera Phone vs. digital camera use among U.S. households. *PMA Data Watch,* Jun 7.

[29]Eastman Kodak Company 2009 Annual 10-K Report.

[30]Eastman Kodak Company 2008 Annual 10-K Report.

[31]Eastman Kodak Company 2007 Annual 10-K Report.

[32]Eastman Kodak Company 2006 Annual 10-K Report.

[33]Eastman Kodak Company 2009 Annual 10-K Report.

[34]*Consumer Reports Buying Guide 2010*.

[35]www.kodak.com. News.

[36]*Consumer Reports Buying Guide 2009*. Based on tests posted on ConsumerReports.org in May 2008.

LIST OF EXHIBITS

EXHIBIT - 1   COMPARISON OF 5-YEAR CUMULATIVE TOTAL RETURN ON EQUITY

EXHIBIT – 2   HISTORY OF KODAK'S SLIPPING STOCK PRICE (MONTHLY CLOSE, IN CURRENT US$) DURING CEO ANTONIO PEREZ ERA (2006 – 2010)

EXHIBIT – 3   HISTORY OF KODAK'S SLIPPING STOCK PRICE (MONTHLY CLOSE in CURRENT US$) DURING CEO DANIEL CARP ERA (2000 – 2005)

EXHIBIT – 4   HISTORY OF KODAK'S SLIPPING STOCK PRICE (MONTHLY CLOSE, IN CURRENT US$) DURING CEO GEORGE FISHER ERA (1993 – 1999)

EXHIBIT – 5   DIVIDENDS DECLARED (IN CURRENT US$) BY EASTMAN KODAK CEOs (1993-2010)

EXHIBIT – 6   EXECUTIVE OFFICERS OF EASTMAN KODAK IN 2009

EXHIBIT – 7   ANALOG AND DIGITAL CAMERA SALES WORLD-WIDE IN 1999-2003 (In million units)

EXHIBIT – 8   STRATEGIC LEADERS AT EASTMAN KODAK SINCE INCEPTION IN 1884

EXHIBIT – 9   DIFFUSION OF DIGITAL CAMERA AND CAMERA PHONES USE IN U.S.

EXHIBIT – 10   SUPPLY-CHAIN METRICS AND SELECTED RESULTS ACHIEVED

EXHIBIT – 11   RESULTS OF CONTINUING OPERATIONS BY SEGMENTS (2004-09)

EXHIBIT – 12   EARNINGS (LOSS) FROM CONTINUING OPERATIONS BY SEGMENTS (2005 - 2009)

EXHIBIT – 13   CONSOLIDATED RESULTS OF CONTINUING OPERATIONS (For the Year Ended Dec 31)

EXHIBIT – 14   NET EARNINGS (LOSS) PER SHARE AND DIVIDENDS

EXHIBIT – 15   CONSOLIDATED FINANCIAL ASSET AND LIABILITY POSITION

© *2010 Dr. R. RAY GEHANI*

EXHIBIT – 1 COMPARISON OF 5-YEAR CUMULATIVE TOTAL RETURN ON EQUITY AT KODAK

As on	Eastman Kodak	Dow Jones US Indl. Avg.	S&P 500	S&P Consumer Discretionary
12/2004	100.0	100.0	100.0	100.0
12/2005	74.1	101.7	104.9	93.6
12/2006	83.4	121.1	121.5	111.1
12/2007	72.0	131.9	128.2	96.4
12/2008	22.6	89.6	80.7	64.1
12/2009	14.5	110.1	102.1	90.6

Source: Adapted from Eastman Kodak 2009 Annual Report, p 22 based on Standard & Poor, www.researchdatagroup.com/S&P.htm.

EXHIBIT – 2 HISTORY OF KODAK'S SLIPPING STOCK PRICE (MONTHLY CLOSE, IN CURRENT US$) DURING CEO ANTONIO PEREZ ERA (2006 – 2010)

Month	2010	2009	2008	2007	2006
Dec	na	4.22	6.58	21.87	25.80
Nov**	4.83	4.05	7.57	23.48	26.02
Oct	4.70	3.75	9.16*	28.66*	24.40*
Sep	4.20	4.78	15.38	26.76	22.40
Aug	3.50	5.32	16.19	26.67	21.27
Jul	3.97	2.97	14.64	25.25	22.25
Jun	4.34	2.96	14.43	27.83	23.78
May	5.64	2.61	15.32*	25.36*	24.11*
Apr	6.13	3.05	17.89	24.91	26.96
Mar	5.79	3.80	17.67	22.56	28.44
Feb	5.94	3.19	16.98	23.87	28.05
Jan	6.05	4.53	19.92	25.86	25.10

Source: Adapted from www.Yahoofinance.com.
Notes: *: Months when dividends declared; ** Year 2010 is until Nov. 7.

EXHIBIT – 3   **HISTORY OF KODAK'S SLIPPING STOCK PRICE (MONTHLY CLOSE in**

CURRENT US$) DURING CEO DANIEL CARP ERA (2000 – 2005)

Month	2005	2004	2003	2002	2001	2000
Dec	23.40	32.25	25.67	35.04	29.43	39.38
Nov	23.97	32.71	24.36	36.92	30.27*	42.00*
Oct	21.90*	30.28*	24.43*	32.95*	25.57	44.88
Sep	24.33	32.22	20.94	27.24	32.53	40.88
Aug	24.37	29.58	27.89	30.54	44.67*	62.27*
Jul	26.74	26.49	27.63	30.78	43.31	54.88
Jun	26.85	26.98	27.35	29.17	46.68	59.50
May	26.28*	26.18*	30.64*	33.27*	47.33*	59.75*
Apr	25.00	25.79	29.91	32.21	43.50	56.38
Mar	32.55	26.17	29.60	31.17	39.89	54.31
Feb	33.99	28.54	29.60	31.50	45.00	57.31*
Jan	33.09	28.41	30.30	28.40	43.62	61.88

Source: Adapted from www.Yahoofinance.com.
Notes: *: Months when dividends declared; ** Year 2010 is until Nov. 7.

EXHIBIT – 4 HISTORY OF KODAK'S SLIPPING STOCK PRICE (MONTHLY CLOSE, IN CURRENT US$) DURING CEO GEORGE FISHER ERA (1993 – 1999)

Month	1999	1998	1997	1996	1995	1994	1993	1992***
Dec	66.25	72.00	60.56	80.25	67.00	47.75	56.25	40.50
Nov	61.88*	72.62*	60.63*	81.12*	68.25*	45.50*	60.88*	41.88*
Oct	68.94	77.50	59.88	79.62	62.63	48.13	62.88	40.80
Sep	75.62	76.87	64.94	78.50	59.25	51.75	59.38	44.50
Aug	73.44*	78.12*	65.37*	72.50*	57.75*	49.75*	61.00*	43.25*
Jul	69.12	83.87	67.00	74.62	57.63	48.38	53.63	43.50
Jun	67.75	73.06	76.75	77.75	60.63	48.13	50.00	40.13
May	67.62*	71.37*	82.87*	74.37*	60.38*	46.88*	51.75*	39.88*
Apr	74.75	72.19	83.12	76.50	57.50	41.50	48.75	39.63
Mar	63.88	64.87	76.00	71.00	53.25	44.38	54.25	40.63
Feb	66.19*	65.62*	89.75*	71.50*	51.00*	43.00*	53.65*	44.63*
Jan	65.37	65.25	86.75	73.37	49.00	44.13	49.88	50.50

Source: Adapted from www.Yahoofinance.com.
Notes: *: Months when dividends declared; *** Year 1992 for CEO Kay Whitmore is given for comparison.

EXHIBIT – 5   DIVIDENDS DECLARED (IN CURRENT US$) DURING 3 CEO ERAS AT

EASTMAN KODAK (1993-2010)

YEAR	DECLARATION DATES AND DIVIDENDS			

CEO ANTONIO PEREZ LEADERSHIP YEARS (2005 – 2010)

Year				
2010*		09/25: $0.00	06/25: $0.00	03/25: $0.00
2009	12/25: $0.00	09/25: $0.00	06/25: $0.00	03/25: $0.00
2008		10/30: $0.25	05/28: $0.25	
2007		10/30: $0.25	05/30: $0.25	
2006		10/30: $0.25	05/30: $0.25	
2005		10/28: $0.25	05/27: $0.25	

CEO DANIEL CARP LEADERSHIP YEARS (2000 – 2005)

Year				
2004		10/28: $0.25	05/27: $0.25	
2003		10/30: $0.25	05/29: $0.90	
2002		10/30: $0.90	05/30: $0.90	
2001	11/29: $0.45	08/30: $0.44	05/30: $0.44	02/27: $0.44
2000	11/29: $0.44	08/30: $0.44	05/30: $0.44	02/28: $0.44

CEO GEORGE FISHER LEADERSHIP YEARS (1993 – 1999)

Year					
1999	11/29: $0.44	08/30: $0.44	05/27: $0.44	02/25: $0.44	
1998	11/27: $0.44	08/28: $0.44	05/28: $0.44	02/26: $0.44	
1997	11/26: $0.44	08/28: $0.44	05/29: $0.44	02/27: $0.44	
1996	11/27: $0.40	08/29: $0.40	05/30: $0.40	02/28: $0.40	
1995	11/29: $0.40	08/30: $0.40	05/25: $0.40	02/23: $0.40	
1994	11/25: $0.40	08/26: $0.40	05/25: $0.40	02/23: $0.40	01/04:$11.72
1993	11/24: $0.50	08/26: $0.50	05/25: $0.50	02/23: $0.50	

Source: Adapted from www.Yahoofinance.com. Note:* Year 2010 is until Nov. 7.

EXHIBIT – 6   EXECUTIVE OFFICERS OF EASTMAN KODAK IN 2009

NAME	AGE	POSITIONS HELD	EXECUTIVE OFFICE	YEAR FIRST ELECTED TO CURRENT POST
Antonio M. Perez	64	**Chairman of the Board, Chief Executive Officer**	2003	2005
Philip J. Faraci	54	President and Chief Operating Officer	2005	2007
Frank S. Sklarsky	53	Chief Financial Officer and Executive Vice President	2006	2006
Eric H. Samuels	42	Chief Accounting Officer And Corporate Controller	2009	2009
Joyce P. Haag	59	General Counsel and Sr. Vice president	2005	2005
Robert L. Berman	52	Sr. Vice President	2002	2005
Brad W. Kuchten	49	Sr. Vice President	2009	2009
Terry R. Taber	55	Vice President	2008	2008

Source: Adapted from Eastman Kodak 2009 Annual Report, p. 18. Executive officers are elected annually in February.

EXHIBIT – 7   ANALOG AND DIGITAL CAMERA SALES WORLD-WIDE IN 1999-2003
(In million units)

EARLY YEARS	2003	2002	2001	2000	1999
Analog Still Cameras					
Americas	16.0	19.0	19.0	20.6	16.8
Europe	17.0	19.0	20.0	20.6	20.1
Japan	2.0	3.5	4.0	5.7	6.0
Rest	22.0	21.5	23.0	24.1	24.1
Total	57.0	63.0	66.0	71.0	67.0
Digital Still Cameras					
Americas	17.0	11.5	6.5	4.3	2.0
Europe	18.0	9.0	4.6	2.3	1.1
Japan	9.0	6.7	5.9	3.6	1.8
Rest	6.0	3.3	1.5	0.8	0.6
Total	50.0	30.5	18.5	11.0	5.5

Note: 2003* numbers were projected in November 2003.
Source: www.pmai.org

EXHIBIT – 8   STRATEGIC LEADERS AT EASTMAN KODAK SINCE INCEPTION IN 1884

PERIOD	NAME	TITLE
2005 – Present	**Antonio M. Perez**	**CEO**
2000 – 2005, May 31	Daniel A. Carp	CEO
1993 – 1999	George M. C. Fisher	CEO
1990 – 1993, Oct. 27	Kay R. Whitmore CEO	
1983 – 1990	Colby H. Chandler	CEO
1972 – 1983, May	Walter A. Fallon	President and CEO
1969 – 1972, May 17	Louis K. Eilers	President and CEO
1960 – 1968	William S. Vaughn	President and CEO
1952 – 1960	Albert K. Chapman	President
1941 – 1952	Thomas J. Hargrave	President
1934 – 1941	Frank W. Lovejoy President	
1925 – 1934	William G. Stuber President	
1921 – 1925, Apr. 7	**George Eastman**President	
1884 – 1919, Jul. 26	Henry A. Strong	President

Source: Adapted from various Eastman Kodak documents and websites.

EXHIBIT – 9   DIFFUSION OF DIGITAL CAMERA AND CAMERA PHONES USE IN U.S.

Year	Camera Phones In Use (million)	Households Own camera phone %	Households Own Film Camera %	Households Purchased Film %
2005	44	25.9%	72%	56%
2006	69	36.8	66	42
2007	92	45.6	55	28
2008	120	57.6	46	31
2009	141	61.0	38*	27*

Source: Adapted from *Photo Industry 2010: Review and Forecast Report*. Based on Digital Imaging Surveys. *Estimated.

EXHIBIT – 10   SUPPLY-CHAIN   METRICS   AND   SELECTED   RESULTS ACHIEVED

	METRICS	RESULT HIGHLIGHTS
Cost	Warehousing Costs (3PL)	Reduced
	Transportation Costs	Reduced
	Total Acquisition Costs	Reduced 13 – 15%
Inventory	Central inventory	Reduced by 32%
	Field Inventory for all parts	Reduced by 66%
	Field inventory days of supply	Reduced by 48%
Serviceability	Priority shipments	Reduced by 22%
	First-call completion rate	Maintained as before
	Call Duration	No adverse effect
	Service level metrics	Improved

Source: Adapted from Brienze and Kekre (2005).

EXHIBIT – 11   RESULTS OF CONTINUING OPERATIONS BY SEGMENTS (2004-09)

Reportable Segments	2009	2008	2007	2006*	2005	2004
Consumer Digital Imaging Group (CDG), Total	2,619	3,088	3,247	3,013	3,215	2,366
- Inside USA	1,618	1,811	2,011	1,910	2,034	1,440
- Outside USA	1,001	1,277	1,235	1,103	1,181	926
Film Photofinishing & Entertainment (FPEG) Group, Total	2,257	2,987	3,632	4,254	5,325	7,051
- Inside USA	508	835	1,054	1,366	1,767	2,476
- Outside USA	1,749	2,152	2,578	2,888	3,558	4,575
Graphic Communications Group (GCG), Total	2,726	3,334	3,413	3,287	2,990	1,344
- Inside USA	831	1,036	1,178	1,231	1,079	587
- Outside USA	1,895	2,298	2,235	2,056	1,911	757
Health Group, Total				divested*	2,655	2,686
- Inside USA					1,052	1,114
- Outside USA					1,603	1,572
All Other, Total	4	7	9	14	83	70
- Inside USA	5	7	10	12	47	41
- Outside USA	(1)	-	(1)	2	36	29
Consolidated Sales, Total	7,606	9.416	10,301	10,568	14,268	13,517
- Inside USA	2,962	3,689	4,254	4,519	5,977	5,658
- Outside USA	4,644	5,727	6,047	6,049	8,289	7,859

Source: Adapted from Eastman Kodak Annual Reports, 2009, 2008, . 2006* Health Group divested.

EXHIBIT – 12   EARNINGS (LOSS) FROM CONTINUING OPERATIONS BY SEGMENTS (2005 - 2009)

(in US$ millions)	2009	2008	2007	2006	2005
Consumer Digital Imaging Group	35	(177)	(17)	(206)	(131)
Film, Photofinishing & Entertainment Group	159	196	281	309	540
Graphic Communications Group	(42)	(31)	104	70	(41)
Health Group					370
All Other	(13)	(17)	(25)	(22)	(231)
Total All Segments	139	33	343	161	507
Restructuring costs, Rationalization And other	(258)	(149)	(662)	(698)	(1,118)
Post-employment Benefit changes	-	94	-	-	
Other operating Income (expenses), Net	88	766	96	59	
Adjustments to Contingencies and Legal reserves/ Settlements	3	(33)	(7)	2	(21)
Interest expense	(119)	(108)	(113)	(172)	(211)
Other income (Charges), net	30	55	86	65	(44)
Profit (Loss) from Continuing operations Before income taxes	(117)	(874)	(257)	(583)	(799)

Source: Adapted from Eastman Kodak Annual Reports, 2009, 2008,

EXHIBIT – 13   CONSOLIDATED RESULTS OF CONTINUING OPERATIONS
(For the Year Ended Dec 31)

In US$ Millions	2009	2008	2007	2006	2005
Net Sales	7,606	9,416	10,301	10,568	11,395
- Cost of Goods Sold	5,838	7,247	7,757	8,159	8,864
= Gross Profit	1,768	2,169	2,544	2,409	2,531
Selling, Gen. & Admin	1,302	1,606	1,778	1,950	2,240
Research & Developmt.	356	478	549	578	739
Restructuring and Rationalization costs	226	140	543	416	665
Other Operating income (expenses), net	(88)	766	(96)	(59)	(40)
Loss from continuing ops. Before interest, income Taxes, and others, net	(28)	(821)	(230)	(476)	(1,073)
Interest expenses	119	108	113	172	139
Other income (charges)	30	55	87	65	4
Loss from continuing ops. before income taxes, and others, net	(117)	(874)	(256)	(583)	(1,206)
Provision (benefit) for income taxes	115	(147)	(51)	221	449
Loss from continuing ops.	(232)	(727)	(205)	(804)	(1,657)
Earnings from discontinued operations, net of income taxes	17	285	881	203	451
Extraordinary item, net of taxes	6	-	-	-	55
NET EARNINGS (LOSS)	(209)	(442)	676	(601)	(1,261)

Source: Adapted from Eastman Kodak Annual Reports, 2009, 2008, 2007 etc.

EXHIBIT – 14   NET EARNINGS (LOSS) PER SHARE AND DIVIDENDS

In US$ Millions	2009	2008	2007	2006	2005
NET LOSS	(209)	(442)	676	(601)	(1,261)
Basic and diluted Net earnings (loss) Per share, Total	(0.78)	(1.57)	2.35	(2.09)	(4.38)
-continuing operations	(0.87)	(2.58)	(0.71)	(2.80)	(4.70)
-discontinued operations	0.07	1.01	3.06	0.71	.52
- cumulative effect of Accounting change					(.20)
Cash dividends per share	$ 0.00	0.50	0.50	0.50	0.50

Source: Adapted from Eastman Kodak Annual Reports.

EXHIBIT – 15 CONSOLIDATED FINANCIAL ASSET AND LIABILITY POSITION

In US$ Millions	2009	2008	2007	2006	2005
ASSETS					
Current Assets, Total	**4,303**	**5,004**	**6,053**	**5,557**	**6,096**
Cash & cash equiv.	2,024	2,145	2,947	1,469	1,665
Receivables. net	1,395	1,716	1,939	2,072	2,760
Inventories, net	679	948	943	1,001	1,455
Deferred income taxes	--		120	108	100
Other current assets	205		104	96	116
Assets fr. discont. Ops.	--		-	811	
Property, plant & equip.	1,254	1,551	1,811	2,602	3,778
Goodwill	991	896	1,657	1,584	2,141
Other Long-Term Assets	1,227	1,728	4,138	3,509	3,221
Assets from discont. Ops.	--			-	1,068
TOTAL ASSETS	**7,691**	**9,179**	**13,659**	**14,320**	**15,236**
LIABILITIES AND SHAREHOLDERS' EQUITY					
Current Liabilities, Total	**2,896**	**3,462**	**4,446**	**4,554**	**5,489**
Accounts payables, others	2,811	3,267	3,794	3,712	4,187
Short-term borrowings And current portion of long-term debt	62	51	308	64	819
Accrued income & other Taxes	23	144	344	347	483
Liabilities of discont. Ops.	--		-		341
Long-term debt, net of Current portion	1,129	1,252	1,289	2,714	2,764
Pension & other post-Retirement liabilities	2,694	2,382	3,444	3,934	3,476
Other long-term liabilities	1,005	1,122	1,451	1,690	1,225
TOTAL LIABILITIES	**7,724**	**8,218**	**10,630**	**12,930**	**12,954**
Shareholders' Equity	**5,987**	**7,009**	**8,793**	**7,191**	**8,095**
Common stock, $2.50 par value*	978	978	978	978	978
Additional paid in capital	1,093	901	889	881	867
Retained earnings	5,676	5,879	6,474	5,967	6,717
Accumulated other Compr. Income (loss)	(1,780)	(749)	452	(635)	(467)
Treasury stock at cost**	(6,022)	(6,048)	(5,764)	5,803	5,813
Total Liabilities & Share--holders' Equity	**7,691**	**9,179**	**13,659**	**14,320**	**15,236**

Sources: Adapted from Eastman Kodak Annual Meetings, 2009, 2008. See notes for details.

* Common stock 950 million shares authorized; 391,292,760 shares issued as of Dec. 31, 2008, 2007, and 2006; 268,169,055 & 287,999,830 shares outstanding as of Dec. 31, 2008, 2007, 2006.

** Treasury stock, 133,123,705 shares as of Dec. 31, 2008 and 103,292,930 shares as of Dec. 31, 2007, and 103,959,637 shares as of Dec. 31, 2006.; 104,069,437 shares as of Dec. 31, 2005.

**EXHIBIT - 16   COMPACT POINT & SHOOT DIGITAL CAMERAS –
TOP RANKINGS (BY SELECTED CRITERIA), 2010**

RANK/ BRAND & MODEL	Price US$	Overall Score	Image* Quality	Vers- atile*	Mega Pixels	Wt. OZs	Life - Shots	Zoom
1. **Canon** – PowerShot G10	500	74	VG	E	15	14	400	5X
2. **Canon** – PowerShot A1000 IS	150	71	VG	E	10	7	450	4X
3. **Panasonic** – Lumix DMC-M	400	70	VG	E	12	6	340	4.6X
4. **Nikon** – Coolpix P6000	400	70	VG	E	14	10	260	4X
5. **Panasonic** – Lumix DMC-L585	120	68	VG	VG	8	6	550	4X
6. **Kodak** – EasyShare M1033	130	68	VG	VG	10	5	220	3X
7. **Canon** – PowerShot D10	330	68	VG	VG	12	8	220	3X
8. **Canon** – PowerShot A2000 IS	160	67	VG	E	10	8	500	6X
9. **Fujifilm** – FinePix F601d	230	67	VG	VG	12	6	230	3X
10. **Panasonic** – Lumix	200	66	VG	VG	10	6	280	5X
...								
20. **Kodak** – EasyShare M380	150	66	VG	VG	10	5	310	5X
...								
30. **Kodak** – EasyShare	140	64	VG	VG	10	5	220	3X

Source: Adapted from *Consumer Reports Buying Guide 2010*, p. 210.
*Scale Used: E=Excellent; VG=Very Good; G= Good; F=Fair; P=Poor.

**EXHIBIT – 17   SUBCOMPACT POINT & SHOOT DIGITAL CAMERAS –
TOP RANKINGS (BY SELECTED CRITERIA), 2010**

RANK/ BRAND & MODEL	Price US$	Overall Score	Image* Quality	Vers- atile	Mega Pixels	Wt. Ozs	Life - Shots	ZOOM
1. **Sony** – CyberShot DSC W300	200	73	VG	E	14	7	300	3X
2. **Canon** – PowerShot SD880 IS	300	72	VG	E	10	6	310	4X
3. **Canon** – PowerShot SD1200 IS	200	71	VG	VG	10	5	260	3X
4. **Canon** – PowerShot SD900 IS	400	70	VG	E	15	6	280	3.7X
5. **Fujifilm** – FinePix F200 EXR	320	70	VG	VG	12	7	230	5X
6. **Canon** – PowerShot SD970 IS	380	70	VG	VG	12	7	270	5X
7. **Casio** – ExSlim Card EX-512	200	69	VG	VG	12	5	270	3X
8. **Sony** – CyberShot DSC-G3	500	68	VG	VG	10	7	200	4X
9. **Nikon** – CoolPix S710	300	68	VG	VG	15	6	250	3.6X
10. **Canon** – PowerShot SD780 IS	230	68	VG	VG	12	5	210	3X

Source: Adapted from *Consumer Reports Buying Guide 2010*, p. 211.
*Scale Used: E=Excellent; VG=Very Good; G= Good; F=Fair; P=Poor.

**EXHIBIT – 18   SUPERZOOM POINT & SHOOT DIGITAL CAMERAS –
TOP RANKINGS (BY SELECTED CRITERIA), 2010**

RANK/ BRAND & MODEL	Price US$	Overall Score	Quality	Image*	Vers-atile	Mega Pixels	Wt. OZs	Life - Shots	Zoom
1. **Canon** – PowerShot 5X10 IS	360	78	VG	E		10	24	600	20X
2. **Kodak** – EasyShare Z1012 IS	230	75	VG	E		10	13	300	12X
3. **Canon** – PowerShot 5X10 IS	560	75	VG	E		10	24	420	20X
4. **Casio** – Exilim EX FH20	430	73	VG	E		9	21	430	20X
5. **Panasonic** – Lumix DMC-F228	300	72	VG	E		10	15	460	18X
6. **Kodak** – EasyShare Z980	350	71	G	E		12	19	400	24X
7. **Canon** – PowerShot 5X200 IS	350	71	VG	E		12	9	280	20X
8. **Kodak** – EasyShare Z1015 IS	250	71	VG	E		10	15	270	15X
9. **Sony** – CyberShot DSC-H20	250	71	VG	VG		10	10	290	10X
10. **Sony** – CyberShot DSC-H20	180	71	VG	VG		8	11	310	10X

Source: Adapted from *Consumer Reports Buying Guide 2010*, p. 213.
*Scale Used: E=Excellent; VG=Very Good; G= Good; F=Fair; P=Poor.

EXHIBIT – 19   SINGLE LENS REFLEX (SLR) BASIC DIGITAL CAMERAS –
TOP RANKINGS (BY SELECTED CRITERIA), 2010

RANK/ BRAND & MODEL	Price US$	Overall Score	Image* Quality	Vers- atile	Mega Pixels	Wt. OZs	Life - Shots	Speed fps**
SINGLE LENS REFLEX (SLR) BASIC								
1. **Canon** – EOS Rebel TLi	850	69	E	VG	15	19	400	3.4
2. **Nikon** – D5000	730	67	VG	E	12	22	510	4.0
3. **Pentax** – K2000	700	67	VG	VG	10	24	400	2.8
SINGLE LENS REFLEX (SLR) ADVANCED								
1. **Nikon** – D300	1,600	78	E	VG	12	32	1,000	6
2. **Olympus** – E3	1,250	77	VG	VG	10	32	610	5
3. **Canon** – EDS400	900	76	E	VG	10	29	800	6.5

Source: Adapted from *Consumer Reports Buying Guide 2010*, p. 216.
*Scale Used: E=Excellent; VG=Very Good; G= Good; F=Fair; P=Poor. Speed = Max frames/second.

EXHIBIT - 20 **TOP RANKINGS OF RIVAL DIGITAL PICTURE FRAMES, 2010**

RANK AND BRAND	Model	Price US$	Overall Score	Picture* Quality	Ease* Of Use	Memory Capacity Mega Bytes
1. HP	df800	170	75	P	E	128
2. Samsung	SPF83V	190	71	VG	VG	64
3. SmartParts	SPX8	180	71	VG	VG	256
4. Prarrot	Photo-Viewer 7"	240	64	VG	G	64
5. Ceiva	LF4008	230	62	VG	G	0
6. Pandigital	PAN80-2	150	56	G	E	128
7. Kodak	SV811	150	56	G	E	128
8. Digital	NT-200	180	55	G	VG	128
9. Digital	MV-800+	180	48	G	VG	256
10. Mustek	PF-i700	100	41	F	VG	0

Source: Adapted from *Consumer Reports Buying Guide 2009*. Based on tests posted on ConsumerReports.org in May 2008.
*Scale Used: E=Excellent; VG=Very Good; G= Good; F=Fair; P=Poor

EXHIBIT – 21   TOP   RANKING   RIVAL   PHOTOFINISHING   ONLINE PROCESSORS

RANK AND AND SITE	Price/Print 4x6 $	8x10 $	Overall Score	Print* Quality	Managing Albums	Editing
1. **Kodak EasyShare** Kodakgallery.com	**0.15**	**3.99**	**86**	E	**VG**	E
2. Shutterfly Shutterfly.com	0.19	3.99	84	E	E	VG
3. Target Photo Center Target.com	0.15	1.99	84	E	VG	E
4. Yahoo Photos Yahoo.com	0.15	1.99	84	E	VG	E
5. Webshots Webshots.com	0.19	3.49	83	E	VG	G
6. Ritzpix Ritzpix.com	0.19	3.89	81	E	VG	VG
7. EZ Prints Ezprints.com	0.19	1.99	79	E	G	G
8. Costco Photo Center Costco.com	0.17	1.49	71	VG	VG	E
9. Snapfish Snapfish.com	0.12	2.99	71	VG	VG	E
10. Walgreens Photo Ctr. Walgreens.com	0.19	3.99	71	VG	VG	E
11. Sam's Club samscclub.com	0.11	1.58	68	VG	VG	VG
12. Wal-Mart's Digital Photo Center Walmart.com	0.12	1.96	65	VG	G	VG

Source: Adapted from www.ConsumerReports.org.
   Scale used: E= Excellent, VG=Very Good, G=Good, F=Fair, P=Poor

..

GOOGLE:

SEARCHING STRATEGIES TO SUSTAIN INNOVATIVE GROWTH IN 2010

Dr. R. RAY GEHANI

Institute for Innovation and Technology Leadership (IITL)
Akron, Ohio.

"To organize the world's information and make it universally accessible and useful."
- Google Mission.

"You Can Make Money Without Doing Evil."
- Google philosophy.

ABSTRACT

This case tracks the phenomenal growth of the search engine giant Google, from its conception, to incorporation, and market leadership. Can the founders and strategic leaders sustain their growth achieved through serial innovations and trust of their valued employees? Or will they have to change as Google grows into a more mature big-business enterprise?

Disclaimer:

This draft case-in-progress is meant strictly for classroom discussion and learning. It must not be considered as a comment on this firm's strategic management decisions or actions.

SEARCH ENGINE INNOVATION

Google claims to offer its users a "more intelligent" Internet search engine to navigate the vast amount of data spread across the global Internet. With Page Ranking and innovative text-matching technologies, Google offers the capability to most rapidly search and retrieve the most relevant information. People around the world use Google search engine to read breaking news, do electronic literature search, make e-purchases, and other related activities. This widespread public use of Internet started in 1994 with the launch of **Netscape Navigator**. The number of global Internet users sky-rocketed from 360 million in 2000, to approx, 1,600 million Internet users out of a total world population of about 7,000 million people in 2009.

SEARCH-BASED ADVERTISING

The exponential growth in the use of Internet search engine caused a disruptive shift in advertising to potential consumers. What is amazing is that within ten years of Google's innovative advertising business model, generating one nickel at a time, Google was amassing more than US$10 billion. In 2008, Google's search engine produced $21.8 billion in revenue and over $4.2 billion in profits. As the number of Google searchers increased, Google's search engine was easily scalable, adding very little additional fixed cost while generating higher profit margins.

The global Internet advertising is expected to steadily grow from approx. $21 billion in 2007 to estimated $37 billion in 2011. In the U.S., Internet advertising was estimated at $9 billion in 2007. The next wave of growth is likely to come from mobile phone searches.

BIRTH OF A SEARCH STAR

Google was innovated by **Sergey Brin** and **Larry Page, the American Business Idols of Internet Age,** when they were post-graduate students at **Stanford University**. They adopted the name Google as a distortion of Googol, which is 1×10^{100}.

Larry Page comes from a Michigan based family of computer scientists. His mother taught computer programming whereas his father taught computer science and artificial intelligence at Michigan State University.

Sergey Brin comes from a Jewish Russian family. His parents emigrated to the United States in 1979. Sergey's mother is an economist whereas his father is a mathematician.

In 1995, a 24 year old Larry Page met 23 year old Sergey Brin at Stanford University. Larry and Sergei shared their passion to efficiently retrieve most relevant information from massive data available online. They recognized that the search engine that is the fastest in retrieving the most relevant information would generate the most wealth. The two, however, frequently differed in many other areas.

As a result of their phenomenal exponential growth, these two techno-vators did not finish their doctorate degrees, but instead became two of the world's youngest billionaires within ten years of taking their company public. They own a 767 Boeing plane for personal travel, and they are financial supporters of Tesla Motors, for pioneering electric automobiles.

THE INVENTION OF SEARCH ENGINES

PREDECESSORS TO GOOGLE SEARCH ENGINE

Gerald Dalton developed SMART information retrieval system at **Cornell and Harvard**. This was before the wide public access in 1995 to Internet, and the invention of the World Wide Web by Briton Tim Barners-Lee in 1991. The open access led to the invention of other "family" members, **"Jughead," "Veronica," and** Gopher. An undergraduate student at the **McGill University** in Quebeck, Canada, developed Archie archival knowledge and retrieval system in 1990.

The 'Excite" web-based search engine was started by Stanford undergraduates in 1991. The number of documents stored online was significantly increased in 1994 by "Yahoo! Directory." This added complexity to online searching. Lycos followed suit in the same year.

GOOGLE SEARCH THEORY

Larry Page developed an innovative **PageRank algorithm** based on a quantitative weight assigned to each element of the hyperlinks connecting different online documents. The PageRank patent is assigned to the Stanford University and credited to Larry Page. This ranking, inspired by academic peer citations, assigned a priority and relative importance to each data set.

When an Internet searcher types in a search inquiry in the search box of Google.com, the Google's search engine computes an equation with 500 million variables to generate a hierarchically ranked list of best-matched results. Within a fraction of a second Google's server farms located around the world scan an index of more than 1 trillion websites.

Based on the **PageRank algorithm**, Larry and Sergey collaborated to innovate a prototype search engine **BackRub**. This search engine examined the number of back link votes pointing to a web site to rate each web site for its relevancy. The number of "votes" for various web sites assigned each web site a priority based on the frequency with which it was linked. Larry and Sergey wrote an extensively cited research paper, titled: "The Anatomy of a Large-Scale Hypertextual Web Search Engine." It caused great excitement on the Stanford University campus, and was a top-10 most accessed scientific research paper (*Mantle, 2008. in Companies That Changed the World*).

Before launching this search engine, Page was already well known on Stanford campus for building a working printer using Lego pieces. In his dorm room, he put together the hardware needed to actually execute the search engine technology. He bought a terabyte of storage disks at bargain prices. He was forced to max out his credit card limit.

Their first search engine was launched as google.Stanford.edu, through the website of Stanford University. Their proprietary domain name google.com was registered on September 14, 1997.

SEARCHING FOR AN INNOVATIVE BUSINESS MODEL

Sergey considered licensing their search engine technology to other Internet search engine service providers. Even though the Silicon Valley was experiencing the frenzy of internet boom, there were no major takers for licensing the **BackRub** disrupting technology. The potential investors argued that most of their customers did not care for the speed and accuracy of the search process.

One of the Yahoo founders, **David Filo**, motivated Larry and Sergey to launch their own search-engine venture. He later contributed financially to Google.

Page and Brin became almost penniless investing every dollar they had in perfecting and demonstrating their innovative search engine technology. Fortunately, they were introduced by Stanford professor

David Cheriton to **Andreas "Andy" von Bechtolsheim**, who co-founded Sun Microsystems (after Stanford University Network), while he too was still in his Ph.D. program at Stanford. Andy had amassed a fortune from this venture.

Page and Brin sent Andy an e-mail one late night. Andy responded back immediately that he was willing to listen to their presentation the next morning at 8 am. Andy saw the market potential of the demonstration immediately. He interrupted their presentation and offered to write them a check. Larry and Sergey requested US$ 50,000, but Andy suggested that they needed twice that amount, and wrote a check for US$ 100,000 payable to Google inc. for 2 weeks.

Google Inc. was hurriedly established so that Larry and Sergey could open a bank account, and deposit the big amount. Based on this success, other friends and family members also came forward to contribute financially. Larry and Sergey raised one million dollars from these friends and family members by the end of Sept. 1998. All these early investors soon became multi-millionaires. Andy and David became billionaires from their investments.

LAUNCHING GOOGLE BUSINESS

Larry and Sergey sought leave from their doctoral programs at Stanford University in 1998. They were running out of work space in Larry's dorm room. A spare room at a friend's 5-bed room house in Menlo Park, California was rented to set up Google. Their access was through the proverbial Silicon Valley "garage." Their third employee was Craig Silverstein. All of them worked informally – trying to change the Internet world.

Even with access to such newly acquired money, Larry and Sergey were frugal from the start. They used discounted computer components to build their main servers.

The speed and accuracy of Google search engine, based on PageRank algorithm, gradually improved. By end of 1998 they attracted close to 10,000 inquiries per day from many loyal followers from California's online community. Within a few months, Google search engine was covered by PC Magazine and USA Today. The former listed Google as one of the Top 100 search engines and websites (*Mantle, 2008: 204. In Companies That Changed the World*). See the Exhibit for search engine market shares.

SCALING UP GOOGLE

As Google's popularity increased, and it was handling 500,000 searches per day in 1999, Larry and Sergey had 25 employees at their University Ave., Palo Alto office. In early 1999, **Red Hat** became Google's first major search customer. In mid-1999 they received additional $25 million investment from the leading venture capitalist firms, **Sequoia Capital** and **Kleiner Perkins Caufield and Buyers**.

By the time Google reached 3 million searches per day, and growing, they decided to move to their **Googleplex headquarters in Mountain View**, California. They used open-plan offices, with lava lamps. Their employees were allowed to bring to work their pet dogs. They also enjoyed a gourmet chef who earlier served the Grateful Dead music band, and played roller hockey games. See the Exhibit - 3 on the Top 10 Things at Google.

In 2000, Google noted the growth of search inquiries by non-English speaking customers, and started developing its first of 10 foreign-language search engines. The company innovated the Google toolbar plug-in that allowed searchers to search the Internet without visiting a Google Portal or its homepage. Google started selling advertisements based on search keywords.

By the end of 2000, Google search engine was processing more than 100 million search inquiries per day. This was barely two years after its launch in September 1997 or 1998.

DAWN OF THE 21st CENTURY AT GOOGLE

In 2001, Google appointed **Eric Schmidt**, a seasoned Silicon Valley leader. Initially he defined his role as 'adult supervision' of young founders Larry and Sergey. Schmidt helped Google grow internally and expand by acquiring partners worldwide. The web documents that Google search engine processed increased from 1.4 billion in 2001 to 3.0 billon at the end of 2001, and to 4.28 billion by 2004 (*Mantle, 2008:204. In Companies That Changed the World*).

Google rapidly innovated and added **Google News, Google Scholar, Google Product Search, and Google Local**. By 2004, its web page index was expanded to 8 billion, with 150 country domains. Google innovated **Short Message Service (SMS)** to search requests to **Google (46653)** via mobile phones.

GOING PUBLIC INNOVATIVELY IN HARD TIMES

Larry and Sergey decided to take Google public on April 29, 2004 with a target to raise $3.6 billion by issuing 25.7 million shares. They chose to use Dutch Auction to carefully choreograph initial public offering with smaller underwriting fees. This generated US$ 23 billion. Close to 1,000 Google employees became millionaires within one day of trading of Google stock. The net worth of Brin and Page skyrocketed to over $3.8 billion each.

The public issue increased Google's liquid assets by $4 billion. These funds were made available to finance further growth and make aggressive acquisitions. In 2005, **Google Earth** was innovated and launched based on Google's acquisition of digital mapping company **Keyhole in 2004**. Its companion technology **Google Map** allowed Internet searchers to view any location in the world, including Taj Mahal, Mount Everest, and their own residence, from a satellite in space. Street view images were added to these.

Between 2005 and 2008, **Google News** was expanded to include archives up to 1900, and **Book Search** was innovated.

Gmail e-mail software, and web-based spreadsheet and document applications were added. To these was added a translation feature into 28 languages and **Picasa Web photo album**. Google users also received **Google Talk**, an **Instant Messaging service** (IMS) free for PC to PC local and long distance calls. Many new applications were offered to mobile phone users, such as **Gmail, Mobile Web Search, Maps for Mobile, Google News**, and much more.

GROWTH BY DIVERSIFICATION

Since 2004, as Google size increased to 8 billion web pages, Google bought **Keyhole Corporation**, and launched **Google Earth**. In 2006, **dMarc** was acquired to bid for radio advertising spots. Google acquired **YouTube** for US$ 1.6 billion, and **Double-Click** webpage advertising company for US$ 3.1 billion. Google outbid Microsoft by more than US$ 1 billion. New advertising revenues were generated through in-stream video advertising and banner ads. In 2008, Google strategic leaders were still figuring out how to best integrate these acquisitions with it pre-existing capabilities.

Google also collaborated with **Apple's iPhone** to provide Internet access over the mobile phone. They joined hands with **Simon Fuller**, the creator of **Pop Idol**. Google has also explored internet television.

Google was rapidly diversifying into video sharing, online graphical mapping, email, and book publishing. Rival search engines such as **Yahoo, MSN, and AOL** are lagging far behind Google.

Google has grown from a dorm room in 1997 to 450,000 servers on low-cost information farms scattered around the world. More than 2 million searchers access Google every day.

In 2008, Google launched its **Android operating system** for mobile phones. This allowed wireless phone makers **Nokia, LG, HTC and others** to have internet features similar to that of **Apple's iPhone**. This was expected to generate additional banner ads for Google.

Google's **"cloud computing" Chrome software** launched in 2009 allowed enterprises to run their software applications or store files using Google's data centers. This facilitated collaborating with other partners needing access to same information. Market for cloud computing was estimated to grow to $95 billion by 2013.

A major challenge was the recessionary slowdown in the U.S. economy in 2008 and 2009. Whereas Google's revenue growth slowed down, Google surged ahead in its net income growth.

EVOLVING INNOVATIVE BUSINESS MODEL

Google's strategic leaders have continually evolved Google's business model as it grew in size and stature. In 2000, innovation of keyword-targeted advertising helped generate revenues from the placement of targeted ads to users defined by their browsing behavior. This helped jump revenues from $220,000 in 1999 to exceed $86 million in 2001.

In 2005, Google started charging advertisers fees for advertising with its 650 media partners, such as newspapers, magazines etc. In early 2009, Google withdrew from print and radio advertising. Google Checkout launched in 2008 helped Google receive 2% fee of the value of a transaction for purchases at participating e-retailer websites.

Please review the Google's financial performance in Exhibits 5, 6, and 7.

GOOGLE SEARCHING STRATEGY FOR GROWTH

1. Internet Advertising

Google' overall strategy is to dominate in Internet advertising. Google has done this by its corporate-level acquisitions since its IPO in 2004, and by focusing its R&D in alignment with this goal. Innovating additional innovative features such as Google Maps, Gmail, Book Search, Local search, airline travel search, Blogger, and others have helped increased searcher traffic to Google sites.

Sometimes, however, Google's innovative efforts have not produced the desired results. Google's highly expensive acquisition of **YouTube**, and more than 5 billion video downloads, produced not even $200 million in revenue in 2007. Google's proprietary social networking site, **orkut**, is performing much behind the rival networking sites such as myspece.com and facebook.com.

2. Search-based Advertising on Mobile devices

Google's strategic intent to dominate search-based advertising on mobile devices, such as with the acquisition of **Android operating system**, had been highly successful. More than 63% searches were performed on Internet-enabled phones in 2008. Google offered Android operating system, with core applications of Gmail, Earth Maps, Wi-Fi capability, and GPS etc., to any phone maker interested in offering mobile devices with Internet capabilities. In September 2008, **T-Mobile** started marketing an **Android operating system** equipped phone **G1**, for the price of $179, more affordable than **iPhone**. G1 offered better keyboard than iPhone. In 2009, **Nokia, LG,** and others were also planning to launch their mobile phones with Android operating system and affiliated applications.

3. Cloud Computing

Google's founders and other strategic leaders strongly believe that in the short-term most businesses would migrate their computer software programs from local hard-drives or Intranets to Internet, and use "cloud computing" to reduce lower support costs and software acquisition costs. By 2013, "cloud computing" was expected to grow to $95 billion worldwide. A prototype beta version **Google Apps** based on "cloud computing" was test-marketed in 2006, and then re-launched in 2008 to directly compete with **Microsoft Office**. Google Apps, hosted in Google's data center, included all the typical capabilities, from Gmail to

GPS, and the needed file storage space. Whereas the site license fee for **Microsoft Office and Outlook** was $350 per user per year, **Google Apps** was licensed to corporate customers for only $50 per user per year. In 2008, the revenues from sale of **Google Apps** to corporate customers were only $4 million. Microsoft's Office sold approx. $17 billion and 98% market share in 2008.

Chrome's browser (since Sep. 2008) and **Chrome operating system** (since Jul. 2009) were innovated to allow users run word processing, spreadsheets, and video-editing.

GOOGLE'S RIVALS

Google was not the first mover into the Internet search engine market. But, in 2009, Google sites dominated the search engine market with 65.0% market share in June 2009, compared to only 18.4% for Yahoo, and 8.4% for Microsoft sites (see Exhibit – 5).

YAHOO.COM

Yahoo pioneered the Internet search engine in 1994. Google offered its search engine capabilities to Yahoo in 1997. In December 2002, Yahoo invested US$ 235 million to acquire **Inktomi** with search technology. In less than a year, Yahoo spent US$ 1.6 billion to acquire **Overture Services** with more search engine related technologies in July 2003. These hefty investments were made to replace the technological capabilities that Google could provide Yahoo. Furthermore, Yahoo sued Google for infringing on some Overture patents. The two former collaborators settled the lawsuit in August 2004 with Google licensing the Overture technologies with its 2.7 million stick shares.

Yahoo had 142 million unique visitors who set up their Yahoo portal in 2008. They could use these Yahoo portals to maintain an e-mail account, check breaking news, coordinate a personal calendar, get maps, monitor stock portfolio, store an online photo album, and search job listings or personal ads. Yahoo hosted for small businesses and retailers their websites.

Yahoo formed strategic partnerships with 20 mobile phone operators and had 35% market share of searches performed using mobile phones.

By 2004, Yahoo had grown to US$ 3.6 billion in revenues and US$ 836.9 in earnings; both growing at over 150% a year.

In 2005, Yahoo's web portal helped almost 4 million unique worldwide visitors every day in 2005. It was available anonymously to its users, or Yahoo helped users register to maintain their e-mail accounts, stock profiles, and check local news, weather, TV programs and more. Whereas most of this information came from public Internet sources in public domain, in 2005, Yahoo commissioned some financial experts for some original content. Yahoo also agreed to participate in the **Open Content Alliance**, to scan and provide access to books that were out-of-copyright timeframe.

In collaboration with **SBC, Yahoo** provided wireless service to its small businesses and e-commerce retailer Internet users. The two collaborators were developing a wireless connection to the entire Yahoo content. Yahoo's strategic moves drove its market space.

Yahoo received revenues for banner ads on Yahoo.com, Yahoo! Mail, Flickr, and its mobile phone customers.

In June 2008, **Yahoo** avoided a hostile takeover by **Microsoft**. Later Yahoo entered an agreement with **Google**, allowing Google to install Google search ads on Yahoo sites. This was expected to generate $800 million annually to Yahoo. This was terminated when Google strategic leaders received a notification from the U.S. Justice Department that their agreement with Yahoo perhaps violated prevailing laws.

MICROSOFT MSN SEARCH

Microsoft kept a close eye on Google's rise and success in search engine. In November 2004, after 18 months of development and US$ 150 million, Microsoft launched its MSN Live Search engine, www.search.msn.com. Its home page had a feel and look quite similar to that of Google, and it linked to its text-ads in more than 10 languages, similar to compete with that of Google.

MSN extended the functionality provided by Google to allow searchers to make queries in common languages. Users could ask, "How did Thomas Jefferson commission the Louisiana purchase?"

In 2003, chairman Bill Gates of Microsoft cautioned his employees that most Google job announcements were quite similar to their own job announcements (*Fortune, 2005*). By 2005, Google snagged the chief architect of Windows and more than 100 other Microsoft employees. Most of them were working in the operating system area. Gates suspected that Google was developing a competing product and planning to give to its Internet users free software products and services such as Word, Office, Power Point, Excel and Access. By doing so, Google would generate increasing revenues from advertisers.

Microsoft started offering mapping capabilities based on satellite pictures, to compete aggressively with Google in December 2005. The company also offered with MSN Search engine additional Voice over Internet Protocol (VoIP) in collaboration with **MCI**. This cut the cost of making local and long-distance calls to under 2 cents per minute, using a personal computer. This could be integrated into **Microsoft**'s other applications such as **Internet Explorer, Outlook**, and more.

In 2008, Microsoft acquired **Powerset**, developer of a semantic search engine, for $100 million. Semantic search engine evaluated the meaning of each word, and was likely to surpass the efficiency of relevance-based Google search engine. But, this required additional few seconds, and Microsoft limited its use for certain specific searches only.

Microsoft reported $60.4 billion revenues and $17.7 billion net income in 2008. The company sold computer software, video game hardware, online services, and consulting services. More than half of Microsoft's 2008 revenue, and almost all of its 2008 operating profits came from **Microsoft Office 2007 and Windows Vista**. Microsoft's online services, including banner ads, search-based ads etc., reported sales of $3.2 billion and operating loss of $1.2 billion. In 2008, Microsoft's Live Search engine cornered only 15% of online searches.

AMERICA ON LINE (AOL)

AOL had aggressively pursued potential consumers by shipping free **AOL** discs, to build its brand. By 2005, more than 20 million U.S. households and 6 million households in Europe subscribed to **AOL, Netscape, and CompuServe**.

In 2004, AOL merged with **Time Warner Inc.**, generated US$ 8.8 billion from its **Internet Service Provider (ISP)**. AOL offered a broadband service with partners. AOL connected on average close to 4 million unique visitors a day with sites such **as AOL Instant Messenger, Mapquest.com, Love.com, Moviefone.com, and others**.

AOL users, on average, spend more than 5 hours per month, significantly more than average of 4 hours per month for Yahoo, and more than 3 hours per month for Microsoft sites. AOL site was the stickiest rival on the Internet.

AOL leveraged all these users to lure large advertisers, who could also advertise with its Time Warner partner. In 2004, merged **AOL-Time Warner** had revenues of US$ 42 billion, with AOL accounting for 21% of revenues, and US$ 934 million in operating profits.

AOL had entered in agreement with Google for search engine services. The partnership generated US$ 300 million in revenues for AOL.

GOOGLE'S CULTURE

The mission of Google is "to organize the world's information and make it universally accessible and useful." In 2005, more than 10,600 Googler employees were based in Googleplex headquarters, and offices around the world. Google employees get generous share options that rise with the growth of the company. The company allows employees to use 20% of their time flexibly on their pet projects. This has given birth to a series of new products and search services.

GLOBALIZING GOOGLE

By 2005, more than a majority of Google's searches were originated from outside the United States. But, only 39% of Google's advertising revenues were global. To get closer to its Latin American advertisers, in 2005, Google opened its operations in Mexico and Brazil.

China had potential to be the world's second largest market. Rival Yahoo entered China in 1999. Google delayed from entering China, because of the state censorship on free speech. This censorship contradicted Google's core philosophy. Google started offering Chinese-language search results in 2000. In 2002, the Chinese government blocked Google's Internet users. Chinese government reopened Google site but censored some linked sites that had political criticized the Chinese government. Finally, to get closer to the Chinese searchers and advertisers, in 2004 Google invested 2.6% equity stake in Baidu, China's leading search engine (Wall St. Jl., 2005).

In 2005, the Chinese government coerced Google's rival Yahoo to disclose the private e-mail records of a journalist who criticized the Chinese government. Cautiously, Google induced Microsoft's key employee in China, and started setting up an office in China. To brand locally, Google launched a local website with ".cn"suffix, though this demanded agreeing to censorship by the Chinese regulators (Wall St. Jl., 2005).

SOCIAL RESPONSIBILITY

As a result of Google's meteoric rise, it was inevitable that some unexpected controversies arose. These included Google's intent to scan popular books and make these copyrighted documents openly available to searchers. Other critics have questioned Google regarding its privacy of searchers' search habits and web addresses. Google was also attacked for cooperating with the Chinese government, contrary to its domestic policy of opposing self-censorship.

SUSTAINING INNOVATIVE GROWTH

The worldwide Internet users exploded from about 360 million in 2000 to estimated 1,600 million in 2009. The United States had 74.4% penetration of the Internet. Asians in 2009 had only 17.4% Internet access, but 657 million Asian users were growing at the fastest rate in the world. How can Google's strategic leaders leverage these opportunities?

Whereas the U.S. economy was in a decline in 2009, and most companies had declining sales, Google reported small positive growth. To sustain Google's growth in its core and new businesses, **CEO Eric Schmidt** committed Google to stay focused on investing in technical innovation (Google Press Release, 2009, Jul. 16). Can Google sustain in the future its past phenomenal growth based on series of innovations?

ADDITIONAL READINGS AND REFERENCES: GOOGLE

Gamble, John E. Google Inc. in 2006: Can the Strategy Support the Lofty Stock Price. Case 18 in Thompson Jr., Arthur A., Strickland III, A.J. and Gamble, John E. 2006?? 15th Ed. *Crafting Executive Strategy: The Quest for Competitive Advantage*. New York: McGraw-Hill/Irwin.

Gamble, John E. Google's Strategy in 2009. Case 8 in Gamble, John A. and Strickland Jr., Thompson. 2011, 2009. 2nd Ed. *Essentials of Strategic Management. The Quest for Competitive Advantage*. New York: McGraw-Hill / Irwin.

Google's Corporate Information. www.google.com/corporate/history.html..

Google Corporate Information. Our Philosophy. www.google.com/corporate/tenthings.html.

Google Inc. Form S-1.

Google Press Release, 2009, Jul. 16. Google Announces Second Quarter 2009 Results.

Fortune. 2005. Gates vs. Google. April 18.

Fortune, 2008. Nov. 5. With Google Gone, Will Microsoft Come Back to Yahoo?

New York Times. 2005. Governments Tremble at Google's Bird-Eye View. December 20.

Mantle, Jonathan. 2008. *Companies That Changed the World. From the East India Company to Google Inc.* London; Quercus.

Page, Larry and Brin, Sergey. year *The Anatomy of a Large-Scale Hypertextual Web Search Engine*.

The Wall Street Journal Online. 1999. High-Tech Search Engine Google Won't Talk About Business Plan. June 4. (Xref#1)

The Wall Street Journal Online. 2004. The Grownup at Google. March 29: B1. (Xref#3, #4).

The Wall Street Journal Online. 2004. For Some Who Passed on Google Long Ago, Wistful Thinking. August 23. (Xref#8)

The Wall Street Journal Online. 2004. Slice of PI: New Google Mystery Centers on $4 Billion Share Sale. August 19. (Xref#9)

The Wall Street Journal Online. 2005. As Google Pushes into China, it Faces Clashes with Censors. December 16: 1.

The Wall Street Journal Online. 2005. Google's Wireless Plan Underscores Threat to Telecom. October 3: 1.

. . .

GOOGLE SEARCHING STRATEGY IN 2009: LIST OF EXHIBITS

Exhibit – 1.   **KEY MILESTONES FOR GOOGLE**

Exhibit – 2.   **MARKET SHARE OF RIVAL SEARCH ENGINES**

Exhibit – 3.   **THE 10 ELEMENTS OF GOOGLE PHILOSOPHY**

Exhibit - 4.   **GOOGLE'S REVENUES FROM DIFFERENT SOURCES (Rounded $ million)**

Exhibit – 5.   **FINANCIAL PERFORMANCE OF GOOGLE (Rounded to $**
million)

Exhibit – 6.   **GROSS AND NET INCOME (Rounded to $million); INCOME PER SHARE**

Exhibit – 7.   **GOOGLE'S FINANCIALS (CONTD.)**

Exhibit – 8.   **REVENUES OF GOOGLE BY GEOGRAPHIC REGION (2006-**
08, Dec. 31)

Exhibit – 9.   **LONG-LIVED ASSETS OF GOOGLE BY GEOGRAPHIC REGION (2006-08, Dec. 31)**

Exhibit – 1.   KEY MILESTONES FOR GOOGLE

1973	Larry Page is born in Michigan, USA
1973	Sergey Brin is born in Russia
1995	Larry meets Sergey at Stanford University
1997 Sep. 14	The domain google.com is registered
1999	Googleplex headquarters are set up
2001	Eric Schmidt is appointed as CEO of Google
2004	Google goes public
2005	Google launches Google Earth
2006	YouTube is acquired by Google
2007	Google acquires DoubleClick
	Google Stock exceeds $700.

Exhibit – 2.   MARKET SHARE OF RIVAL SEARCH ENGINES

	2004	2006 July	2009 June
Google	47%	43.7%	65.0%
Yahoo	21	28.8	19.6
MSN	14	12.8	8.4
AOL	—	5.9	3.1
Ask.com	n.s.	5.4	3.9
Others	18	3.4	n.s.
Total	100	100	100

Source: Adapted from Nielsen/Net Ratings in Fortune Online, April 18, 2005, and ComScore.com.

Exhibit – 3.   THE 10 ELEMENTS OF GOOGLE PHILOSOPHY

1. Focus on the User and All else will follow.
Google believes in providing the best user experience, by offering (1) a clear and simple interface, (2) instantly loading pages, (3) with advertisers offering relevant content without distraction, and (4) never sells search results to anyone else.

2. It's Best to do One Thing Really, Really Well.
Google uses its huge research and development tea to focus on developing the world's best search engine. They leveraged what they have learned into additional related services, such as Google Maps, Gmail, Google Desktop, and more.

3. Fast is Better Than Slow.
Google tries hard to provide the fastest, and most instant gratification to its searchers.

4. Democracy on the Web Works.
Google avoids relying on a few editors and instead basis its business on a vast number of website providers available worldwide.

5. You Don't Need to be at Your Desk to Need an Answer.
Google believes in enhancing people's mobility by providing its search services through a variety of distribution channels.

6. You can Make Money Without Doing Evil.
Google generates revenue by seeking advertisements, without these ads distracting the search effort on Google's results page (unless the sponsored links are related to the search results). Advertisers are clearly and ethically identified as "Sponsored Link."

7. There's Always More Information Out There.
Google tries hard to creatively retrieve difficult to find information. Documents in diverse formats are integrated with relevant images.

8. The Need for Information Crosses All Borders.
Google maintains offices and Internet domains around the globe to retrieve information in 35 languages. A translation service allows users to refer information in other languages.

9. You can be Serious Without a Suit.
Google puts its employees first and believes in facing challenges while having fun. An informal ambiance allows sharing and ease of communication.

10. Great Just Isn't Good Enough.
Google anticipates what its customers' needs and is not able to articulate clearly. It then tries to innovate what works well and iterates to go beyond.

Exhibit - 4. **GOOGLE'S REVENUES FROM DIFFERENT SOURCES**
(Rounded $ million)

	Advertising Revenues Google Web site	Google Network Web site	Total Advertising Revenues	Licensing and other Revenues	Net Reve- nues
2001	67	--	67	19	86
2002	307	12	319	29	348
2003	792	629	1,421	45	1,466
2004	1,589	1,554	3,143	46	3,189
2005	3,377	2,688	6,065	74	6,139
2006	6,333	4,160	10,493	112	10,605
2007	10,625	5,788	16,413	181	16,594
2008	14,414	6,715	21,129	667	21,796

Source: Various Google 10-K and S-1 Reports.

Exhibit – 5. **FINANCIAL PERFORMANCE OF GOOGLE**
(Rounded to $ million)

Year Dec 31	Revenues Revenues	Cost of Goods	R&D	Sales & Marketing	General & Admin.	Total Cost	Income fr Ops.
2001	86	14	17	20	12	75	11
2002	440	136	32	44	24	253	186
2003	1,466	626	91	120	57	1,123	342
2004	3,189	1,458	226	246	140	2,549	640
2005	6,139	2,577	600	468	387	4,121	1,465
2006	10,605	4,225	1,229	850	758	7,055	3,078
2007	16,594	6,649	2,120	1,461	1,279	11,511	4,204
2008	21,796	8,622	2,793	1,946	1,803	15,164	4,227

Exhibit – 6. GROSS AND NET INCOME (Rounded to $million) AND INCOME PER SHARE

Year Dec 31	Income from Ops	Interest income (expense)	Income Tax	Net Income	Income/share Basic Provision	Diluted
2001	11	(1)	3	7	$0.07	$0.04
2002	186	(2)	85	100	$0.86	$0.45
2003	342	4	241	106	$0.77	$0.41
2004	640	10	251	399	$2.07	$1.46
2005	2,017	124	676	1,465	$5.31	$5.02
2006	3,550	461	934	3,078	$10.21	$9.94
2007	5,084	590	1,470	4,204	$13.53	$13.29
2008	6,632	316	1,627	4,227	$13.46	$13.31

Exhibit – 7. GOOGLE'S FINANCIALS (CONTD.)

Year Dec 31	# Shares Basic Mil.	Marketable Diluted Mil.	Total Securities	Total Current Assets	Total Assets = liabilities	Total Current Liab.	Stock Equity
2001	95	187	na	na	na	na	na
2002	115	221	89	232	287	90	174
2003	138	257	186	560	871	235	589
2004	193	273	2,132	2,693	3,313	340	2,929
2005	276	292	8,034	na	10,272	na	9,419
2006	301	310	11,244	na	18,473	na	17,040
2007	311	316	14,219	na	25,336	na	22,690
2008	314	318	15,846	na	31,768	na	28,239

Source: Various Google Financial Statements.

© 2010 Dr. R. RAY GEHANI

Exhibit – 8.   REVENUES OF GOOGLE BY GEOGRAPHIC REGION
(2006-08, Dec. 31)

In $ million (Rounded)	Revenues		Rest of The World	Total Revenues
	U.S.A.	U.K.		
2006	6,030	1,604	2,971	10,605
2007	8,698	2,531	5,365	16,594
2008	10,636	3,039	8,121	21,796

Exhibit – 9. LONG-LIVED ASSETS OF GOOGLE BY GEOGRAPHIC
REGION (for 2006-08, Dec. 31)

In $ million (Rounded)	U.S.A.	Rest of The World	Total L.L. Assets
2006	5,071	363	5,433
2007	7,335	712	8,047
2008	9,783	1,807	11,590

KEVLAR MIRACLE POLYMER:
A CASE STUDY IN BREAKTHROUGH INNOVATION AT DU PONT

Dr. R. RAY GEHANI

Institute for Innovation and Technology Leadership (IITL)
Akron, Ohio.

Abstract

This case reviews the progress and evolution of a radical innovation in a major technology-driven U.S. corporation. The senior management in the Executive Committee (X-Committee) is faced with a strategic dilemma of funding $332 million for a 50 million pound Kevlar plant expansion in 1974. The Textile Fibers Department requested this approval to generate economies of scale needed to compete in the tire cord reinforcement market invaded by steel radial belt tires, and a reluctant aerospace reinforced composite market.

Analyze the case to develop your decisions and recommendations for funding the larger new plant.

KEVLAR: THE SUPER-STIFF MIRACLE POLYMER

Kevlar®, an aromatic amide (para-aramid) forms a fiber that is a high-strength, lightweight synethtic polymer fiber. It has 5 times the tensile strength of steel per pound.

Thousands of policemen and policewomen protect their lives in the line of their duty. These highly desirable properties helped Kevlar aramid fiber become an indispensible material in the lightweight bullet-resistant vests, fire-resistant and fire-blocking fabrics, canoes, mooring ropes, fiber-optic cables, and sails for yachts. Kevlar® is also found in fiber reinforcement in automobile tires, brake linings, and high performance composites for aerospace and many more applications.

But in February 1974, Du Pont's Textile Fibers Department was not so sure while submitting a request for $332 million capital expenditure to build a 50 million pounds of Kevlar Aramid fiber per year plant to Du Pont's Executive Committee. This committee was known inside Du Pont as X-Committee. If the X-Committee approved the proposal, it would allocate first of four $82 million to fund the partial design of the plant, and better estimation of cost of construction.

The journey for the breakthrough technological innovation of this Kevlar aramid started in the early 1960s with DuPont's need for a high performance next-generation fiber. The development moved forward because of new ways of creative thinking, inter-disciplinary teams, and sustained sponsorship by senior leadership. Many unexpected events demanding unconventional wisdom occurred during the journey of this breakthrough innovation.

The story of Kevlar innovation spanned from early 1960s, to invention of aromatic amide polymer and fiber in 1965, followed by a scale-up and a steady growth in the production capacity of this synthetic polymer fiber. In 1971, after a presentation on the invention, properties, and anticipated markets for aramid Fiber B1, the X-Committee allocated $8.9 million for a Market Development Facility (MDF) to produce enough Fiber B1 to estimate the manufacturing cost and conduct its market research. Since January 1, 1971, Fiber B1 development was reclassified as a New Venture Development. The cost incurred thereafter was not included in the income statement of the Textile Fibers Department. In 1972, Du Pont built a 1 million pound/year market development plant. Full commercialization was reached by 1982, with a 45 million pound/year plant.

PREAMBLE TO ARAMID INNOVATIONS

During the early 1960s, Du Pont was encouraged by the invention and block-buster commercial success of the first synthetic nylon polymer and a series of better polymer fibers. In response to this need the senior management at Du Pont research organization identified a need for developing super polymer fibers with the conflicting and unusual requirements of high stiffness of glass, and the high thermal resistance of asbestos.

The research route for achieving such breakthrough super polymer fiber was through synthesizing breakthrough polymers. Another scientific conflict involved the spinning and fiber-formation of candidate polymers. Because of the extreme insolubility and intractability of certain potential polymers, previous experimental attempts of spinning such polymers into fibers had failed.

Complimentary Nomex-related Competencies

In 1950, Du Pont researchers identified a need to synthesize a stiffer and more thermally stable polyamide for application in fire-fighting garments, airplane upholstery and others. Such a polymer was synthesized in 1950 at the interface of two immiscible liquids and room temperature. Researchers continued to improve this process, and in 1953 some polymers were synthesized from a single-phase solution at low temperatures. In 1959, a group of researchers including **Stepahanie Kwolek, Paul Morgan, and Wilfred Sweeney**, working at Wilmington Experimental Station, used solution polymerization to form an aromatic polyamide with sufficiently high molecular weight to form a fiber. They ran a number of trials to further simplify the polymerization process for a patentable polymer. In 1961, the X-Committee authorized the Textile Fibers Department to build a 1-million pound pilot plant in Richmond, Virginia to produce aramid fiber and paper in place of the closed down rayon manufacturing facility. In 1963 this was trademarked as Nomex aromatic polyamide or aramid. In the same year, the Richmond pilot plant produced Nomex paper, substituting natural mineral mica for electrical insulating applications. Approval of the Underwriter's Laboratory (UL) was obtained for Nomex paper as an insulating material. Boeing and Lockheed got interested.

In 1965, Du Pont's X-Committee authorized construction of a 9 million pounds per year commercial plant for Nomex in Richmond, Virginia. The commercial Nomex plant was commissioned in 1967.

Pre-commercial R&D expenses for developing Nomex exceeded $50 million, an unprecedented amount for a development project at Du Pont. The sales of Nomex were much below expectations, and the Nomex plant operated below its rated capacity for six years. The development of Nomex fiber progressed slowly because aramid was harder to dye with light-stable dyes. The Nomex plant saw many operating hurdles, and needed modifications for wider market diffusion and acceptance. This was typical for industrial products, where industrial customers were reluctant to replace tried and tested materials with unproven newer products. For first 4 years, Nomex generated only marginal operating earnings, and lost money. Du Pont had to commit $100 million before making any profit from the new polymer.

Other New Polymer Innovations In the Pipeline

After the block-buster success of **nylon**, **Dacron** polyester fiber, and **Orlon** acrylic fibers in the market-place, Textile Fibers Department in Du Pont had launched in the 1960s the commercialization of a number of new polymer products. These included Qianna nylon, Reemay spunbonded polyester, Typar spunbonded polypropylene, Tyvek spun-bonded polyethylene, and Nomex aramid fiber. These polymer innovations required heavy investments in high pre-commercialization R&D, high capital expenses in plants to a total estimated at more than $300 million. These innovations also produced high operating losses, estimated at over $400 million, in their early years after commercialization. The X-Committee called them "problem children." (**See Exhibit - 1**). Only Lycra spandex fiber from this group became a profitable success in a short time after its commercialization. The polymer fibers commercialized earlier, such as nylon, Dacron Polyester, and Orlon acrylic fibers were seeing a slowdown in their sales because of increasing competition from new rivals entering the synthetic fiber industry.

EXHIBIT – 1
DUPONT's MAJOR NEW TEXTILE FIBER PRODUCT INNOVATIONS

Fiber Type	Discovery	Commercialization	Years
Lycra Spandex Fiber[1]	1953	1962	9
Nomex Aramid Fiber	1954	1967	13
Reemay Spunbonded polyester	1958	1965	7
Typar Spunbonded Polypropylene1	1958	1966	8
Tyvek Spunbonded polyethylene[2]	1958	1967	9
Qiana Nylon	1960	1968	8

[1]Lycra R&D costs were $25 million; cumulative losses prior to commercialization by 1973 amounted to $115 million.
[2]Cumulative pre-commercial losses increased to $265 million by 1973.
[2]Other fibers cost $25-60 million (average $45 million) pre-commercial R&D.

This was the time when the Textile Fibers Department requested Du Pont X-Committee for $332 million allocation for Kevlar plant.

Unspinnable Opaque Aramid Polymer Solution

In 1965 **Stephanie Kwolek**, was working under **Gene Magat**, Research Manager responsible for the research effort, and with Paul Morgan. Born in New Kensington, Pennsylvania, in 1946 Stephanie Louise Kwolek received her Bachelor of Science degree in chemistry from the Carnegie Institute of Technology. Same year, she joined E.I du Pont de Nemours & Company as a chemist at the Buffalo, New York facility. In 1950, she moved to the pioneering Research Laboratory at Du Pont's Experimental Station in Wilmington, Delaware. [Note #1. Kwolek retired from Du Pont as a research associate in 1986, but continued to consult with the company. She was inducted to the National Inventors' Hall of Fame in 1995. She also served on the committees of the National Academy of Sciences and the National Research Council.]

After synthesizing the polymer and preparing an opaque, watery solution of an aromatic polyamide polymer, Stephanie Kwolek discovered that it could not be either clarified by filtration or thermal distillation. She discovered that when the opaque watery solution was stirred, it became opalescent. This seemed like a dead end for fiber formation research. The conventional understanding of polymer science would make one believe that the aramid polymer solution probably had a viscosity too low to be spinnable into forming fibers. Further, that the opaque polymer solution probably had some very fine suspended particles which would instantly plug the microscopic holes in the fiber forming spinneretes. Stephanie Kwolek, if she had followed the conventional understanding of the state of polymer science knowledge, should have discarded the opaque polymer solution flowing like water. However, she did not stop there. By conducting crude spinnability test, such as dipping a spatula in the polymer solution and lifting it. She was surprised to see that the watery opaque solution gave a 'honey-like' steady flow instead of dropping as droplets. This was rather strange.

Persistence Pays Off

Instead of rejecting such opaque watery polymer solution, Stephanie Kwolek persisted with spinning the fiber. This persistence paid off. The watery opaque polymer solution spun into fibers with ease and with amazing properties. She discovered an amazing new branch of polymer science – liquid crystalline polymers (anisotropic). She was awarded patent number 3,819,587; Re. 30,352 for "optically anisotropic aromatic polyamide dopes and oriented fibers there from."

Discovering Science for Technological Innovation

Stephanie noted that in certain polymer solutions, depending on the molecular structure of the polymers, a degree of order intermediate between the isotropic disorder of a liquid and the perfect order of a solid was formed. This was called the liquid-crystalline state. Generally the liquid-crystalline structure was formed by polymers with rigid rod-like molecules. (See **Exhibit - 2**). These liquid-crystalline phases were further classified as Smectic (Type S), Nematic (Type N), or Cholesteric (Type C) liquid-crystals. The Type S smectic liquid crystal had the highest order, with rod-like molecules arranged in layers. In the Type N nematic phase the rod-like molecules were oriented parallel, but their centers of gravity were positioned in a disorganized manner. The Type C cholesteric liquid crystalline phase, with a helical structure, occurred only in optically active substances. (**See Exhibit - 2**). Furthermore, the liquid-crystals were also classified as lyotropic Type L when induced by the concentration of solution, and thermotropic Type T when induced by temperature.

EXHIBIT – 2: STRUCTURE OF MATERIALS

ISOTROPIC

NEMATIC LIQUID-CRYSTAL

SMECTIC LIQUID-CRYSTAL

CHOLESTERIC LIQUID-CRYSTAL

Source: Gehani, R. Ray. 1985. Aramid – New Generation High Performance Fiber, <u>Synthetic Fibers</u>, July/September, Volume 14, No. 3.

A 15% solution of para-aromatic polyamide, dissolved in sulphuric acid, manifested lyotropic liquid-crystalline behavior. Such liquid-crystalline solutions retained the high degree of orientation in fibers that was imparted in the spinning stage. Such as-spun fibers were likely to be extremely strong without requiring additional orientation. On the other hand, in the conventional flexible-chain polymers, the orientation imparted by spinning was relaxed rapidly.

After extended and systematic research, **Stephanie Kwolek** and other polymer researchers established that the solution was not due to suspended fine particles but due to the formation of polymer liquid crystals in aromatic polyamide solutions. In the spinnerete, as the polymer solution was forced through the microscopic holes, the long liquid crystalline polymer molecules oriented, resulting in breakthrough spinnability and high strength in the spun fibers. The as-spun fibers from aramid liquid-crystalline solutions recrystallized easily on brief heat-treatment at temperatures above 300 ^{0}C. This improved perfection of lateral order of the rigid polymer chains in the fiber, with tenacity as high as 18 grams per denier, and modulus higher than 1,000 grams per denier. Like Nomex, the fibers were heat resistant and stable at high temperatures. But amazingly, these miracle fibers were very strong and stiff, unlike Nomex.

The aramid fibers were more than 7 times stiffer than commercially available Dacron polyester fibers. Unlike nylon and polyester fiber, the aramid fibers manifested mechanical properties, like tensile strength and modulus, much closer to their calculated theoretical limiting properties. (**See Exhibits – 3 and 4**).

The as-spun fibers formed from aromatic polyamide solution were tested for physical characteristics by the Du Pont physical testing laboratory. They were shocked to see the results. The mechanical characteristics were so high that they thought they had made some mistake. Others did not believe the extraordinary results easily. The test laboratory technicians ran the stress-strain tests a number of times, to replicate the results, often in front of a number of observers. The aromatic polyamide fiber had four times higher stiffness than that of glass, and a breaking strength that was radically many times more than that of the fibers known at that time. And, therefore a perfect new candidate for use as a tire reinforcement, and in high performance composites used in aircraft.

In 1969, the Textile Fibers Department started sending small sample quantities of aramid fiber with code name Fiber B, to selected tire companies and an aircraft manufacturer. The tire companies had to use a special adhesive dipping treatment under severe conditions (high tension) to stretch and bond the Fiber B cords to rubber. They were, however, able to make about 200 test tires, which showed most superior product performance of all competing products. But, the severity of the dipping conditions was likely to limit the appeal of Fiber B as a tire reinforcement to many tire manufacturers.

The luck also ran out soon thereafter on other fronts. Du Pont researchers discovered that the raw materials and intermediates required were too expensive for scaling-up the production to multi-million pound quantities needed to demonstrate the commercial viability of the innovation super fiber concept based on aromatic polyamide. Particularly, for the tire cord reinforcement application.

These two obstacles seemed insurmountable in 1970. Du Pont researchers in the Pioneering Research Laboratory and managers did not give up. They launched a major research initiative to understand physical chemistry and synthesis to produce a variety of liquid crystalline solutions. The outcome of this research initiative, after two years, was a body of new knowledge that helped develop a liquid crystalline polymer from more economic ingredients. This was called **PPD-T polymer**. This was a breakthrough discovery of low-cost raw materials to make a polymer that produced a fiber with unprecedented great properties. This would pave the way to enormous economic prosperity for the Du Pont enterprise. The improved fiber, named Fiber B1, had high thermal resistance, slightly higher stiffness, and a 50% improvement in tensile strength.

Another obstacle had emerged in realizing this breakthrough technological innovation to its commercial success. The liquid crystalline polymer solutions required the fiber spinning in extremely corrosive 100% sulfuric acid solvent. The polymer solutions were found to be too viscous to spin at commercially economical speeds. This liquid crystal fiber spinning process was discussed with the engineers and production managers who would design, construct, and operate the polymer production and fiber spinning plants. They found that the production yields of the sulfuric acid spinning process were too low and required very high investments. The polymer dissolving, mixing, and fiber spinning was run at room temperatures because the conventional wisdom suggested that corrosivity as well as polymer degradation were expected to increase exponentially if the fiber spinning was performed at higher temperatures. The production engineers therefore concluded that spinning super-strong fiber from the liquid crystal aromatic polyamide in sulfuric acid solution was not practical, and therefore worthy of rejection and discontinuation of further efforts.

Another Du Pont researcher, **Herb Blades,** took this challenge and went against the conventional wisdom prevailing at that time, that **PPD-T** liquid crystalline polymer would be degraded significantly if used with sulfuric acid solution at high temperature. Herb Blades proceeded by heating a liquid crystalline polymer solution in 100% sulfuric acid. The polymer solution formed a liquid-crystalline complex and did not degrade as expected by the nay-sayers. The innovators persisted their efforts with this breakthrough discovery by developing an innovative new fiber spinning technology using dramatically higher polymer concentrations than those tried earlier. They demonstrated to the engineers and production managers that the fiber spinning yields and economics improved dramatically with the development of the new technological innovations.

Multi-disciplinary Production Scale-Up Team

When the engineers and production managers fully grasped the proposed innovative production technology, and the risks associated with this, they agreed to participate in a core multi-disciplinary team for scale-up from laboratory scale process to a scaleable commercial scale. Effectively doing this is one of the toughest obstacles for a technology-driven enterprise.

Du Pont management formed a new business unit for the scale-up and further development of production technology for the super-stiff aromatic polyamide fiber. A multi-disciplinary task force of dozens of engineers and scientists was chartered to do the needed task of developing the basic manufacturing data and scale-up knowledge. Some of the researchers in the Du Pont Experimental Station at Wilmington, Delaware, were physically moved to report at a new plant site in Virginia.

Scale-Up Obstacles. A number of new obstacles emerged from time to time and were successfully tackled. The spent sulfuric acid used in the liquid-crystalline polymer solution had to be economically recovered and disposed of after fiber spinning. A creative solution emerged based on converting the spent sulfuric acid into gypsum (calcium sulfate) used by cement and wallboard manufacturers.

Another scale-up obstacle, encountered unexpectedly, was related to the solution used in polymerization, hexa-methyl-phosporamide. This was discovered to be animal carcinogen by Du Pont Haskell laboratories in their lifetime exposure study with experimental rats. Emergency measures were taken to ensure that the workers, the community, or the customers were not exposed to this hazard. A crash technological initiative was started to discover an alternate bio-safer solvent for polymerization.

Du Pont managers had developed a high level of confidence in problem solving capability of the multi-disciplinary core development team. With sustained support from Du Pont's strategic leadership, the multi-disciplinary team could overcome any obstacle with creative breakthrough thinking.

Even though the production technology involved was complex, the progress was rapid. From laboratory discoveries of Herb Blades, in less than 2 years, a **1 million pound/year market development plant** started shipping Kevlar® to potential customers of this super-stiff polymer fiber. A **15 million pound/year market development plant** was commissioned 5 years later.

Market Commercialization

Management approval for a full-scale commercial plant for this breakthrough technological innovation involved a financial commitment of US$ 400 million. A prerequiste for this financial commitment was to demonstrate the market potential of Kevlar®. This market development effort to discover viable and practical new applications of Kevlar® was required to be carried out in parallel with the efforts required for product development and production development of super-stiff poly-aramid fiber.

For commercial success of Kevlar®, this super-stiff fiber had to offer competitive price with a superior value-adding higher than that of DuPont's incumbent polymer fiber such as polyamide nylon, and other competing reinforcing fibers such as steel, fiberglass, and carbon.

Du Pont researchers had already discovered that the super-stiff Kevlar® fiber would not fit the existing conventional applications. The miracle fiber required to search its own market. Initially applications in tires, ropes, cables, composites, asbestos replacement and more were evaluated.

RISK-TAKING SENIOR MANAGEMENT

In early 1971, Textile Fibers Department requested X-Committee to allocate a $32 million Market Development Facility (MDF) in Richmond. They did this on the basis of the favorable results of tests run on Fiber B by the tire companies, but without specifically testing the improved Fiber B1 with the tire makers and aerospace companies. Already 5 years had passed since Stephanie Kwolek had spun Fiber B, and the Textile Fibers Department had spent $5.7 million on this project in the laboratory. By December 1971, the Fiber B1 Market Development Facility was commissioned, using previous equipment design (rather than commercial scale equipments) with a starting capacity of 125 pounds per hour.

The Fiber B1 thus produced was sent to the potential customers. The next step involved designing a larger MDF-II, with the critical process technologies needed in the future commercial scale production plant. The larger MDF-II with 6 million pound capacity, would generate more accurate cost data. In April 1972, the X-Committee approved the appropriation, and provided additional funds in May 1973. The MDF-II, with an initial capacity of 900 pounds per hour was commissioned in the fourth quarter of 1973. Capacity could be further increased by a factor of 2-3. Over a million pounds of Fiber B1 were produced in MDF-I and MDF-II, at the average cost of $20 per pound. The R&D department had made more process improvements to produce a better Fiber B1, now trademarked as Kevlar Aramid Fiber.

The original cost projections, based on crude laboratory equipments, had postulated that a 20 million pound plant would cost $112 million, and if run on 90% sales/capacity ratio, would yield a 10-20% return on investment. These needed to be modified somewhat by a conventional amount, as the 90% capacity utilization could not be achieved until the 5th year of commercialization. To penetrate the tire cord reinforcement markets and fiber reinforced composite market at competitive prices, Du Pont concluded that more economies of scale were needed, and plant capacity must be raised higher.

1. TIRE CORD REINFORCEMENT MARKET

Du Pont was a pioneer in the tire cord reinforcement business. In the mid 1930s, in cooperation with Goodyear, Du Pont displaced cotton tire cord with cellulosic rayon tire cord. By early 1940, rayon tire cord had replaced cotton tire cord. (See Exhibit – 5).

After World War II ended, and the military demand for nylon started slowing down, Du Pont introduced nylon tire cord. Nyon tire cord had many advantages including better tensile strength, tensile modulus, and elongation to break than rayon tire cord. Nylon, however, had a major disadvantage. Overnight, when the tire was not moving, it got cold and loaded on one point for extended period of time. This caused flat-spotting on the tire at the point of contact with ground. After the rest period, when the automobile was driven, the flat spot in the tires produced a 'thumpy' ride until the tire was heated and rounded. Du Pont spent millions of dollars in R&D but could not eliminate the flat spotting caused by nylon tire cord. Finally, Du Pont developed polyester tire cord with no flat spotting, but needed a special adhesive dipping treatment. The Big Automakers, using huge quantities of tires as original equipment (OE), were afraid that the auto owners would not buy their cars fitted with nylon tires. Du Pont and other rivals invested aggressively to develop and produce nylon and polyester tire cords for different tire market segments.

Radial Tire Invasion

In the late 1960s, another major technological assault came from Michelin of France in the form of Radial tire. Most of the tire reinforcement was provided by a belt, which ran circumferentially around the tire, in the direction of the motion. Only one third of tire cord was needed, as radial bands plied perpendicular to the belt circumference or the direction of motion. Neither nylon nor polyester tire cords had the needed mechanical properties to reinforce tire as the radial belts. Fiberglass had the needed mechanical characteristics, but poor flex life, adhesion to rubber, and durability. Some new steel reinforcement wires had the needed characteristics for use in the radial belts. The core-competencies and competitive advantages of Du Pont were in chemical and polymer related technologies, and not in fiber-glass or steel manufacturing. With the rise of radial tires, Du Pont was facing a likely threat of losing its tire industry market.

At first, the American tire makers and the Big auto makers were reluctant to shift to radial tires. In 1970, about 40% of tires used in Europe were radial, whereas in the United States only 1% of radial tires were used. General Motors, however showed interest in introducing radial tires in its cars by about 1975. The super strong Aramid Kevlar fiber was Du Pont's hope to compete with the rising demand for steel wire reinforced radial belts. Kevlar was 4-5 times stronger than steel pound-for-pound. Kevlar's tensile strength and tensile modulus were better than those of steel wire. Kavlar's elongation to break was inferior to steel, but still acceptable. In thousands of bias-belted and radial tires, Kevlar had performed extremely well. And, fortunately for Du Pont, in the United States, the steel tire cord manufacturers were reluctant to enter in this labor intensive market, or expand their steel cord capacity.

Kevlar was lighter than steel, thereby providing fuel-efficiency and a smoother ride. Unlike steel, Kevlar could be processed and run on the processing equipment developed and used for rayon, nylon, and polyester tire cords. Kevlar did not pose the difficulties that tire makers experienced while producing large radial truck tires with steel belts. Du Pont estimated that for Kevlar to compete and gain market share, it could not be priced more than 4.8 times the price of steel. This was the replacement ratio for the two competing materials. The total market for Kevlar belt tire cord was estimated to reach 500 million pounds by 1980.

The major tire makers were willing to adopt Kevlar aramid as tire cord in their higher performance tires, and replace rayon belts with Kevlar. Goodyear launched its Double Eagle super-premium radial tire, belted with Flexten, a Kevlar based proprietary tire reinforcement. World-wide, 8 tire makers sold Kevlar belted radial tires as their highest performance tires. More companies made thousands of truck tires reinforced with Kevlar. With such market success, MDF-II plant making Kevlar was unable to fully meet the heavy demand. With full capacity utilization, it was hard to make product and process improvements on this facility. The Textile Fibers department, therefore estimated that a 50 million pound plant would generate the economies of scale needed to effectively compete with its substitute steel tire cord. Hence the department's request to the Du Pont X-Committee.

EXHIBIT - 3
PHYSICAL PROPERTIES OF HIGH PERFORMANCE FIBERS

TYPE OF FIBER	Specific Gravity	Young's Modulus GN/m^2	Tensile Strength GN/m^2	Elongation to Break %
1. Polyamide 6,6	1.14	5	0.9	13.5
2. Polyester	1.38	12	1.0	10.5
3. E-Glass	2.6	70	2.5	4.0
4. Steel	7.8	200	4.0	2.0
5. Aramid Kevlar 29	1.44	59	2.7	4.0
6. Aramid Kevlar 49	1.45	127	2.9	2.6
7. Hi Strength Carbon	1.75	260	2.6	1.0
8. Hi Modulus Carbon	1.95	400	2.0	0.5

Source: Gehani, R. Ray. 1985. Aramid – New Generation High Performance Fiber, Synthetic Fibers, July/September, Volume 14, No. 3.

EXHIBIT – 4
MAXIMUM CALCULATED THEORETICAL MODULUS AND STRENGTHS OF FIBERS

	Modulus Grams/denier	Strength Grams/denier
1. Polyester	950	200
2. Polyamide 6,6	1780	215
3. para-aramide	1500	165
4. Polyethylene	2060	250

Source: Gehani, R. Ray. 1985. Aramid – New Generation High Performance Fiber, Synthetic Fibers, July/September, Volume 14, No. 3.

EXHIBIT - 5
TIRE CORD SUBSTITUTION
(In millions of pounds)

Type of Tire Cord	1970	1971	1972	1973
Rayon	86	113	94	73
Nylon	265	276	291	274
Polyester	150	179	222	242
Fiberglass	35	36	37	34
Steel	3	5	24	60
Kevlar	-	-	-	1
Total	**539**	**609**	**668**	**683**

EXHIBIT – 6
SALES AND EARNINGS OF Du PONT COMPANY AND TEXTILE FIBERS DEPARTMENT
(In US$ millions)

	Fibers Department		Du Pont Company	
	Sales	Earnings	Sales	Earnings
1960	712	124	2,143	251
1962	815	159	2,407	309
1964	972	180	2,761	343
1966	1,087	163	3,159	372
1968	1,299	175	3,455	362
1972	1,885	184	4,961	418
1973	2,283	243	6,008	579

2. FIBER REINFORCEMENT COMPOSITE MARKET

In the 1960s and early 1970s, the fiber – reinforced composite materials were used in industrial and aerospace applications requiring the strengths of aluminum and steel, but with much lower weight. Airframe manufacturers valued weight savings at $50 per pound, compounding further with advantages in design and fuel carrying capacity, to about $150 per pound. Fiberglass reinforced composites were routinely used using 50-60% fiberglass in a plastic matrix of phenolic or epoxy polymer resins. However, the fiberglass reinforced composite materials were weak in transverse direction, and strong only along the axis of the fiber glass

© *2010 Dr. R. RAY GEHANI*

reinforcement. Fiberglass reinforced composite plastics (known as FRP) had low impact resistance, and lower fatigue strength than metals.

Du Pont's Nomex was adopted by Boeing and Lockheed in non structural parts of aircraft panel composites. Du Pont was hoping to leverage that success by introducing Kevlar for reinforcement in the structural airframe components. Kevlar had about same tensile strength and a higher modulus than glass fiber reinforcements, with significantly lower density than glass. Substituting glass fiber with Kevlar fiber could generate at least 25% reduction in weight. This implied an added-value of $25 per pound of compsoite material in aircraft applications. There was a high demand potential for Kevlar fiber if it was priced between $10 and $15 per pound. Kevlar also absorbed radar waves, a distinct advantage over using metal parts in fighter aircrafts and other military aerospace and missile applications.

Carbon fibers and boron fibers were other reinforcements used in aircraft and aerospace applications. Carbon fibers were supplied at $50-$500 per pound by a number of U.S. companies, such as Union Carbide, Hercules, British companies such as Courtaulds, and Japanese companies such as Toray. Carbon fiber composites were three times stiffer than Kevlar composites, but Kevlar had weight and strength advantages. Carbon fibers were so fine that they penetrated skin while handling in making fiber reinforced composites. Hybrid composites reinforced with carbon and Kevlar fibers seemed to produce the optimum properties and handling in aircraft and aerospace markets. Boron fibers, with double the stiffness of Kevlar, were also potential reinforcements, but cost $200-300 per pound. Economies of scale was likely to reduce this price by a factor of two to three.

Du Pont was also aware that in aircraft and aerospace applications, the material certifications took ver long periods of testing. This made estimating demand for Kevlar quite unceyrtain. They estimated that by 1980, about 11 million pounds of Kevlar may be required in aircraft and aerospace applications.

EXHIBIT - 7

FINANCIAL PERFORMANCE OF DU PONT COMPANY
(US$ million)

Year	Sales	Operating Income	Operating Investment	% Net ROI Op.	Long-term Debt
1947	783	78	1,016	7.7 %	0
1950	1,298	187	1,408	13.3	0
1953	1,750	153	1,866	8.2	0
1956	1,888	255	2,252	11.3	0
1959	2,114	288	2,745	10.5	0
1962	2,407	305	3,341	9.1	0
1965	3,400	419	5,238	8.6	43
1968	3,931	380	6,784	6.4	114
1971	4,371	357	7,700	4.9	236
1974	6,910	404	10,521	4.2	793

MANAGEMENT DECISION IN 1974

Du Pont's Executive Committee was also well aware that once they approved $332 million in four installments to build the 50 million pound plant to gain economies of scale to enter radial tire and aerospace composite markets, they would also have to bear operating losses for several years. Du Pont however was seeing a steady decline in earnings since 1968 on rising sales (**See Exhibits – 6, 7 and 8**). This was due to its funding of many new ventures during this period, and some members of senior management viewed these ventures as failures. In 1973, Du Pont invested record capital expenditure of $781 million, up from a record spending of $561 million in 1972. In 1974, more requests for capital spending, exceeding $1 billion, were pouring in for approval of the X-Committee. In the past, the X-Committee had approved all the capital requests. This was when Du Pont's cash reserves were running at a historical low for the first time in many years.

If you were in the X-Committee, would the Textile Fibers Department get the needed $332 million to build the 50 million pounds per year Kevlar fiber plant or not?

EXHIBIT – 8
INVESTMENT AND DIVIDENDS FOR DU PONT

Year	Sales Income	Op. Inv.	Op. Expenses	Capital Payout	% Div. /Employee	Investment
1947	783	78	1,016	116	83%	14,000
1950	1,298	187	1,408	114	82%	18,000
1953	1,750	153	1,866	135	78%	20,000
1956	1,888	255	2,252	157	80%	25,000
1959	2,114	288	2,745	174	79%	33,000
1962	2,407	305	3,341	245	79%	37,000
1965	3,400	419	5,238	369	68%	42,000
1968	3,931	380	6,784	355	69%	49,000
1971	4,371	357	7,700	474	68%	64,000
1974	6,910	404	10,521	1,038	67%	77,000

POST SCRIPT: OIL SHOCKS AND THE AFTER-EFFECTS

With the rapid rise in petroleum oil prices in the 1970s and 1980s, production of synthetic fibers stagnated and profits were squeezed because of increase in the cost of raw materials and stiffer market competition (Gehani, 1985).

The centers of production gradually shifted from industrialized countries in the West to emerging economies of South Korea, Taiwan and others in East Asia with lower labor costs. For 1975-1985, the output of synthetic fibers grew annually by about 1.5%, mainly for specialty fibers, in the U.S., lower in Japan, and no growth in Europe. On the other hand, there was 12% growth in other countries, mostly in South Korea and Taiwan. In 1982, bal production of man-made fibers fell by 6.7%, cellulosic yarn and fiber output increased by less than 0.6%, while the synthetic fibers grew by 7.5%.

The industrialized countries concentrated on developing more added-value sophisticated products. They used their knowledge accumulated from producing rayon, nylon, polyester, and acrylic fibers to developing flame and heat resistant fibers, and higher performance aramid and carbon fibers. These were based on longer-term persistent research and study of structure and properties of polymeric fibers.

REFERENCES: DU PONT KEVLAR PARA-ARAMID FIBER

Tanner, David. 1997. Total Creativity in Business and Industry, Des Moines, IA: Advanced Practical Thinking Training Inc.

Magat, Eugene E. 1996. In the Pursuit of Strength – The Birth of Kevlar ®, Internal DuPont Publication, planned for issuance by Management of Advanced Fiber Systems.

Tanner, David; Fitzgerald, Jim A., and Phillips, Brian R. 1988. Kevlar – From Laboratory to Marketplace Through Innovation, the Du Pont Company Advanced Materials Conference, Wilmington, DE, November.

Tanner, David; Fitzgerald, Jim A., and Phillips, Brian R. 1989. The Kevlar Story – An Advanced Materials Case History, Angev, Chem. Adv. Mater., 101(5).

Christensen, Clayton M. 1999. Innovation and the General Manager, New York: Irwin – McGraw Hill.

Gehani, R. Ray. 1985. Aramid: A New Generation Fiber with Structure Designed for High Performance, Synthetic Fibers, Volume 14, No. 3, July/September.

Hounshell, David A. 1992. Du Pont and the Management of Large-Scale Research and Development. Chapter 9 in Galison, Peter and Hevly, Bruce. (eds.) Big Science: The Growth of Large-Scale Research, Stanford, California: Stanford University Press.

Hounshell, David A. 1989. The making of a New Industrial Fiber: The Case of Du Pont's Kevlar, 1950-1980. Paper presented at the Business History Seminar, Harvard Business School, April 17.

Hounshell, David A. and Smith Jr., John Kenly. 1988. Science and Corporate Strategy: Du Pont R&D, 1902-1980. New York: Cambridge University Press.

SILICONE POLYMER-FILLED BREAST IMPLANTS:
PRODUCT LIABILITY AND POLYMER APPLICATIONS IN MEDICAL IMPLANTS

Dr. R. RAY GEHANI

Institute for Innovation and Technology Leadership (IITL)
Akron, Ohio

"Let me make very clear that Dow Corning remains satisfied that Dow Corning implants produced over the years have filled an important medical need for thousands of women, and did not and do not represent an unreasonable risk. Based on past experience, we believe that the vast majority of women who have our implants will remain satisfied with the device. Our reasons for not resuming production and sales, therefore are not related to issues of science or safety but to the existing condition of the marketplace.

Keith McKinnon,
Chairman of the Board and Chief Executive Officer.
Dow Corning Corporate News, March 19, 1992.

ABSTRACT

This case reviews the decision-making processes at Dow Corning for the innovation of silicone polymer filled Cronin breast implants. We review the high persistent demand for medical implants driven by a deep-rooted American value for looking perfect. The demand for reconstructive and augmentation surgical procedures, therefore, stayed high even after the media frenzy about risks associated with rupture of silicone breast implants.

Caveat:
The purpose of this educational case material is to stimulate student discussion for learning important educational concepts, and intended to comment or judge the managerial decision-making at the concerned enterprises and other organizations.

INNOVATION THAT TURNED AROUND

Barely two weeks after his appointment as the CEO of Dow Corning, on February 19, 1992, **Keith R. McKennon was** called to testify before the Food and Drug Administration's (FDA) Advisory Committee on the safety of Dow Corning's silicone gel breast implants. Though, there were other manufacturers of silicone breast implants, Dow Corning became the "poster-boy" for the controversy - having pioneered the invention of silicone breast implants.

Until March 19, 1992, when Dow Corning withdrew from the breast implant market, the company was the market leader. The company's silicone polymer-filled breast implants accounted for estimated 20% market share according to the American Medical News, and 35% of the market according to other sources. In about three decades, these manufacturers had implanted silicone polymer prosthetics in close to 2 million women. Silicone breast implants, accounted at best for about 1% of Dow Corning's total sales revenue from hundreds of other innovative applications of silicone polymer chemistry.

In the spring of 1994 a group of U.S. breast implant manufacturers, led by Dow Corning Corporation, agreed to pay US$ 4.2 billion to women who alleged that their implants had caused them ill health. Of this, approximately US$ 1 billion was expected to go to attorneys, and the rest to be shared by approximately 440,000 plaintiffs who claimed headaches, pains, hair loss, all the way to autoimmune diseases such as lupus, rheumatoid arthritis, and scleroderma. Even this mammoth amount was not likely to be sufficient, as there were thousands of more plaintiffs who were suing implant manufacturers independently, and had opted out of the settlement agreement.

This case raises many strategic issues for chemical, biopolymer, and health care industries. How did a miraculous man-made molecular innovation come to cause so much controversy and cost? What implications did the silicone breast implant controversy have on the future development and innovations in medical implants? Where did the corporation and its strategic leadership go wrong? How could they have managed their innovation differently? What were the responsibilities of other stakeholders beside the implant manufacturers: the customers/clients, plastic surgeons who recommended the breast implants, the plaintiffs' lawyers who were making chunk of money, media, and the American society at large?

THE AMERICAN "ME" GENERATION

During the1990s, there was a huge media frenzy over alleged hazards of silicone breast implants. Yet, by the end of the American 20th Century, millions of Americans resumed their love-affairs with the elective surgeries. These reconstructive and cosmetic surgeries using silicone polymers helped them look better and love themselves more in the intensely competitive 1980s and 1990s. Not so long ago, in the 1960s and 1970s, there was a stigma attached to elective surgery. Only aspiring starlets, Broadway and TV celebrities, or the very rich and famous women past middle age secretly chose the surgeries to improve their looks. Not in the New Millennium. The image conscious American women and increasing number of men from all walks of life, with a wide range of income levels, and all ages (including the teenagers), searched for man-made augmentation for perfectly sculpted beauty. Breast implants led this augmentation movement (referred as "augs").

THE BREAST-IMPLANT IN QUEST FOR AMERICAN BEAUTY

The Cronin silicone-filled breast implants were invented and commercialized in 1964 by **Senior Surgeon Tom Cronin** working at **Dow Corning**. Dow Corning Corporation soon became the world's largest manufacturer of silicone gel-filled breast implants. The customers and their doctors resisted the thick gel and shell, and a modified design with seamless envelope and softer silicone gel was launched in 1969. An ex-employee of Dow Corning contended that the silicone gel was too fluid in the second-generation breast implant. This may have caused a higher incidence of leakage failure rate than the first-generation breast implants.

INNOVATION OF SILICONE BREAST IMPLANTS

The British chemists **F.S. Kipping** coined the term silicone for a family of synthetic polymeric compounds derived from silicon (Si) found abundantly in nature in sand, quartz and more. The silicone polymers (or polysiloxanes are based on long polymeric chains, with very stable, alternating silicon (Si) and oxygen (O) atoms in the backbone of the long-chain (See Exhibit-1). A wide range of organic groups in the side chains are attached to the polymeric backbone to modify the properties of the basic silicone polymers. More catalysts and additives are added to get the characteristics most desired in an application.

EXHIBIT 1
CHEMICAL STRUCTURE OF SILICONE POLYMERS

A.   **Poly-di-methyl-siloxane**

$$
\begin{array}{ccccccc}
CH3 & & CH3 & & CH3 \\
| & & | & & | \\
\text{------[--- Si -- O -- Si -- O -- Si - O...]---} \\
| & & | & & | \\
CH3 & & CH3 & & CH3 \\
\end{array}
$$

B.   Modified Poly-di-methyl-siloxane

To reduce hardening and crystallization, substitute a small (5-10%) of $-CH_3$ groups in the side chains with much more bulky $-R_1$ and $-R_2$ groups, such as a phenyl group to produce phenyl-methyl-siloxane, or di-phenyl-siloxane.

$$
\begin{array}{ccccccc}
CH_3 & & R_1 & & CH_3 \\
| & & | & & | \\
\text{---[--- Si - O -- Si -- O -- Si - O...]---} \\
| & & | & & | \\
CH_3 & & R_2 & & CH_3 \\
\end{array}
$$

Source: Adapted from Charrier, 1991. Polymeric Materials and Processing, Munich: Hanser Publishers.

Corning Glass Works, based in Corning, Upstate New York, extensively used silicon in its glass-molding operations. Over the years, Corning researchers explored and investigated the structure, processing and properties of their key raw material. In the 1930s, Corning researchers developed a number of resins, gels, and rubbers from silicon that could withstand very cold and very hot temperatures. Corning Glass Works approached Dow Chemical, headquartered in Midland, Michigan, with a proposal for launching a joint venture. A small plant near Dow's plant in Midland, MI started the trial production of silicones for industrial applications. This start-up plant produced a wide variety of products including the silicone sealant that helped the ignition systems of Allied fighter aircrafts withstand the severe thermal conditions at high altitudes.

In the uncertain environment of the World War II in 1943, Dow Chemical Company and Corning Glass Works entered into a 50:50 joint venture to produce and commercialize silicones. The goal of the new firm was to develop and produce polymeric materials and applications based on silicone chemistry. Corning Glass provided knowledge and expertise of silicone chemistry, while Dow Chemical contributed their chemical processing, engineering, and manufacturing knowledge. Both companies also deputed key employees. The two partners called the new venture Dow Corning, which produced products for use in radio and radar systems, on Navy ships, and war material factories for the US military.

In 1943 Dow Chemical begins first of 157 industrial toxicological tests of silicone compounds on contract for Dow Corning. The last of these tests was completed in the 1970s (Reisch, 1995).

At the end of the World War II, the high demand for military applications of silicones started dwindling. In 1948, Dr. Bass of Dow Corning and Dr. Rowe and Dr. Spencer of Dow Chemical published a Dow Chemical research report announcing the biologically inert characteristic of silicone.

After the War ended Dow Corning diversified to develop civilian applications for silicones. By about 1955, Dow Corning introduced a wide variety of more than 600 new silicone products, including sealants, specialty lubricants, and resins for industrial applications. A number of consumer products, such as Silly Putty, construction caulk, and adhesive labels were also successfully launched. In that period, the company grew six times, becoming the fastest growing firm in the booming chemical industry.

In the 1950s, Japanese bar girls, to please their GI and Allies customers, self-administered injections of industrial grade silicones to enlarge their breasts. Japanese doctors noted and reported in medical journals the complications caused by the migration of silicones to other parts of bodies, allegedly causing painful infections, lumps, and other diseases including cancer.

By the mid 1950s, scientists at Dow Corning started exploring medical applications of silicones. Suitable grades of silicone polymers can be physio-biologically quite inert and with low toxicity. These materials were expected to be well tolerated by body tissues and therefore were good candidates for implants (Charrier, 1991). Dow-Corning used silicones to develop many different implantable medical devices, including a heart pacemaker (and a hydrocephalic shunt).

In 1959 Dow Corning created a Center for Aid to Medical Research to help doctors developing experimental medical silicone applications. Plastic surgeons at Baylor University developed first silicone breast implants in 1962.

In the early 1960s, **Thomas Cronin**, a physician/surgeon working for Dow Corning got interested in using silicone to make a breast prosthesis for mastectomy patients who lost their breast(s). Cronin worked with engineers to encapsulate a firm high-density silicone gel in a rubbery silicone elastomer bag. The silicone envelope holding the silicone gel eliminated the need to inject silicone directly into a human body. Thus, the first prototype of a silicone gel-filled breast implant was invented. Dow maintained that the silicone envelopes were durable enough to stay intact within a woman's body throughout her life.

In 1963-64, the Cronin implant was launched in the market – exclusively for reconstructive surgery after mastectomy of a breast cancer patient. Alleged complications from early implants included scarring around the implant, because the body treated and rejected the implant as a foreign object. There was some alleged leakage of silicone-gel from the envelope in some cases.

Dow Corning was not required by law to prove the safety of its implants. But the management tried to assess the safety of medical devices before releasing them for sale. Food and Drug Research Laboratories, an independent contractor, was hired in 1964 to study the safety of injecting several medical-grade silicones, including the ones used in breast implants, in test animals. No major evidence that silicones caused cancer was found except in one study where silicones injected in dogs caused persistent, chronic inflammation. Dow Corning scientists classified this as typical "foreign body reaction" in the animal, and concluded that the evidence was not material specific to the silicone used.

After another study by the same outside contracting laboratory, Dow Corning was reported in 1969 that silicone fluids injected into mice spread widely to their lymph nodes, liver, pancreas, spleen, and other organs. Dow Corning did not advocate direct injection of silicone, and therefore did not worry about these adverse findings. The company maintained that silicones were biologically inert and safe for internal use in human body.

According to Dow Corning's documents, in 1969 Dow Corning, Dow Chemical, and Gruppo Lippitt (an Italian subsidiary of Dow

Chemical) conduct joint research on biologically active silicone compounds for pharmaceutical use. Gruppo Lippitt starts distributing Dow Corning implants in Europe and Latin America. This relationship lasts from 1969 to 1992.

CHANGING ORGANIZATION STRUCTURE

The company also developed a high reputation as an innovator – not only a leader in research and development but also an innovator of its organizational design. In 1967, Dow Corning was experimenting with an innovative new organization structure. From its conventional divisionalized organizational structure, Dow Corning reorganized to a "multi-dimensional" global-matrix form of organization structure, organized by geographical regions. The new decentralized organization structure, drew significant attention from outsiders. It had ten profit centers, each with a Business Board and a manager. Under each profit center, individual product families were assigned to a cross-functional product management group (PMG). Most members reported to their functional managers as well as their business group. Authority and decision-making was decentralized down, with a stress on cross-functional teamwork and open informal communication.

In 1969, a modified breast implant design with seamless envelope and softer silicone gel was introduced.

RISING COMPETITIVE RIVALRY

Five young scientists and salesmen left Dow Corning in 1972 to join *Heyer-Schulte*, a small medical devices company based in Goletta, California. They leveraged their experiences to develop a competing breast implant. In 1974, *Donald K. McGhan* led the whole group to form *McGhan Medical Corporation*, and based it in Santa Barbara, California. McGhan wished to improve the basic Cronin breast implant technology developed by Dow Corning over the past ten years, by making a softer, and more interactive silicone-filled implants. In 1974 Dow Corning's breast implant business faced serious competitive rivalry from Heyer-Schulte and McGhan Medical for the first time. The rivals quickly gained trust of plastic surgeons, and Dow Corning's market share steadily eroded to 35%. (See Exhibit – 2 for the list of implant manufacturers).

EXHIBIT 2
PARTIAL CHRONOLOGY OF BREAST IMPLANT REGULATION

1976, May 28: The FDA receives Congressional authority to regulate medical devices including breast implants.

1978: The FDA General and Plastic Surgery Devices Panel recommended placing breast implants in class II regulation requiring general controls and performance standards.

1982, Jan 19: Breast implants placed on class III FDA regulation (requiring stringent safety and effectiveness controls) because of some adverse reports appearing in the medical literature.

1988, Jun 24: All breast plants classified by FDA into class III regulation. After a 30 month waiting period, FDA required manufacturers to submit premarket approval applications (PMAs) with data demonstrating the safety and effectiveness of these devices.

To compete with the new rivals' softer and pliable breast implants, Dow Corning management formed a cross-functional mammary task force of about 20 men, to develop, produce, and launch the next generation of breast implant that was softer and more interactive. They were given a short deadline of June 1975. The new breast implants would have multiple profile shapes, and more sterile packaging. Comprehensive medical testing for safety was skipped because there was no time, and because the materials were considered quite similar to the original breast implants. The scientists were aware that more pliable "flo-gel" silicone with softer touch was also more likely to have excessive bleed through the elastomer envelope shell.

SUPER-FAST MAMMARY PRODUCT DEVELOPMENT

On January 28, 1975, the task force leader *Arthur Rathjen* reminded the members of the mammary task force that only two weeks were available before the flo-gel silicone would be formulated and filled in breast implants. Whether the flo-gel would significantly bleed more through the elastomer envelope was still not clear. On February 4, 1975, the two product engineers *William Larson and Thomas D. Talcott* reported inconclusive results from their short 2-3 week study, and noted that the bleed from flo-gel was not significantly more than from the control values from the old gel.

The biomedical tests with insertion of flo-gel silicone in experimental rabbits were outsourced to an independent laboratory. On February 26, their early reports indicated mild to occasionally moderate acute inflammatory reaction around the place where the gel was injected. The pathologist concluded it was not due to the flo-gel silicone but insertion trauma. The mammary task force also outsourced biomedical tests on monkeys to check migration of flo-gel silicone. The result from the test laboratory indicated some migration of the flo-gel silicone formulation. The mammary task force concluded that the bleed of flo-gel did not bleed significantly more than the older silicone gel standard.

The mammary task force leader **Arthur Rathjen** complimented the task force members for their open channels of communication, and shared with them that the group received accolades from the members of the management Business Board. On March 7, the leader Arthur Rathjen suggested Thomas Talcott's objections by stating that they were beyond the point of discussing about bleed through envelopes, and that he should instead improve the envelope if he could.

By March 31, 1975, six-week ahead of the original schedule, the new flo-gel silicone formulation was filled in 10,000 breast implants, ready to be packaged and shipped to the California Plastic Surgeons meeting on April 21, 1975. Early demonstrations on the West Coast in May 1975 showed oily surfaces and bleeding on the velvet in the showcase one day after the flo-gel breast implants were manipulated by different customers for a while. The task-force members concluded that it was not a product problem, and that the surgeon in the operating room would not see any appreciable oiling when the breast implant was removed from its package. Talcott and Larson were reassigned to test the high bleeding flo-gel samples. A marketing representative on the mammary task force advised the sales force to change the demonstration samples often, making sure that the samples were dry and clean before customer detailing.

The flo-gel breast implants were given the approval to put to commercial production. The mammary task-force shifted its focus from development and production to strategies for marketing the flo-gel implants aggressively to recover Dow-Corning's market share from 35% to 50-60%. They considered price discounts for big-volume using surgeons, and free samples for surgeons performing cosmetic breast augmentations. The task-force wanted to get aggressive for the forthcoming peak mammary season in June and July.

Dow Corning scaled up production fast, and by September, 1975 was producing 6,000-7,000 breast implants per month. By early 1976, the older Cronin implants were phased out. But, the reject rate for flo-gel silicone implants was a high 50%, due to weak envelopes, thin spots, breakage and contamination of implants with dirt. Despite the high rate of returns, surgeons liked the more pliable and softer flo-gel breast implants. The flo-gel silicone implants seemed more natural to touch, and were easier to implant requiring smaller incisions and less traumatic surgical procedures.

Task-force member Thomas Talcott resigned his job of 24 years, unhappy with the way Dow Corning commercialized a breast implant with inadequate testing for proving its safety. Later, Talcott testified as expert witness for the plaintiff women suing Dow Corning for liability from selling them unsafe product.

FACTORS CONTRIBUTING TO GROWTH IN DEMAND

The demand for breast implant surgery grew rapidly in the late 1970s and the 1980s. Availability of softer, pliable breast implants requiring smaller incisions and less invasive surgeries helped sell the product to reluctant customers. But many other environmental factors also contributed to its growth. Availability of large number of skilled plastic surgeons who were able and willing was an important pre-requirement.

RETURN OF THE MILITARY PLASTIC SURGEONS

One important factor for the growth in demand for plastic surgeries was the increasing availability of plastic surgeons. Early in the 20th century, procedures to graft healthy tissue from one part of the body to a damaged or mutilated part were developed. But, only during the World War II in the 1940s, military surgeons pioneered many innovative reconstructive surgeries for the wounded soldiers. After the World War II, these surgeons returned home as civilians starting their plastic surgery practices. Within two decades, plastic surgery practice became the fastest growing specialty of medical profession in America. Between 1960 and 1983, when the US population grew by 31%, the board-certified plastic surgeons increased by approximately 400% - much faster than any other medical specialty. The reconstructive surgery was not growing as fast, and elective cosmetic surgeries were not fully insured by health care insurance providers.

The growing numbers of board certified plastic surgeons needed new demand for their medical services. In 1982-1983, the *American Society for Plastic and Reconstructive Surgery (ASPRS)*, a professional association representing 97% of board-certified surgeons, sought permission from the US Food and Drug Administration (FDA) to launch a major "practice enhancement" advertising campaign. Other plastic surgeons also placed ads offering well-endowed body by a prominent local plastic surgeon, just like a sleek Ferrari automobile. The plastic surgeons campaigned with FDA to reclassify female flat-chestedness (referred as "miromastia") as a disease or a deformity producing feeling of inadequacy and lack of confidence or self-perceived femininity. They therefore recommended that enlargement of the underdeveloped female breast was often very necessary to "insure an improved quality of life for the patient." (ASPRS Communication, 1982; Rigdon, 1992; Faludi, 1991). Later, ASPRS officially retracted this perspective.

SHIFTING DEFINITIONS FOR FEMINITY

In the 1970s, the role models for women were tall, boyish looking females wearing men's suits for success. In the 1980s, the cultural standards for feminine beauty changed dramatically. Some observers call the 1980s as the decade of social conservatism, and a "backlash" against feminism and female liberation. Actresses like Cher openly spoke about their surgical augmentations. By 1990, about 80% of breast implant surgeries were for breast augmentation rather than for reconstruction after mastectomy. (Lawrnece, 1993).

BREAST IMPLANT CONTROVERSY

In 1977, several cases of ruptured breast implants went to court. Some settlements of approximately $170,000 were awarded. Unfortunately, as the breast implant surgeries increased in the 1980s, so did the number of sick women claiming pain from the implants. Some of them sued. *Maria Stern of Nevada* claimed that her breast implants caused fatigue, weight loss, pain in her joints and swollen lymph glands. In 1982, San Francisco lawyers obtained Dow Corning internal documents. They alleged that the company did not perform the basic research work body's reaction to long-term implantation of silicone gel implants. In 1984 a San Francisco court jury awarded her $1.7 million, and alleged that Dow Corning had committed a fraud by marketing its silicone breast implants as safe. This was the first verdict with punitive damages. The case while waiting to go to trial on appeal, was settled in 1987 for an undisclosed amount, and the court records were sealed.

Following the Stern case, Dow Corning modified its package insert and included a warning regarding possible capsular contracture, silicone migration following rupture, and immune system sensitivity.

After Maria Stern's landmark court verdict, increasingly larger number of women started speaking publicly about their pain resulting from breast implants.

What was the responsibility of the U.S. government in all this?

REGULATION OF MEDICAL BREAST IMPLANTS

In the 1950s, the medical devices and even implants were mostly not regulated. This was unlike pharmaceutical drugs, which were regulated since 1906 under the Pure Food & Drug Act, and its various amendments. The Food and Drug Administration acquired the authority to inspect manufacturing sites where medical devices were manufactured under the Food and Drug, and Cosmetics Act of 1938. Under this law FDA could even seize wrongly labeled and adulterated medical devices. But, FDA could not demand a manufacturer of medical devices to provide pre-market approval (PMA) for safety or effectiveness of its product. FDA could order recall of a medical device only after demonstrating that the manufacturer had broken the law. (Office of Technology Assessment, 1984).

On May 28, the **Medical Device Amendments (MDA) amendment law of 1976** was passed to give responsibility for regulating safety of medical devices such as breast implants to the Food, Drug and Cosmetics Act of 1938. This empowered the U.S. Food and Drug Administration (FDA) to regulate medical devices through the establishment of Pre Market Approval (PMA). The MDA law mandates manufacturers of new medical devices to scientifically demonstrate that they are safe, properly labeled, and effective before these devices are offered to customers or launched into the market. See Exhibit – 3.

The U.S. Food and Drug Administration (FDA) classified medical devices into Class I, II, and III regulatory categories. The first two classes were for medical devices with well-established safety and effectiveness.

Class I regulation category was for simple medical devices when manufacturing processes can control the risks of the devices.

Class II regulation category was for medical devices requiring additional "special controls" to reduce risks, such as performance standards, postmarket surveillance studies, and other measures such as education of users.

Class III regulation category requires premarket review of medical devices with lack of information about its safety and effectiveness. These medical devices may be either medical breakthroughs, with innovative new technologies, or they may be devices with questionable or poorly established effectiveness and safety.

Breast implants, such as silicone gel-filled and saline-filled breast plants, developed and in use before MDA 1976, were granted permission to stay on market – but were expected to eventually demonstrate safety, effectiveness, and proper labeling.

Allegedly, to take shelter under the grandfather clause, the makers of breast implants rushed to get their product to market to beat the FDA deadline.

On June 24, 1988, FDA classified all breast implants as class III FDA regulation. After a 30 month waiting period, FDA required manufacturers to submit their Pre-Market Approval (PMA) applications with data demonstrating the safety and effectiveness of these devices.

Polyurethane foam used as coating on certain types of silicone gel-filled breast implants, was shown by an unpublished study in March 1989 to degrade and release 2-toluene diamine (TDA). This chemical, under high temperature and alkalinity was known to cause cancer in animals. FDA asked the manufacturers to provide specific information for polyurethane foam regarding the safety testing and chemical composition. About 10% of women with breast plants had polyurethane-coated type breast implants when the manufacturers removed them from the market.

On May 17, 1990, FDA issued a proposed 515(b) regulation – requiring safety and effectiveness data for silicone gel-filled implants, in the *Federal Registrar*. On April 10, 1991, FDA published a final 515(b) regulation, requiring manufacturers of silicone gel-filled implants to submit pre-market approval application (PMA) with data showing the effectiveness and safety of the implants. The manufacturers were instructed to do so by July 1991. In June 1991, under the new post-market surveillance authority of the new Safe Medical Devices Act of 1990, FDA required the manufacturers of polyurethane-coated silicone-gel breast implant to conduct research on the material. On July 31, 1991, the FDA General and Plastic Surgery Devices Panel reviewed FDA's risk assessment of polyurethane foam coating of silicone gel-filled breast implants. The Panel concluded that the alleged risk of cancer appeared minimal, and was less than the surgical risk of removing a polyurethane-coated breast implants.

In August 1991, Bristol-Myers Squibb officially withdrew from the breast implant market due to persistent litigation.

PLASTIC IMPLANT INDUSTRY

As a result of regulatory action by the FDA and rising wave of litigation, in 1992 most major US manufacturers of breast implants, except **McGhan Medical Corporation**, a subsidiary of **Inamed Corporation** based in Carpinteria, California, and **Mentor Corporation** headquartered in Santa Barbara, California, discontinued production of breast implants. Both these U.S. companies were based in California. Prior to that, in early 1992, beside **Dow Corning**, the silicone breast implants were also produced by **Surgitek, a subsidiary of Bristol-Myers Squibb** headquartered in New York city, and **Bioplasty** of Roseville, Minnesota.

Globally, major competitors (beside **Inamed** and **Mentor**) included **Laboratories Sebbin, L.P.I., Novamed, P.I.P., and Silimed**. Many of them received FDA approval to market saline breast implants in the US, but accounted for less than 3% of sales of breast implants in 1998. (Medical & Healthcare Marketplace Guide, 1999).

Given below is a brief description of some of major players in the breast implant manufacturing industry. See Exhibit 3.

Exhibit 3
MANUFACTURERS OF BREAST IMPLANTS

MANUFACTURER (Some have gone out of business)	IMPLANTS MANUFACTURED
Baxter Healthcare Corporation 1385 Centennial Drive Deerfield, IL 60015	Silicone Gel-filled Implants 1-800-323-4533
Bioplasty, Inc. 1385 Centennial Drive St. Paul, MN 55113	*Silicone Gel-filled Implants* 1-800-328-9105
Dow Corning Corporation P.O. Box 994 Midland, MI 48686-0994	Silicone Gel-filled Implants 1-800-442-5442
McGhan Medical Inc. 700 Ward Drive Santa Barbara, CA93111-2936	Silicone Gel-filled Implants Saline-filled Implants 1-800-624-4261
Medical Engineering Corporation (A Bristo-Myers Squibb Company) 2317 Eaton Lane Racine, WI 53404	Silicone Gel-filled Implants (414) 632-3717
Mentor Corporation 5425 Hollister Avenue Santa Barbara, CA 93111	Silicone Gel-filled Implants Saline-filled Implants 1-800-235-5731
Porex Technologies 500 Bohannon Road Fairburn, GA 30213	Silicone Gel-filled Implants 1-800-241-0195
Surgitek (replaced by Medical Engineering Corp.) 3037 Mt. Pleasant Street Racine, WI 53404	Silicone Gel-filled Implants

1.   SURGITEK, A BRISTOL-MYERS SQUIBB SUBSIDIARY

In the 1980s Bristol-Myers Squibb was a broadly diversified pharmaceutical and health care company headquartered in New York City. The company manufactured and marketed nonprescription health products (including baby formula milk, toiletries, beauty aids) and household products. It also produced and sold cardiovascular and other pharmaceutical products, and medical devices such as orthopedic implants and surgical instruments.

In April 1991, **Surgitek** voluntarily suspended selling its Meme and Replicon polyurethane foam-coated silicone gel-filled breast implants. This was done in response to the preliminary data in a 1991 FDA study that suggested that such foam might degrade into 2-toluene diamine (TDA). TDA had been shown to cause cancer in laboratory animals. Surgitek requested doctors and surgeons using its products to delay using such implants until the FDA evaluated laboratory and risk assessment data for a potential relationship between cancer and the polyurethane foam. A toll free telephone number was set up for patients and physicians making inquiries about its products.

Bristol-Myers Squibb officially withdrew from the implant market in August 1991, while the litigation against the company was still pending.

2.   INAMED / McGHAN CORPORATION

In 1974, this company was started as **McGhan Medical Corporation**, a manufacturer of silicone implant products for reconstructive plastic surgery. (Medical & Healthcare Marketplace Guide, 1999). **Minnesota Mining and Manufacturing (3M)** acquired the business in 1977. The assets of 3M's silicone implant business were reacquired as a new **McGhan Medical Corporation**. The name of its holding company was changed in 1986 to **Inamed Corporation**, for its increasing involvement with innovations in medical field. McGhan developed, manufactured, and sold a number of implantable products, such as mammary prostheses, facial implants, and tissue expanders for plastic and reconstructive surgery. The company also offered custom prostheses for a wide range of other surgical procedures and applications. Its 1991 product offerings included many different models, sizes, and shapes of implants including gel-filled, saline, double-lumen mammary and other implants. It offered its patented low-bleed **Biocell**^{TM} implants, and patented textured surface implants. **McGhan** and other **Inamed** subsidiaries manufactured saline-filled mammary prostheses.

With demand for saline products unaffected by the FDA's moratorium, and expecting a somewhat increase, the company increased its production levels in the second half of 1991. The company also filed application to the FDA for permission to continue implant production and operations. For the year ending December 31, 1991, McGhan reported sales of $42 million, with a net loss of $2.8 million or about 35 cents per share. The loss was attributed by the company to the $4.4 million write-off accrued in relation to the FDA regulation of the silicone gel-filled implants. The company shared that a number of Inamed subsidiaries were included as defendants in about 130 pending lawsuits either for general or/and punitive damages.

The company, in its News Release dated January 7, 1992, stressed that its strategic plan for 1992 emphasized the marketing of saline-filled implants to achieve "a leading world-wide market share." The company increased its inventory of saline-filled implants in anticipation of an increase in demand due to the litigation against the silicone gel filled implants.

In a News Release on May 18, 1992, Donald K. McGhan, Chairman of the Board regretted that they were still unable to manufacture or market gel-filled breast implants but added that,

"Our customers are accepting the Company's saline-filled implants for most applications. The Company does expect to renew manufacturing and shipping of gel-filled implants as soon as the FDA allows."

The company either discontinued or sold a few product lines related to the US plastic surgery business. **Inamed** company consolidated operations of **CUI Corporation** and **Flomatrix Corporation** into **McGhan Medical**. (Medical & Healthcare Marketplace Guide, 1999).

Approximately 90% of Inamed's consolidated sales in 1998 consisted of breast implants and related tissue expander products. These products were used for augmentation in cosmetic surgery or for reconstruction after partial or total removal of tissue due to breast cancer. In August 1999, Inamed agreed to acquire Collagen Aesthetics Inc. for approximately $142 million, or $16.25 a share in cash. The consolidated company, with estimated $225 million in sales, was expected to become a global leader in plastic surgery and aesthetic medicine. Its portfolio of products included saline and silicone gel-filled implants for breast reconstruction and augmentation, devices to treat obesity, Zyderm ® and Zyplast ® collagen implants for correcting facial scars and wrinkles. These products met the needs of reconstructive plastic surgeons, cosmetic surgeons, dermatologists, and other aesthetic practitioners. (Medical & Healthcare Marketplace Guide, 1999).

Thus, **Inamed** marketed and distributed its silicone gel-filled gel implants only outside the US, and its saline-filled breast implants in the US and abroad until 1997. From April 1998 onwards, as part of an adjunct study for reconstructive and revision surgery, **Inamed** started selling certain styles of its silicone gel-filled breast implants in the US.

3.   MENTOR CORPORATION

Established in 1969, **Mentor Corporation** was headquartered in Santa Barbara, California, with manufacturing and research facilities in California, Massachusetts, Minnesota, Missouri, and Texas.

The company developed, produced, and marketed specialized medical products for plastic and reconstructive surgery, urology, and ophthalmology. These included an extensive product family including primarily silicone gel-filled breast implants, saline-filled implants, mammary prostheses, and skin/tissue expanders for breast augmentation and reconstruction related to congenital deformity, cancer-related surgery or other purposes. They also supplied some other surgically implantable prostheses for plastic cosmetic and reconstructive surgery. Certain disposable urologic products were supplied for the management of selected urinary or gastronomical disorders. Surgical and diagnostic equipments such as coagulators were provided to regulate bleeding during ophthalmic surgery or other microsurgery.

Mentor Corporation saw and embraced the opportunity created by the withdrawal of **Dow Corning** and other manufacturers from the implant market. According to Mentor's Annual Report for 1992, in the year ending March 31, 1992, plastic surgery business accounted for about 30% of its revenue. The company was looking forward "to serve the needs of the market while working with the medical profession and the FDA to increase our knowledge and advance the technology of breast implants." The report also stated that they purchased the silicone gel used in their implants from an outside supplier (**Dow Corning**), and that they "believe that it is the responsibility of that supplier to defend it and indemnify us against claims of injurious effects on the body." In accordance with the **FDA** guidelines, **Mentor** filed for pre-market approval, and resumed shipment of gel implants.

In the first quarter ending June 30, 1992, Mentor reported record sales and earnings. In a news release dated July 16, 1992, the company attributed the sales growth primarily to "the resurgence in plastic surgery sales following the lifting of the FDA moratorium on breast implants," and to strong international sales, and a strong performance from urological surgical products.

In subsequent years, the mammary prostheses comprised approximately 90% of Mentor's total plastic surgery revenues. The saline-filled breast implants accounted for about 80% of mammary prostheses sold in FY 1999. (Medical & Healthcare Marketplace Guide, 1999).

Mentor sold a product family of patented tissue and skin expanders used for growing additional tissue for reconstruction and skin graft procedures. Tissue expansion is applied to a great extent for post-mastectomy reconstruction, and removing disfiguring due to facial deformities, burns, and scars.

Mentor started marketing a line of facial implants in April 1997, supplied by **Implantech**. Following the US FDA approval in July 1997, in September 1997 Mentor started marketing the Contour Genesis, an ultrasound assisted product used for liquefaction and aspiration of soft tissues in reconstructive, plastic or general surgery. This system was also being developed for liposuction. (Medical & Healthcare Marketplace Guide, 1999).

In FY 1999, Mentor made equity investment in Byron Medical Inc., a privately owned supplier of wide range of specialty products for liposuction and body contouring. (Medical & Healthcare Marketplace Guide, 1999).

4.   BIOPLASTY

Bioplasty, based in Roseville, Minnesota, produced and marketed medical products.

In 1991, after the US FDA claimed that Bioplasty did not have enough data to prove their products' safety, the company withdrew its PMA application for Misti Gold implants.

In January 1992, the Chief Executive Officer of Bioplasty Arthur Beisang, in an interview with the *Minneapolis-St. Paul City Business Journal*, shared that the company was waiting for the US FDA approval to allow them to start marketing its non-silicone implants made of an inorganic polymer. Unlike silicone, this polymeric material was excreted by the human body if there was a rupture in the implant. In early 1992, Bioplasty withdrew from the implant market after the US FDA's moratorium and its panel recommendation to restrict the use of silicone gel-filled implants.

5.   DOW CORNING

The breast implant business was fast growing but an insignificant part of Dow Corning's total revenue. At its best, the breast implant business contributed to less than 1% of the firm's total sales revenues.

In early February 1992, Keith R. McKennon, executive vice president and head of domestic operations at Dow Chemical Company, was appointed chairman and chief executive officer of Dow Corning. At Dow Chemical, McKennon had led the company's response to charges alleged against Dow's Agent Orange (a defoliant sprayed in Vietnam) that this product had caused chronic health problems for the US military veterans. He also defended the company against allegations that its anti-nausea drug Benedectin caused birth defects. He had earned the reputation of a "seasoned troubleshooter," and served on the Board of Directors of Dow Corning for 6 years prior to his appointment as its CEO.

AMERICAN VALUES AND POPULARITY OF PLASTIC SURGERY

For many adult Americans, cosmetic surgery was fast becoming as routine as the medical check-ups. Baby boomers, accounting for more than 40% of the plastic surgery market, wanted to live 100, but never look older than 35. (Kalb, 1999). Many women boomers felt pressure to keep up appearances to hold their jobs or be more competitive in the job market. They felt that other people judged them by their appearances. They got face-lift or other augmentations as often as they felt the pressure. (See Exhibit 4, 5, 6).

Men too were electing surgery in increasingly large numbers. Sometime simple vanity motivated them to look lean and muscular. Other times, they wanted to stay competitive with the new crop of twenty-something, or because they were reentering the dating scene after a divorce. (See Exhibit 5).

Increasingly younger young adults were considered appropriate for elective surgery. Highly impressionable teenage girls, under enormous peer scrutiny, and media-marketing pressure, begged their parents for breast augmentation and liposuction. Should girls not old enough to order an alcoholic drink, or buy a pack of cigarettes, be allowed to order silicones or saline implants? The plastic surgeons wanted to avoid government regulation, and keep cosmetic surgery as a judgement call for the teenagers and their families. They suggested that the choice of plastic surgery should not depend on the chronological age of the girl, but depend on the stage of her development. As judged by her or her parents.

PLASTIC SURGERY MARKET

The plastic surgery segment of the medical and healthcare market consists of medical services related to aesthetic and cosmetic procedures indicated in Exhibit – 4 and 6. According to Banc Boston, the plastic surgery segment generated a revenue of $4.4 billion in 1997, increasing to $5 billion in 1998, and $5.8 billion in 1999, growing at 15-20% per year. (Medical & Healthcare Marketplace Guide, 1999).

The growth in plastic surgery has been attributed to a number of factors: (A) Influence of fashion and media opinion leaders; (B) Aging baby boomers hoping to extend their youth; (C) Increasing public acceptance for elective cosmetic surgery; and (D) Reassurance of improved technology.

Most health care insurers classified such cosmetic medical procedures as elective, and therefore excluded these from their coverage. A patient therefore usually had to pay privately for cosmetic plastic surgery. Breast augmentation cost from between $4,000 and $8,000, whereas liposuctions and chemical peels usually cost on average about $2,500. Exhibit - 4 shows some of the typical prices for various procedures for men and women.

In 1992, the American Society of Plastic and Reconstructive Surgeons (ASPRS) started registering cosmetic and reconstructive surgeries. The statistics by the ASPRS National Clearinghouse of Plastic Surgery provides the overall trends for such procedures. In 1998, certified surgeons performed more than 2.2 million procedures of plastic surgery, with 44% annual growth. Between 1996 and 1998, the growth in cosmetic surgery was 50%. (Medical & Healthcare Marketplace Guide, 1999).

Exhibit – 4
GROWING DEMAND FOR PLASTIC SURGERY PROCEDURES
(In '000, rounded)

		1992	1998	Change
1.	Breast augmentation	32.5	132.4	306%
2.	Breast reduction		70.4	
3.	Breast Reconstruction		69.7	
4.	Cosmetic surgery	1,045.8		
5.	Liposuction	42.4	172.1	264%
6.	Eyelid Surgery		120.0	
7.	Facelift		70.9	
8.	Chemical Peel		66.0	
9.	Reconstructive Surgery		1,169.4	
10.	Tumor Removal		509.5	
11.	Hand Surgery		160.7	
12.	Lacerations		72.8	
	All Plastic Surgery Procedures	1,538.0	2,215.2	44%

Source: Adapted from the American Society of Plastic and Reconstructive Surgeon statistics, April 28, 1999.

BREAST IMPLANTS PROCEDURES

Breast reconstructive surgery is the procedure when a surgeon reconstructs a woman's breast after a mastectomy. Aging and increasing awareness of American women was expected to increase the need for mastectomy and breast reconstructive surgery. In 1992, about 29,000 such breast reconstructive procedures were performed, increasing to about 50,000 similar procedures in 1998. In October 1998, a new federal law mandated unprecedented insurance coverage for reconstructive surgery after a mastectomy. (Medical & Healthcare Marketplace Guide, 1999).

Breast Augmentation is a medical procedure by which a surgeon puts breast implants to enhance the shape or size of a woman's breast for cosmetic purposes. Typical patients are women between the ages of

18 and 50, with moderate to high income. In 1992, approximately 32,000 breast augmentation surgeries were performed, increasing to 122,000 women in 1997. In the near future, demand for cosmetic breast augmentation was expected to grow faster corresponding to the US population of 25-40 year old women.

Surgeons position breast implants either in **subglandular position** under a woman's breast tissue, or in **submuscular position** under a woman's **pectoralis muscle**.

All breast implants consist of a silicone elastomer shells filled with either silicone polymer gel or saline solution. The saline-filled implants are usually implanted empty, with the advantage of requiring only a small incision, and then filled and positioned. The small incision can be made quite inconspicuously, as (A) infra-mammary incision in the fold of the breast; or as (B) peri-areolar incision around the nipple; or as (C) a trans-axillary incision under the arm. When the incision is made under the arm, endoscopic probe fitted with a tiny camera may be used to help visualize the creation of the surgical pocket (Medical & Healthcare Marketplace Guide, 1999).

The breast implants can be shaped either as round or anatomical – depending on what the patient desires. Both shapes increase the size of breast. The finished implants may be a smooth silicone or a textured surface.

A surgeon usually performed the breast implant surgery in an outpatient room. In 1990, surgeons performed 82% of all breast augmentation procedures on an outpatient basis. This was done either at a hospital or the surgeon's office. Breast augmentation surgery is done with general anesthesia, though local anesthesia is an option, usually lasting 1-2 hours. An incision creates pocket for the implant, and stitches and tapes close the incision. Breast reconstructive surgery is usually performed in a hospital, and often requires more than one operation over several months.

Exhibit – 5

MOST COMMON RECONSTRUCTIVE AND AUGMENTATION SURGICAL PROCEDURES FOR MEN AND WOMEN

Procedures For Females	Procedures For Males
In 1998: 946,784 procedures (91%)	In 1998: 99,031 procedures (9%)

Top 5 Female Procedures:	Top 5 Male Procedures:
1. 16% Liposuction	1. 20% Liposuction
2. 14% Breast augmentation	2. 16% Eyelid surgery
3. 11% Eyelid surgery	3. 13% Nose reshaping
4. 7% Face-lift	4. 9% Breast reduction
5. 7% Chemical Peel	5. 6% Face-lift
45% Others	36% Others

TRUSTWORTHY MEDICAL IMPLANT REGISTRY

By February 2000, about 25 million Americans had medical implants. Many of them did not have a clear idea about what was inside their bodies. Only their doctors had the complete record of their implants. Therefore, in case of a recall of medical implants, many patients may never know. If there was an implant registry started earlier, then corrective action could have been taken much faster.

Some implant patients believed that the voluntary registries created by manufacturers of breast implants were not effective. Their information was not widely shared (Rouhi, 2000). Some patients who got a jaw joint implant, experienced severe pains in their head every day (Rouhi, 2000). They may or may not link the two.

Some observers recommended a mandated implant registry by FDA, NIH, and private and public institutions. They argued for reliable checks and balances in recording the information so that patients as well as the manufacturers can trust the registered information. Federal agents argued that a national registry of all patients with different patients was not feasible. The proponents of the national implant registry, on the other hand have pointed out that if 100 million cars can be registered in case of a brake recall, then 25 million patients with medical implants can be registered too.

Independent industry observers suggested that the device manufacturers and medical clinicians should have "womb-to-tomb responsibility for their devices" (Rouhi, 2000). They also suggested that retrieval and analysis was critical for quality control of the medical devices. A registry of patients with implants will help manufacturers to take early action in case their products cause complications.

In the absence of such implant registry, no one can estimate what proportion of patients can experience implant related complications.

Exhibit – 6

TYPICAL COSTS OF RECONSTRUCTIVE AND AUGMENTATION SURGICAL PROCEDURES FOR MEN AND WOMEN

Procedures For Females In 1998: 946,784 procedures (91%)		**Procedures For Males** In 1998: 99,031 procedures (9%)	
Forehead lift:	$2,526	Scalp reduction (baldness):	$2,776
Laser skin resurfacing (full face):	$2,770	Eyelid surgery (both):	$2,942
Fat injection (face and neck):	$1,093	Cheek implant:	$2,135
Collagen Injections/1 ml:	$315	Ear Reshaping:	$2,501
		Nose reshaping:	$3,434
Breast augmentation:	$3,077	Anti-wrinkle injection:	$3,434
Breast lift:	$3,426		
Breast reduction:	$5,471	Liposuction:	$1,872
		ultrasound assisted:	$3,817
Upper-arm lift:	$2,820		
Fat Injection–extremities:	$917	Calf implant:	$4,750
Trunk:	$88		
Buttock lift:	$3,693		
Thigh lift:	$3,817		
Tummy tuck:	$4,095		

THE FDA ADVISORY PANEL HEARINGS

Two weeks after his appointment as the CEO of Dow Corning, on February 19, 1992, Keith R. McKennon was called to testify before the Food and Drug Administration's (FDA) Advisory Committee on the safety of Dow Corning's silicone gel breast implants. Though, there were other manufacturers of silicone breast implants, Dow Corning was the "poster-boy" leader, being the pioneering inventor of silicone breast implants. In about three decades, all the breast implant manufacturers had implanted silicone polymer prosthetics in close to 2 million women. Estimated 35% of these were by Dow Corning.

The silicone gel-filled breast implants were sacks filled with a silicone gel containing catalysts, fillers, and dozens of other ingredients (Luesby, 1995). All these contents could leak if the envelope ruptured. At the FDA hearings, the critics pointed out that the implants leaked silicones into the body, causing severe pain, inflammation, scarring, and autoimmune damage. The autoimmune diseases thus could cause rheumatoid arthritis and scleroderma. They contended that the breast implants blocked the detection of breast cancer by mammography.

Later, plaintiff's lawyers demanded and collected Dow's company's internal correspondence (Dow Papers). The Dow Papers indicated that many Dow employees had expressed their concerns about the lack of tests to evaluate the safety of breast implants in human body, rupture and leakage of the envelope, hardening of tissue around the implant, and migration of the leaked gel to other parts of body. Few jurors were sympathetic to the breast implant manufacturers, when they were told that aluminum and nickel containing silicone gel moved through the brain, heart, or liver but the manufacturers did not conduct any tests to check this effect in human body.

McKennon defended that breast implants met an important medical need for a large number of customers. Hundreds of women have testified to that. He also assured that the breast implants did not pose unreasonable risks to users.

The FDA Advisory panel debated for about 3 hours, and recommended on February 20, 1992, that the breast implants be recalled from the market. Only exception was when a woman wished to correct serious deformities, or needed reconstruction after mastectomy. The recipients of implants were to be enrolled in a controlled clinical study. FDA Commissioner David Kessler was expected to rule on the Advisory Panel's recommendations within 60 days.

CEO McKennon faced a number of important strategic decisions.

1. Would Dow Corning under McKennon's leadership be forced to declare bankruptcy like Manville and A.H. Robins did after a major product recall?

2. Or would Dow Corning reemerge stronger as Johnson & Johnson did after its Tylenol poisoning crisis?

3. Should Dow Corning get out of the breast implant business, and take care of its liability commitment?

4. Will the firm's $250 million insurance cover the entire liability?

5. What was Dow Corning's overriding responsibility to the women with Dow Corning's implants? (Burton and McMurry, 1992).

On January 6, 1992, the FDA commissioner Dr. David Kessler recommended a voluntary moratorium that all US manufacturers of silicone gel-filled breast implants voluntarily stop selling. The surgeons were requested to stop implanting the breast implants until information on safety of the procedures was reviewed. The number of lawsuits against Dow Corning jumped from 100 to more than 1,000. On April 16, 1992, the FDA lifted its voluntary moratorium of January 6, but mandated that silicone gel-filled breast implants be available only under controlled clinical studies. On May 27, The US FDA acknowledged the public health need for breast implants in patients who lost one or both breasts due to cancer or trauma, or have a serious malformation requiring reconstructive surgery.

CLAIMANTS' COMPLAINTS

In 1994, approximately 200,000 claimants were involved in a class-action lawsuit against Dow Corning.

On April 1, 1994, a Settlement Agreement with plaintiffs in the breast implant litigation was approved by the courts. According to this Settlement Agreement, Dow Corning would contribute $2.02 billion per an agreed schedule to a total of $4.2 billion by the various industry participants. About $1 billion was going to attorneys, and the remainder $3.4 billion was expected to be divided between 440,000 plaintiffs. The Settlement Agreements involved more than 30 breast implant manufacturers bearing their total cost of over $5 billion.

© *2010 Dr. R. RAY GEHANI*

SCIENTIFIC EVIDENCE FOR SILICONE'S IMMUNE RESPONSE

The plaintiffs' lawyers often built their case and won huge awards based on some controversial scientific evidence.

SILICONE EXPERT WITNESS

In some of the major settlement cases of breast implants, one expert witness played a major role. **Dr. Nir Kossovsky**, a pathologist at the UCLA Medical Center testified again and again that silicone breast implants can affect a woman's immune system. To prove it he claimed that he has developed a test. He was hired by John O'Quinn, a legendary Houston plaintiff's attorney when he had more than 800 breast implant cases in the pipeline (Taubes, 1995). Since the trial hinged on the scientific legitimacy of the silicone-related diagnosis, O'Quinnn hired several expert witnesses, including Dr. Nir Kossovsky. They showed that silicone could wreak havoc on the human immune system of their clients. One of their clients was 46-year old **Pamela Johnson**, after she had her third set of silicone breast implants removed. The jurors awarded Pamela Johnson $25 million, with $20 million punitive damages. In 1994, Dr. Nir Kossovsky had testified in another judgement against 3M company for #40 million.

Pamela Johnson had her first set of implants from 1976 to 1989. She had that removed because she complained to her husband that her breasts had hardened, apparently due to scar tissue hardening around the implants. Surgeon performed a **closed capsulotomy** procedure, trying to manipulate breast to break up the scar issue. The left implant ruptured and resulted in what popular media often referred as the "runny mess." The surgeon performed a partial mastectomy to replace the old implants with the second set. Johnson found the new implants aesthetically unpleasant and consulted another surgeon. In November 1989, this surgeon replaced the set two implants with set three implants. Until June 1992 Pamela Johnson kept those implants, though she often complained of chronic fatigue, headaches, hair loss, and night sweats. When the physicians suggested that her ailments were caused by silicone in her system, Pamela Johnson had her set three implants removed, and sued the manufacturer of the first two sets of implants, **Medical Engineering Corporation**, a subsidiary of Bristol-Myers Squibb. Houston's legendary plaintiff attorney **John O'Quinn** took her case along with approximately 800 implant cases pending resolution.

Dr. Nir Kossovsky played a strategic role in the breast implant cases. He served as a consultant to the Food and Drug Administration advisory committee that imposed the moratorium on implants after the 1992 hearings. Her lawyer John O'Quinn's firm refers to Dr. Nir Kossovsky as the "senior world authority on the biological properties of silicone." The pathologist, however, does not have a board certification in either rheumatology or immunlogy, the disciplines central to the silicone breast implant controversy (Taubes, 1995).

Nir Kossovsky got interested in silicone as a second-year medical student at the University of Chicago. He read two dozen volumes of a Dow Corning report on silicone. The executive summary made the contention that silicone was ideal material for implant devices because it did not chemically interact with other materials in the body. Since it was inert, the report concluded that silicone could not harm when buried in a living organism for a long time. Kossovsky found inconclusive evidence in the rest of the report, with some silicone induced inflammation and lymphomas in animals and patients. To him, it left "a big question mark" (Taubes, 1995).

Kossovsky's Silicone Immune Response Theory

This doubt prompted Nir Kossovsky to run a few experiments on silicone in guinea pigs with his adviser John Heggers, a microbiologist and immunologist. They published the studies in 1983, claiming that silicone in guinea pigs "could induce a sensitivity to their own blood proteins." Kossovsky postulated that this could act as the first step in a process leading to an autoimmune disorder and diseases such as rheumatoid arthritis. Then the immune system may attack the body's own tissues, and go haywire. Between 1984 and 1987 Korrovsky was trained in pathology at Cornell University Medical Center. Then he transferred to UCLA, where he continued building his speculation into a theory of silicone's effect on immune system.

Kossovsky's theory is based on stickiness of silicone molecule. When silicone leaks from an implant, according to Kossovsky, it is coated with protein molecules from the body, "just as a cherry dipped in chocolate becomes instantly coated with the chocolate" (Taubes, 1995). Proteins are normally coiled, long, knotted chains of amino acids. Kossovsky claims that silicone "denatures" or untangles the protein molecules in a "biophysical phenomena" of surface chemistry, changing their shape.

When the body encounters such unfamiliar substances or antigens (such as bacteria or viruses), body's immune system generates antibodies. These antibodies are launched on the mission to search-and-destroy the antigens with molecular flag markers distinguishing them. Kossovsky hypothesized that the body's immune system and antibodies would attack the denatured blood proteins as well as the body's normal proteins. This could cause autoimmune disorder.

Most researchers agree that when silicone implants rupture, or when a scar tissue hardens and contracts around an implant, the local effects can be quite horrible. They, however, saw no conclusive evidence whether presence of silicone could cause systemic autimmune diseases, particularly rheumatoid arthritis, scleroderma, and lupus.

Marcia Angell, executive editor of the *New England Journal of Medicine*, noted that many women contracted autoimmune disorders without having implants, and therefore the postulated silicone-related associations were very difficult to evaluate. Epidemiologists, such as **Buddy Ratner**, a University of Washington bioengineer, point out that silicone molecules composed of silicon and oxygen pervade our bodies. For instance, most breakfast cereals and antacids use silicones as fillers. Underarm deodorants incorporate silicone probably absorbed through our skin. Silicone is coated on Norplant birth control devices.

In 1990, a woman's advocacy group called Nir Kossovsky, requesting him to examine specimen slides of breast tissue from women with implants and some health problems. Kossovsky noted from minimal biological reactions to gross amounts of silicone and inflammation. The woman's advocacy group, at the top of their newsletter, printed names of Nir Kossovsky and John Heggers as collecting blood samples from women with implants. Women from all over the country sent their blood samples to Nir Kossovsky thinking that they were sending it for some study. Nir passed it to John Heggars for testing. This started getting very expensive, so John asked Kossovsky to hold the rest.

ELISA Test Assay for Antibodies

Kossovsky saw this as a golden opportunity to test his hypotheses about silicone's immune response. He decided to custom design a test "just like an HIV test" to detect the antibodies for silicone-denatured proteins. He designed simple to use but hard to interpret ELISA test assay. He took a polystyrene plastic dish (assay well), which like silicone holds tightly to proteins that contact it. As step-1 he coated the polystyrene dish with the specific antigen (AG) to which he would like to find antibodies (AB). The antigen (AG) sticks to polystyrene. Then in step-2 he added a serum (S) – the fluid component of blood after removing the cells. If the serum has antibodies (SAB) specific to his antigen (AG), they will latch onto the antigen (AG) already stuck to polystyrene. In step-3 he washed away the excess serum. What should be left behind is the antibodies (SAB) stuck to the antigen (AG), that is sticking to the polystyrene (Taubes, 1995: 69).

The ELISA test seems simple, but its mechanisms are complex and hard to control. If in step-1 polystyrene is not completely covered with antigens (AG), then in step-2 all the antibodies in the blood serum (SAB, SBB, SCB, SDB...) including the antibody to your antigen SAB, but also antibodies to other antigens or substances (such as SBB, SCB, SDB...) will also stick to the polystyrene. Because almost everything sticks to polystyrene. So if ELISA test found antibodies in serum (SBB, SCB, SDB ...), it does not imply that you found the specific antibody (SAB) you were looking for. The results also varied significantly with the technician, temperature, humidity, and many other uncontrollable variables.

Kossovsky instead assumed that ELISA test was robust. He quickly trained undergraduate student volunteers to do the tests. They coated the ELISA (polystyrene) wells with silicone. Then they added proteins common in human tissue and blood, such as fibrinogen and collagens. These were expected to be denatured by silicone. Then they poured 249 of the blood samples Kossovsky had kept, to test if it had antibodies that would bind to the silicone denatured proteins.

Kossovsky was not sure why women get denatured proteins. These could be caused by many reasons, including other infections, diseases, or inflammations due to a major surgical operations that implant insertions required. He therefore needed to carry out and compare "blind" tests on blood samples from women who were sick and healthy, with implants and without implants. Only then could he scientifically claim that women with implants and ill-health symptoms only had antibodies (or more antibodies) to the denatured proteins.

In October 1991 Kossovsky collected blood samples from 47 healthy women without implants. A few months later he contacted the *Autoimmune Disease Center at Scripps Research Institute in La Jolla, California*. Intrigued by his theory they agreed to send him in March 1992 "blinded" blood samples from 40 "nonimplanted" women with autoimmune diseases, 10 healthy women without implants, and 11 women with implants and autoimmune diseases (Taubes, 1995: 70). Kossovsky tested the blinded blood samples and in April 1992 sent the test observations to Scripps researchers to find if Kossovsky's test revealed that women with implants and symptoms of autoimmune diseases had (or had more) antibodies to denatured proteins compared to the same in other women without implants. Scripps researchers shared results with Kossovsky that his test may have detected women with autoimmune diseases, but that there were many more better tests available to do that. More importantly, they found that the test failed to distinguish between the set of women with implants from the set with no implants (both sets having autoimmune diseases).

Two years later in 1994, according to **rheumatologist Robert Fox**, Scripps institute started receiving calls from patients, physicians and other institutions with the impression that Scripps had either validated or were offering Kossovsky's test. Fox wrote two letters to Kossovsky refraining him from mentioning Scripps Clinic patient data. Kossovsky did not respond (Taubes, 1995: 70).

Fox did a statistical analysis of Kosovsky's April 1992 test results. He described the results in a letter in 1994 to Stephen Miller, president of the American Association of Plastic Surgeons and a plastic surgeon at Scripps and the University of California at San Diego. Fox shared that ELISA values Kossovsky obtained for his set of healthy nonimplanted women were significantly different from the values for the Scripps set of healthy nonimplanted women. The test did not seem consistent, and that "the entire ELISA (test) must be considered invalid and rerun" (Taubes, 1995: 70).

Kossovsky did not accept Scripps conclusion and Fox's opinion, which he waived as "a very bizzare rambling letter, that didn't make any sense to me." Much before the collaboration with Scripps clinic, in a 1991 California trial Kossovsky testified about the immune response to silicone based in part on the preliminary findings of his study. This helped the plaintiff win a $7 million judgement against Dow Corning.

In 1993 Kossovsky was able to publish a paper based on his own analysis, rejecting Scripps analysis, in the peer-reviewed *Journal of Applied Biomaterials*. Allegedly this acceptance was received after rejections from at least three scientific journals, and that Kossovsky was a member of its editorial board (Taubes, 1995: 71). Researchers who read the paper commented that the study was based on unmatched sample sets, with interpretation of results requiring extra caution. His 249 sick implanted women and 47 healthy nonimplanted women were compared with 39 of the 40 autoimmune patients from Scripps clinic. Kossovsky reported that 9 of his 249 implanted women had much higher ELISA values than other 240 implanted women, or mean scores of 47 healthy women or 39 Scripps women with autoimmune diseases. He therefore implied that the 9 implanted women (representing 4% of 249 implanted set) had an unnatural amount of antibodies to denatured proteins because they were suffering from a silicone-related disease. These 9 implanted women had symptoms little different from the other 240 implanted women.

Critics such as John Butler of University of Iowa noted that Kossovsky was basing his conclusions on the hypothesis itself, and that critical information about his test was not described fully. *The British Medical Devices Agency* concluded that it was "not possible to draw any definitive conclusions from his work."

SBI Laboratories and Decasil Test Service

After publishing the paper, Kossovsky filed a patent application through the University of California, and founded SBI Laboratories in Pittsburgh to market Detecsil blood test service to detect silicone. His partners were wife Beth Brandegee and father Ram Kossowsky (with different spelling). By March 1994, SBI was advertising in *Trial*, a magazine for plaintiffs' lawyers,"

"Representing clients in silicone-related litigation? Consider this: The Detecsil test confirms whether or not an individual has developed an immune response to silicone-associated proteins. Detecsil provides valuable answers to those studying silicone immune reactions in at-risk populations" (Taubes, 1995: 71).

According to SBI, at-risk populations included not only estimated one million women with silicone breast implants but everyone with any silicone prosthesis or occupational exposure to silicone. This included diabetics who injected insulin through hypodermics lined with silicone. Interested customers were required to send $350 per blood sample which SBI will test and inform those that scored high on the Decasil test implying they had an immune response to silicone, and by implication, a good lawsuit. SBI could earn a hefty profit too.

In a June 1984 deposition Kossovsky when asked by the lawyers of implant manufacturers for log books and laboratory records of his research data, he explained that most of it, perhaps all, had been lost during a Los Angeles earthquake. Kossovsky said that the data was piled in stacks on his office floor. During the earthquake,

"...some partially consumed cups of coffee or water or combinations thereof, some of which may have been growing microbiologic species, and some other fluid containers that were lying around also in close proximity to the edge of the desk and the large pile on the floor and a lot of things got very wet and quite disgusting" (Taubes, 1995: 74).

He got two large garbage cans and discarded everything that "looked disgusting or not particularly important."

The Food and Drug Administration (FDA) had little regulatory control because Decasil was not sold as a test kit but was offered as a service. However, FDA looked into its truthful advertising. In July 1994 the FDA pointed out SBI claim that "Decasil is the first and only test to detect an immune response to body proteins damaged by silicone," seemed to imply it as diagnostic tool. This was contradicted by the caveat in its promotional materials that it was "for research purpose only." FDA warned that SBI promotional material was misleading and violating federal regulations until Decasil has proven diagnostic ability (Taubes, 1995: 74).

In court depositions, Kossovsky explained that Decasil was not a detection tool, but "a research tool and a legal tool… to identify patients that really have some evidence of silicon-induced reactions and distinguish them from (other) patients…." In May 1995 SBI Laboratories applied for FDA approval of Dcasil as a medical device, and suspended sales of the test shortly thereafter (Taubes, 1995: 74).

STRATEGIC TECHNO-MANAGERIAL DECISIONS

In 1995 strategic managers like Dow Corning's CEO Keith McKinnon and other CEOs at the various implant manufacturers faced a huge dilemma and uncertainties about the future of the silicone gel-filled and saline-filled implant businesses. How should they block or overcome the building tide of litigations and accusations against them? They were forced to quickly but carefully analyze their past practices, assess their present strategic choices and resources, and develop specific short-term and long-term actions for their growth and survival in the future. They could definitely use all the analytical help and advice available.

REFERENCE LIST AVAILABLE WITH THE AUTHOR

AFTERMATH OF THE SILICONE-FILLED BREAST IMPLANT CRISIS (1995): BANKRUPTCY OF A CHEMICAL GIANT

Dr. R. RAY GEHANI

Institute for Innovation and Technology Leadership (IITL)
Akron, Ohio

LOSING SETTLEMENT AGREEMENT

Thousands more plaintiffs opted out of the silicone filled breast implant settlement. They hoped to sue the implant manufacturers independently to claim bigger bounties.

The insurers of breast implant manufacturers backed out. They refused to cover the claims agreed under the Settlement Agreement, arguing that they would have never agreed to insure the implants if they had seen the Dow's internal correspondence and papers. This was contrary to Dow's defense for many years. That it never designed, made, tested for safety, or gave opinions on the safety of breast implants (#___: Luesby, 1995, FT).

By May 1995, the number of claimants mushroomed to 480,000 (per Medical Journal of Australia). On May 15, 1995, the 1994 Settlement fell apart due to opt-outs, and Dow Corning, the biggest contributor to the breast implant fund, filed for Chapter 11 bankruptcy protection. Legal actions was started against its parent company, Dow Chemical. In a May 17, 1995 article in *The Wall Street Journal*, CEO Richard Hazelton of Dow Corning lamented that the mushrooming US civil litigation practices threaten to crush innovation and new product development in Corporate America.

In September 1995 the Settlement Agreement collapsed and negotiations began on a new settlement.

FRESH PRODUCT LIABILITY AWARDS

In October-November 1995, a Nevada jury awarded **Charlotte Mahlum**, approximately $15 million in damages against Dow Chemical, parent company of the breast implant manufacturer Dow Corning (#___: Luesby, 1995, FT).

Dow Chemical filed post-trial motions seeking to have the Nevada jury's verdict overturned. If that failed, the company had the option to lodge an appeal with the Nevada Supreme Court. The company maintained that there was no medical evidence for any link between their breast implants and their customers' ill health.

Hundreds of other women had won compensation through independent legal action. But, the news of the Nevada case kept more than 440,000 litigants registered under a class action suit hopeful.

One such woman was **Christine McCarthy** living in a mobile home, just outside Maidstone in Kent. Christine claims that on the day before her honeymoon, she woke up to find that she could not walk. She never went for her honeymoon. Her life was horrendous since she was 21 when she had a mastectomy and a breast implant. Her hip was seized, making it hard for her to walk around her mobile home on crutches. She had multiple infections, including in kidneys, which hospitalized her for four days. Dehydration, allergies, rashes, aches, and pains constantly bothered her. Like hundreds of other women, Christine blames silicone breast implants for all her misery. Christine considered the initial settlement offered, ranging from $140,000 to $1.4 million, a blessing. But it was long time before she was going to receive a penny.

Other women claimed even more. **Social worker Lynda Roth**, in Broomfield, Colorado, shared with jury how fast her life changed. One day she was told that she had breast cancer, she saw a plastic surgeon the same day. Next day she had a mastectomy, and a breast implant. From then on, she claimed that she was in constant pain. She has brain damage, due to loss of blood-flow to the brain – cause unknown. She has seizures. The scans prove it.

Lynda and other women said that they did not want to finish off Dow Chemical. They, however, do want an acknowledgement and an apology for the carelessness that led to their suffering. And up to $5 billion to top up the settlement fund (Luesby, 1995. FT).

REVISITING THE FIRST SPACE SHUTTLE CHALLENGER DISASTER: KNOWLEDGE MANAGEMENT AND HIERARCHICAL COMMAND AND CONTROL IN A COMPLES ORGANIZATION

Dr. R. RAY GEHANI

Institute for Innovation and Technology Leadership (IITL)
Akron, Ohio

"I believe that this nation should commit itself, to achieving the goal, before this decade is out, of landing a man on the moon, and returning him safely to the earth. No single space program in this period will be more impressive to mankind, or more important for the long range exploration of space."

President John F. Kennedy

May 25, 1961

"The future is not free: the story of all human progress is one of a struggle against all odds. We learned again that this America, which Abraham Lincoln called the last, best hope of man on Earth, was built on heroism and noble sacrifice. It was built by men and women like our seven star voyagers, who answered a call beyond duty, who gave more than was expected or required and who gave it little thought of worldly reward."

President Ronald Reagan

January 31, 1986.

This Case is Dedicated To the Memory of Columbia Space-Shuttle Crew Members

Commander	*Francis R. (Dick) Scobee*
Pilot	*Michael John Smith*
Mission Specialist One	*Ellison S. Onizuka*
Mission Specialist Two	*Judith Arlene Resnik*
Mission Specialist Three	*Ronald Erwin McNair*
Payload Specialist One	*S. Christa McAuliffe*
Payload Specialist Two	*Gregory Bruce Jarvis*

Abstract

America's Space program started as a technological program of great national pride. The National Aeronautics and Space Agency (NASA) under the visionary leadership of a young charismatic President John F. Kennedy helped America catch-up with the Soviet Union and win the Cold Space War. The Space Shuttle was born when the Vietnam War, the civil riots, and the Nixon Administration took away that privileged position from NASA. Decisions leading to the Space Shuttle Challenger disaster are reviewed to comprehend knowledge management in large complex organizations.

Caveat:

This is a work-in-progress case, primarily to illustrate concepts for educational purposes. There is no intent to comment on the managers, organizations, and the decisions involved.

[Parts of this paper were published in an earlier paper on Applications of Polymers and Composites Technology in Space-Shuttle in 1986].

CHALLENGER SPACE SHUTTLE DISASTER

The image of *Challenger Space-shuttle* exploding in sky on *January 28, 1986* is permanently etched in the minds of hundreds of millions of TV viewers worldwide. Within 76 seconds of its launch 51-L, the space shuttle blew up with its seven passengers. This flight had a particularly devastating effect because its crew included a highly publicized outstanding civilian schoolteacher **Christa McAuliffe from New Hampshire**. Media and millions of young impressionable schoolchildren closely followed her training. They were shocked by the live fatal explosion. The launch was planned for a school day so that she could conduct some lessons for students following her.

DECISION-MAKING PATH TO DISASTER

The Challenger disaster was the result of a hierarchical command and control management in a large complex organization. This hierarchical style of leadership and decision-making is still quite common in many public and private organizations today (Maier, 1992). The Space-Shuttle disaster reflects the obsession of top-down decision-makers relying on sequential analytical decision making process that overlooks the changing contextual conditions. On one hand, the upper echelons of a hierarchical organization often lack the technical knowledge critical to their core 'business.' On the other hand they overlook the knowledge embedded in the front-line engineers, designers, and staff members in the trenches and fringes of a large complex organization. This is done at the expense of their obsession with "Just Do It" and cost-cutting. Passion to rush to become Number One outweighs all the other fact-based technical or engineering objections (Maier, 1997: 953).

Since the Space-shuttle disaster in 1986, many researchers have analyzed the disaster incident from different perspectives.

Chronological reviews of the Challenger disaster are available from Maier (1994) and Vaughan (1996). The research studies include decision-making procedures (Gouran, Hirokawa, and Martz, 1986; Rogers, 1986; Renz and Greg, 1988; Starbuck and Milliken, 1988); technological failures (Bowser, 1987; Westrum, 1986); organizational culture (Schwartz, 1987); risk assessment (Renz and Greg, 1988); organizational design and structure (Vaughan, 1990, 1995); staffing procedures (Kovach and Render, 1987); ethics in decisions (Boisjoly, 1991); and more. Maier (1992, 1994) conjectured that the norms, and procedures at the core of hierarchical "pyramid-like" command-and-control organizations caused the disaster. These norms emerge from masculine work ethic (Maier, Ferguson, and Shrivastava, 1992; Maier, 1992, 1994).

THIS STUDY

In this paper we revisit the Challenger Space-Shuttle disaster as a failure in NASA's techno-managerial decision making process. NASA's Space-Shuttle program, a highly complex technological and managerial venture, has gone through a number of compromising technological changes because of external pressure from tax-paying public and the U.S. Congress. As a result of this outside pressure this pioneering program was made to rely on the technological and managerial expertise of a number of outside suppliers.

SPACE EXPLORATION:
THE PRIDE OF A GLOBAL SUPER-POWER

NASA's Space Flight program, once started, was a great source of pride for America, the post-war Super-Power. The Soviet lead in space, with the launch of *Sputnik I and II* in 1957, was a severe blow to America's self-image as the savior and leader of the free world during the World War II. *President Eisenhower* created *National Aeronautics and Space Administration (NASA)* in 1958 with a broad mandate for action and plenty of resources. The Cold War rivalry between the United States and the Soviet Union that followed the World War II started the Cold Space War. The U.S. Federal government provided lots of funds to a wide variety of science and technology efforts to catch up with the Soviet Union. Resources flowed freely to NASA.

THE SUPER-COLD SPACE WAR

In May 1961, after just 31 months of starting **Mercury Space** project, **Astronaut Alan Sheppard** manually controlled the first US manned space launch. He communicated from outer space as millions watched and listened. He traveled 300 miles and reached an altitude of 115 miles with 5 minutes of weight-lessness. About 16 minutes after lift-off the spacecraft was recovered. The Mercury flight was a success. But the **Russian Cosmonaut Yuri Gagarin** had already orbited the earth in a heavier spacecraft.

The newly elected **President John F. Kennedy** in 1960 admitted, "We are behind. The news will be worse before it will be better. And it will be sometime before we catch up." He asked *Vice President Lyndon Johnson* to head a study of how US can beat Russians in the Space Race. NASA's 10 year plan had the goal of the first manned flight around the Moon. How could the goal be extended to landing on the surface of the Moon?

On May 25, 1961, *President John F. Kennedy* addressed a joint session of the US Congress, to define a new national goal. He proclaimed,

"Now it is a time to take longer strides. Time for a great new American enterprise. Time for this nation to take a clearly leading role in space achievement. Which in many ways may hold a key to our future on earth.
I believe that this nation should commit itself, to achieving the goal, before this decade is out, of landing a man on the moon, and returning him safely to the earth. No single space program in this period will be more impressive to mankind, or more important for the long range exploration of space."

NASA was exhilarated but awed. To land a man on moon and return to earth was perhaps the hardest technical project on earth at that time.

Soon after the untimely assassination of President Kennedy, *President Lyndon Johnson* demanded that NASA develop a proposal for space objectives after the Apollo program. NASA administrators feared that some of their specific programs would invite criticism that the programs were too expensive. Starting in 1966, the budget for NASA started falling every successive year.

Successful landing of man on the Moon by Apollo in July 1969 brought back the United States in lead in the global Space Race. This success in the Space Race, before the Soviets, was the ultimate goal of the nation's senior policy makers. Once achieved, the urgency changed. Some observers suggest that when the Soviet Union did not retaliate America's landing on the Moon with a bigger space program (the US satellites positioned in space were monitoring), the American policy makers became complacent. The spectacular successes with moon landings, made NASA view itself as a unique ideal organization that knew everything, and could achieve anything (Richard Cook, 1991).

After the dramatic and successful Apollo mission to the Moon and back in July 1969, NASA needed a new mission. The 1960s were not easy in America. President Kennedy's assassination, racial riots, America's extended engagement in Viet Nam, and antiwar protests preoccupied the newly installed **President Richard Nixon**. The economic recession and a runaway federal budget did not help President Nixon's popularity.

CALLS FOR COST-CUTTING

A Harris Poll in 1969 indicated that 64% Americans believed that the $4 billion annual budget for NASA was too much, and 56% believed that too much money was spent on the Apollo Moon-landing program (Harris, 1970). Under the **Chairmanship of Vice President Spiro Agnew, President Richard Nixon** appointed a **Space Task Group** to study post-Apollo plans for the space program. In January 1970, **President Nixon** told **NASA Administrator Thomas Paine** that the public opinion and his political advisors indicated a mood for major cuts in NASA's space program. And that even though the President was committed to the space program for the long-term future, he had to make cuts most reluctantly. In 1970, the **Bureau of the Budget, which became the Office of Management Budget (OMB)**, was chartered to save cost and make government programs more efficient. OMB did not see the need for a new space-flight initiative.

DECISION-MAKING IN COMPLEX ORGANIZATIONS

Without the blessing of a President championing the Space program, the NASA administrators were forced to develop a low-cost, economical space transportation, with low development costs and low operational costs. Compared to other government agencies, NASA was new to managing the political decision-making process in their favor. From that point onwards, NASA's every memo and briefing in support of the Space-shuttle was rooted in the economics and cost-benefit analysis of the program. NASA's past mandate, for developing new technological capabilities for working with ease in space, was lost to the new economic considerations.

With lack of support from the White Office and the government, NASA sought allies in Air Force, where **Robert C. Seamans**, a former deputy NASA Administrator was newly appointed as secretary. In exchange for the support, the Space-shuttle program had to accommodate Air Force's vehicle requirements.

The chosen Space-shuttle design rejected many competing designs in favor of a two-stage design. This design was capable of landing on a runway like a conventional aircraft. It was going to be launched like a rocket with the two stages separating from each other near the edge of the earth's atmosphere. The first stage returned to the earth. Under its own power, the second stage flew into earth's orbit, performing its mission objectives. Then it returned to earth, to be tested, refurnished, refueled, and relaunched.

NASA estimated the cost of building the Space-shuttle system at $10 billion a year, and requested $15 billion a year. OMB demanded a new design and a reduction in cost to about $3.2 billion a year for the first five years of the 1970s. NASA desperately needed a successful Space-shuttle for its own survival and growth.

By the fall of 1970, a number of NASA officials under **NASA Administrator Thomas Paine** favored a more economical and less capable Space-shuttle to be upgraded later. Others such as **Deputy Associate Administrator Werner von Braun** favored the best technological program stretched over many years, so that the average cost for one year was less than $3.2 billion.

OMB advocated a new more amicable NASA Administrator who would reduce empire building, and improve internal management with maturity. In September 1970 **Paine** left NASA, and in February 1971 **James Fletcher became NASA Administrator**.

The US Congress, facing political unrest and growing military spending in Vietnam, was vigilantly looking for programs to cut. The **New York Congressman Ed Koch** declared that he could not support funding programs to search for microbes in Mars when there were rats in the Harlem Apartments. Another **Congressman Joseph Karth** led the opposition to the funding of Space-shuttle program because of NASA's sloppy work reflecting a disrespect for the U.S. Congress. OMB administrators recommended NASA to learn from the Department of Defense in terms of looking at funding and designing alternatives.

All this external pressure forced NASA to review its options for Space-shuttle program, and bring the development of the Space-shuttle to under $1 billion for 6-years. NASA also changed its research focus. To analyze the possible uses and potential savings of reusable spacecraft

NASA contracted with three suppliers, **Lockheed, the Aerospace Corporation, and Mathematica**. Lockheed and Aerospace Corporation provided estimates of payload characteristics and future space traffic to Mathematica, who conducted the primary research. These studies by independent outsiders impressed OMB, the U.S. Congress, and the White House. Mathematica suggested a one-and-a-half stage reusable space shuttle vehicle that was more cost effective than a two-stage design. A subsequent study recommended a Thrust-Assisted Orbiter Shuttle (TAOS) that was partially reusable as an economical and acceptable solution that achieved the major objectives.

In the 1970s, the Space Agency sold the Space-shuttle program to the U.S. Congress with 60 projected launch missions a year. The actual number of space missions never reached the sanctioned number of launches. In 1985, the Space Agency boldly committed itself from 9 missions a year to 15 missions in 1986, and to 24 missions a year by 1990. The international Space Race warranted the bravado of accelerated flight schedule despite intensifying warning signals (Maier, 1997: 958). NASA was facing the unrelented pressure to meet an accelerated flight schedule while keeping the costs under control (Rogers, 1986: 153).

By early-1980s, the USSR was launching a spacecraft every third day. Worldwide, about 140 astronauts and cosmonauts had traveled to space and back in 92 spaceflights launched by US and USSR. Their successes and failures had helped develop various technologies and control instruments needed to make the space flight more accurate, predictable, and safer. Over the past few years, many policy makers also had reluctantly come out of their utopian fantasies and fairy tales about the potential of space technology.

With increasing sophistication of advanced new materials available, and the increasing cost of payload in each launch, the space engineers and managers realized that they could no more afford to use spacecrafts for one time missions only. Prior to the development of the Space-shuttle, going to space was like throwing a Rolls Royce away after every commuting trip to work. Yet, it was not easy for NASA to gain approval for the prestigious space shuttle project. They envisaged a space faring ferry ship that could be used many times carrying people and cargo back and forth between earth and space. One major obstacle was the wear and tear of the structures with large fluctuations in temperatures in space and up to 1300 ^{0}C during re-entry.

THE SPACE-SHUTTLE PROJECT INNOVATION

After several years of design, fabrication, modifications, and testing, the first successful reusable spacecraft was launched in the Spring of 1981. On April 14, at 7 AM (Eastern Standard Time), the Columbia Space-shuttle took off, and 54 hours and 21 minutes later at 10:21 AM (PST) on April 17 touched down at Edwards Air Force Base, with millions watching in awe around the world. The Space-shuttle with two crew members orbited about 200 miles away from earth with an orbital speed of about 18,000 miles per hour, and successfully returned to earth after fulfilling its mission objectives beyond everyone's expectations. The Americans went delirious with excitement during the liftOff and touchdown. The success of the Space-shuttle was mainly attributed to the use of advanced polymeric materials in different applications.

To demonstrate the reusability of the Space-shuttle, a second mission was launched from Cape Canaveral on November 12, 1981. It demonstrated the ability of the manipulating arm for placing satellites and other objects in space. A number of scientific experiments were successfully placed in the payload bay of the Space Shuttle.

COMPLEX SPACE-SHUTTLE MISSION

A Space-Shuttle system consisted of the **Orbiter**, an **external tank** containing propellant for the Orbiter's three main engines, and **two solid rocket boosters (SRBs)**. The Orbiter and boosters were reusable, whereas the external tank was lost in each launch. The Orbiter had the size of a commercial DC-9 medium range jetliner. Its 45x18 meter payload cargo area was designed to take single or multi-unit payloads (up to 30,000 kilograms) for launch in orbit. It was also designed to bring back payloads weighing up to 15,000 kilograms. The **Remote Manipulator System** was a 15 meter long arm made of carbon fiber composites. On earth, this manipulator arm could not support its own 400 kilogram weight. But in space, it could handle payload up to 30,000 kilograms weight, and up to 18 meter length and 4.5 meter diameter size.

A typical Space-shuttle mission started with installation of the mission payload into the Orbiter cargo bay. After reaching the appropriate orbit this payload was checked out, serviced, and activated in space.

At liftoff the *solid rocket boosters (SRBs)* and the Orbiter main engines were fired together. At about 28 miles altitude the two solid rocket boosters (SRBs) were jettisoned after burnout. These were recovered from sea with parachute systems. The recovered boosters were inspected, refurbished and refueled for the next flight.

The main engines of the *Orbiter* continued to burn until the Orbiter was just short of its desired orbital velocity. At that time, the main engines were shut off and the external tank jettisoned. It breaks with its tumble. The desired orbit was attained with the help of *Orbital maneuver system*.

The *Orbiter* crew then began their payload operations by performing numerous assigned tasks as per the mission objectives. These tasks included retrieving satellites from the earth orbit, servicing the orbiting satellites, conducting experiments in space, or examining earth's surface or space from the high vantage point.

After completing the mission operations, normally scheduled to take about 7 days, the deorbiting maneuvers were started. The *Orbiter* re-enters the earth's atmosphere at a high angle of attack. As a result of friction temperatures as high as 1300 ^{0}C are generated on the exterior leading edges. The Orbiter is then leveled into horizontal flight at low altitude for an unpowered aircraft-type landing at about 200 miles per hour speeds. After removing the cargo payloads, the Orbiter can be refurbished for another space mission in about two weeks.

ADVANCED POLYMER INNOVATIONS FOR SPACE

The environment in space is very severe for all materials in general but particularly for visco-elastic polymers. Temperatures rapidly fluctuate between very low temperatures and very high temperatures. Enormous thermal shocks are experienced during the explosive launch and equally tough reentry into the earth's surface (in the case of reusable spacecrafts). Due to the intervening long distances for communication with earth, it is important to maintain precise alignment of communication and sensor systems on board. The materials used in space are therefore expected to maintain their dimensional stability under severe physical and thermal shocks.

Spacecrafts must use highly weight critical materials and structures. As a result, ever since the start of the Global Space War in 1957 when former Soviet Union launched Sputnik-I and Sputnik-II in quick succession, several fiber reinforced composites were put to use. First, the traditional glass fiber reinforced composite was tried. In 1960, the **COURIER 1-B Satellite** was launched using glass epoxy composites.

Later lighter metal alloys and high-performance advanced composites were incorporated in structures.

KEY ROLE OF POLYMERS IN SPACE-SHUTTLE

As mentioned before, many key functions of the Space-Shuttle technology system would not have been feasible but for the innovative use of high performance polymers and composites. The tubular **Remote Manipulator Arm** made of carbon-epoxy composites, was equipped with shoulder joints, elbow, and wrist for rotating in the yaw, pitch, and roll modes. Without the use of carbon composite, the boom would have added much more payload weight, and would have become incapable of lifting the heavy payload weights.

Re-entry Nosecap and Leading Wing Edges

For re-entry capability, the Space-Shuttle needed materials to withstand 1500 ^{0}C reentry temperature at the nose and wing leading edges. Carbon-carbon matrix composites were used for the nose cap. This was fabricated in one piece, about 4.5 feet in diameter, 3 feet in length, and about ½ inch thickness. The wing leading edges were made from 44 panels up to 13 feet wide, 30 inches long, and ¼ inch thickness. The carbon phenolic parts were cured at 175 ^{0}C and then carbonized at 825 ^{0}C, and re-impregnated with furfural alcohol resin under vacuum. The pyrolysis – and – alcohol impregnation process was repeated three times, to drive off the residual resin that may pyrolyze during the reentry.

Overall, the Space-Shuttle system is a technological challenge of unprecedented complexity.

"MONDAY MORNING" DISASTER ANALYSIS

President Ronald Reagan, responding to enormous emotional outburst by people for the Challenger accident, passed the Executive Order12546 on February 3, 1986 and appointed a Presidential Commission to look into the tragic accident. The mandate by the President required the Commission members to:

1. Review the circumstances surrounding the accident to establish the possible cause or causes of the accident; and,

2. Develop recommendations for corrective or other action based upon the Commission's findings and determinations.

The Commission divided itself into 4 investigative panels:

A. Development and Production, responsible for investigating the acquisition and test and evaluation processes for the Space Shuttle elements;

B. Pre-Launch Activities, responsible for assessing the Shuttle system processing, launch readiness process and pre-launch security;

C. Mission Planning and Operations, responsible for investigating mission planning and operations, schedule pressures and crew safety areas; and

D. Accident Analysis, charged with analyzing the accident data and developing both an anomaly tree and accident scenarios.

The Presidential Commission interviewed more than 160 individuals, and held more than 35 formal panel investigative sessions. This generated almost 12,000 pages of transcript. Approximately 122,000 pages in 6,300 documents and hundreds of photographs were examined for the Commission's permanent data bases and archives. In open and close sessions 2,800 pages of hearing transcript generated. In addition, more than 1,300 employees from all NASA's facilities, over 1,600 persons from other government agencies, and more than 3,100 persons from NASA's contractor organizations were involved. The military, the Coast Guard and NTSB helped salvage and analyze the Space-Shuttle wreckage.

The Presidential Commission headed by **William. Rogers**, investigating the Challenger space-shuttle disaster, (See Exhibit for members) produced its *Space Shuttle Challenger Accident Report* on June 6, 1986.

The Presidential Commission noted that it was an "accident rooted in the history" of the organizations and its managers involved. In briefing, Rogers Commission noted that NASA's findings in August 1985 at its headquarters (in connection with a previous flight), was "sufficiently detailed to require corrective action prior to the next flight" (Rogers, 1986: 148).

Many factors and earlier decision-making events contributed to the Space-Shuttle Challenger disaster. Let us review the progress of the complex Space-Shuttle program.

PREAMBLE TO A TECHNO-MANAGERIAL DISASTER

In a typical government bidding process, **Morton Thiokol** was selected to exclusively build the **Solid Rocket Boosters (SRBs)** for the Space-Shuttle program. The company had sizeable cost advantage over its bidding rivals. As is common in such bidding process, some observers ranked **Morton Thiokol** lower than other contestants in engineering design capabilities. With this order in hand, NASA became a major customer for **Morton Thiokol**. The company could not afford to displease their client lightly. Doing so would risk follow-on purchase orders, as well as the survival and growth of the firm.

In 1977, nine years before the **Challenger space-shuttle** disaster, the engineers at **NASA's Marshall Space Flight Center (MSFC)** pointed out certain design deficiencies of the reusable Solid Rocket Boosters (SRBs). This was the unit responsible for monitoring the development and performance of the hundreds of thousands of components that go into making the complex technological miracle of the Space-Shuttle.

PRESIDENTIAL PUSH FOR EDUCATOR IN SPACE

The reusable Space Shuttle started making its return trips to space in 1981. After just four test flights, **President Ronald Reagan** was eager to declare the Space Shuttle system fully operational. He announced that, "We have only peered over the edge of our accomplishments!" Even though at that point inspection of the recovered *solid rocket boosters (SRBs)* indicated some deficiencies.

During the 1984 election campaign, **President Ronald Reagan** announced his Civilian-in-Space program. He personally insisted that the first such civilian would be a schoolteacher. From 142 applicants the **New Hampshire school teacher Christa McAuliffe** was personally picked. Prior to the launch of *Challenger* Space-Shuttle, that was scheduled to carry the chosen Civilian, there were many telephone calls from the President's office to the **Kennedy Space Center** regarding launching the Space-Shuttle in time for President Reagan's State of the Union Address on January 28. Postponing the space-shuttle launch by one more day would have switched the flight to a Saturday, not convenient for broadcasting the lessons scheduled to be conducted by school teacher Civilian-in-Space.

LACK OF LEARNING FROM PRIOR EXPERIENCE

The solid rocket boosters (SRBs) from previous space flights were recovered and thoroughly inspected. These inspections showed that hot gases from inside the four (12 feet diameter and 25 feet tall) booster segments of rockets sometime passed the ¼ inch twin *O-ring rubber seals*. There was one primary, and one back-up rubber ring designed to seal joints between the booster segments. The flames passing through the seals eroded the seals partially during the flight. In March 1984 NASA officials had accepted the possibility of erosion of O-rings due to impingement of rocket hot gases (Level-I Review, March 27, 1984). Despite increasing evidence of erosion of O-rings, the space shuttle flights continued. The O-ring erosion was treated as "an acceptable flight risk." Per *Commissioner Richard Feynman* (Rogers Report, 1986: 2469) each successive flight without a catastrophic disaster resulting from total burn-through of O-rings encouraged the NASA program managers in a "Russian Roulette" like mind-set. Any bad news was routinely suppressed by middle-level managers at **Marshall Space Flight Center (MSFC)** and passed on with a positive spin to the upper managers (Maier, 1987b: 273).

In 1985, there were two near-disasters. In January 1985, in a Space-Shuttle launch on a particularly cold day (53 ^{0}F), hot gases burned all the way in one joint through the primary O-ring, and charred the booster's critical secondary seal. Two missions later, there was a complete failure of a primary seal, and the secondary O-ring was partially eroded.

NASA'S RESPONSE

These burn-throughs raised a few eyebrows at *NASA* and *Morton Thiokol (MT)*. The *Morton Thiokol rocket engineer Roger Boisjoly* had inspected the disassembled rockets retrieved from the two missions. He sent a memo to *Robert Lund, the Vice President of Engineering at Morton Thiokol*, warning against flying without fear of failure and the possibility of a catastrophe with potential loss of human life. A *Seal Task Force* was established under the leadership of **Bob Eberling** to look into the matter.

At *NASA*, on the other hand, a newly hired *budget analyst Richard Cook* interviewed engineers at the *Office of Space Flight* in NASA Headquarters to estimate the budgetary implications of the O-ring burn-through. The engineers shared with him that they were afraid that the space shuttle could blow off, and that they held their breath during each launch (Boffey, 1986). Cook wrote a detailed memo about potential failure of O-ring seals, and sent it to his boss. He feared immense impact on budget if the current solid rocket boosters (SRBs) were to be scrapped while new designs were developed. The shuttle flights would be suspended in the meantime.

In August 1985 **Jesse Moore, NASA's top Shuttle official and Associate Administrator** convened a meeting for a comprehensive review of the O-ring matter with senior personnel from **Morton Thiokol** and **the Space Flight Center**. **Morton Thiokol** representatives stressed the critical need for a good secondary seal. They agreed that efforts were needed to eliminate O-ring erosion due to solid rocket motor burn-through.

Every time a Space-Shuttle launch was scrubbed or delayed, the reporters in print and broadcast media were vicious in criticizing NASA. They did not understand or appreciate the delay due to NASA's concern for safety. The journalists who barely understood the intricacies of a complex launch of a Space Shuttle quickly broadcasted sound-bytes that a flawless lift-off was too much of a challenge for *Challenger* Space-shuttle (Maier, 1997: 958).

NASA's decision-making managers, concluded that the O-ring burn-through constituted an "acceptable risk." They recommended against grounding the Space-Shuttle fleet. They opted to continue flying the Space-Shuttle as before. Meeting flight schedules and cutting costs received higher priorities than flight safety. NASA, was under increasing pressure from the U.S. Congress to cut costs.

By the Fall of 1985, organizational inertia was turning the **Seal Task Force at Morton Thiokol (MT)** into a paper tiger. The **Task Force Leader, Bob Eberling** wrote an appeal for "HELP" to **Allan McDonald, Morton Thiokol's SRM Project Director. Joseph Kilminster**, the Vice-President of the Morton Thiokol's Space Boosters Program agreed to meet with the **Seal Task Force**. He insisted that the engineers on the Seal Task Force must follow the established procedures and existing channels of command.

One week prior to the Challenger space-shuttle disaster, on January 21, 1986, NASA announced that it was seeking <u>four competing bids</u> from rival contractors to procure additional rocket boosters. This put for grab Mortan Thiokol's exclusive contract with National Aeronautics Space Agency worth over $1 billion.

THE DAY OF THE DISASTER: JANUARY 28, 1986

In January 1986 the NASA program managers were looking at the most delayed flight in the history of the space shuttle. By January 27 the Challenger shuttle launch had been postponed three times in 6 days. Next day, a cold front was expected in with sub-zero 29 ^{0}F temperature in the morning. This temperature was much below the previous coldest launch temperature of 53 ^{0}F in January 1985. Morton Thiokol, supplier for O-ring joint seal, was expected to recommend aborting the launch at such low temperatures.

On January 27 *Larry Mulloy* and *Stanley Reinartz* met with *Marshall Director William Lucas* at their motel to apprise him of the impending "no-launch" recommendation by O-ring seal supplier Morton Thiokol. *William Lucas* was known among his managers as a tough administrator demanding strict obedience to his orders and personal loyalty (McConnell, 1986: 108). He commented that, "We get a little cold nip, and they (*Morton Thiokol*) want us to shut the Shuttle system down." He demanded to see the reasons for their recommendation. *Mulloy* then suggested that they would not accept Morton Thiokol recommendation "on the basis of some hand-wringing emotion."

To discuss their recommendations, *Morton Thiokol professionals in Utah* and *MSFC personnel in Alabama and Florida* had a conference telephone call in the afternoon of 27th January. Morton Thiokol supplier insisted on opposing the launch if the launch temperature fell below 53 ^{0}F, the previous record low launch temperature. NASA requested Morton Thiokol to fax its data to *Marshall Space Flight Center* and the *Kennedy Space Center* for further evaluation. A follow-up conference telephone call was scheduled at 8:45 PM. *Morton Thiokol* continued to insist on canceling the launch due to the fear for the safety of its seals in the rocket motor joints. Boisjoly's data was rejected by NASA as 'qualitative' gut-feeling, and not logical. This data was strongly challenged by *Larry Mulloy, the NASA Solid Rocket Booster (SRB) Program Manager*, demanding 'quantitative' proof of their concern that the joint seals would fail if the space shuttle is launched. Later he mentioned to the Rogers Commission that, he found in most cases that "engineers, managers or whatever else who have a true conviction in the data that they are presenting..., will hang tough and resent someone probing and penetrating that data," (Rogers, 1986: 1632).

In the meeting, *Mulroy* reacted, "My God, Thiokol! When do you want me to launch? Next April?" Being on-time and on-budget seemed more important to NASA officials than launch safety and other technical criteria. The integrity of the (bureaucratic/institutional) system was considered more reliable than the context-specific technological knowledge input of the people in it responding to changing context (weather conditions and temperature). *Mulroy* pointed out that there was no mutually agreed launch criterion for joint temperature. He was critical of generating new *Launch Commit Criteria (LCC)* on the eve of a space shuttle launch. He pointed out that NASA had successfully launched 24 times with the existing LCC. The *NASA SRB Program Manager* therefore insisted to know if it was "truly logical" to have 53 ^{0}F temperature to launch the delayed Challenger Space-shuttle? (Rogers, 1986: 1541).

SUPPLIER'S DILEMMA

Supplier Morton Thiokol was in a tough spot. Its technical recommendations were being questioned by its major customer for the first time in the history of the Space-Shuttle program. Morton Thiokol management team requested a "time-out" from the telephone conference, to re-evaluate its data.

Roger Boisjoly

Jerry Mason, the Senior Vice President at Morton Thiokol looked to the three vice presidents with him and announced that they had to make a "management decision." This defined the type of decision as well as who was entitled to make that decision. *Roger Boisjoly, and Arnie Thompson*, Morton Thiokol's two senior engineering experts on the O-ring seals program urged their senior managers to insist on their (MT) original decision to cancel the launch at low temperatures. *Arnie Thompson* drew a sketch of the O-ring joint seal to explain the problem to the senior managers. He and his scientific knowledge were brushed away with a cold disciplining glance from **Sr. VP Jerry Mason**. Then, **Roger Boisjoly** showed the photographs from post-flight inspection of previous flights. He literally screamed that the factual empirical data clearly showed that cold temperatures increased the risk of hot gases blowing through the O-ring joint seals. The technical engineers felt that they were being excluded while their senior managers were making the strategic decisions.

Sr. VP Jerry Mason became impatient, and asked his subordinate executives, if he was "the only one who wants the launch?" He asked **Bob Lund, the Vice President of engineering** to "take off your engineering hat and put on your management hat." *Bob Lund* gave in under this pressure. Finally, only the 4 senior managers were polled, and they unanimously supported a launch. In a latter testimony, *Jerry Mason* explained that they listened to engineers' reasons and not to their intensity. Only management people were polled by Mason, "because we had already established that we were not going to be unanimous (Rogers, 1986: 1362). He admitted that "they (executives) found themselves in a position of uncertainty that they were unable to quantify" (Maier, 1997: 953). The senior executives felt no need to heed to the dissenting technical knowledge from lower operational ranks.

NASA NODS FOR LAUNCH

Morton Thiokol executives resumed their conference telephone call with NASA at 11:00 PM, and *Joe Kilminster, Vice President of Space Boosters at Morton Thioko*l announced their reversal of previous opposition to launch. NASA promptly accepted their contractor's green light for launch, and proceeded with the countdown of the fatal flight. Challenger Space-Shuttle was launched a few hours later at 11:38 AM.

The *Level III NASA Managers Larry Mulroy and Stanley Reinartz* did not find it fit to share the original 'No' vote up by Morton Thiokol with the NASA bosses at Level I and Level II. In their testimony to Presidential Commission they insisted that there was no requirement to do so when no launch commit criteria (LCC) were violated. And therefore it was a Level III issue that they had resolved appropriately at their Level III. Similarly, *Marshall Space Flight Center Director William Lucas* did not mention those reservations to higher level launch officials, because it was not his "reporting channel," (Maier, 1997: 955).

Subsequent investigation in the Space-shuttle disaster clearly showed the evidence that the NASA decision-makers were more concerned with the consequences of wrongly holding up a launch, rather than with the possibility of launching under unsafe launch conditions (Maier, 1997: 958). The Presidential Commission investigations focused on whether the procedures were followed or not, who communicated what and to whom, and who had what responsibilities. Much less time and effort was devoted during the investigation to the safety of the lives of the 7 astronauts or the grief of their families.

LIST OF REFERENCES AVAILABLE WITH THE AUTHOR

SELF-REVIEW QUESTIONS

1. What were the major flaws in the decision-making process at NASA that led to the Challenger Space-Shuttle disaster.

2. Identify (build a flow-chart) for the different elements of the Decision-Making Entity for a safe Space-Shuttle launch.

3. Describe the organizational configuration of NASA's Space Shuttle program. How are the different departments organized and inter-related?

4. Discuss and rate the product complexity, the production process complexity, and the market complexity (demand side) for the Space-Shuttle. Relate these to the configurational complexity of NASA.

5. Design and develop an improved decision-making model (flow-chart or protocol) for NASA Space-Shuttle program.

6. Suggest ways to improve the staffing and organizational configuration of NASA.

Exhibit – 1
MEMBERS OF THE PRESIDENTIAL COMMISSION

1. **William P. Rogers, Chairman**
    Former Secretary of State under President Nixon (1969-1973), and Attorney General under President Eisenhower (1957-1961).

2. **Neil A. Armstrong, Vice Chairman**
    Former astronaut, spacecraft commander for Apollo 11, July 16-24, 1969, the first manned lunar landing mission.

3. **David C. Acheson**
    Partner in a law firm

4. **Dr. Eugene E. Covert**
    Educator and engineer. Currently Professor and Head, Department of Aeronautics, at Massachusetts Institute of Technology.

5. **Dr. Richard P. Feynman**
    Professor of Theoretical Physics at California Institute of Technology. Nobel Prize winner in Physics, 1965.

6. **Robert B. Hotz**
    Was the editor-in-chief of Aviation Week and Space Technology magazine (1953-1980).

7. **Major General Donald J. Kutyna, USAF**
    Director of Space Systems and Command, Control, Communications.

8. **Dr. Sally K. Ride**
    Still an active astronaut. First American woman astronaut Mission specialist astronaut on STS-7, launched on June 18, 1983. She also flew on mission 41-G launched on October 5, 1984. Holds a Doctorate in Physics from Stanford University (1978)

9. **Robert W. Rummel**
   Former vice president of Trans World Airlines

10. **Joseph P. Sutter**
    Currently Executive Vice President of the Boeing
    Commercial Airplane Company. Was a principal figure in the
    development of three generations of jet aircraft.

11. **Dr. Arthur B.C. Walker, Jr.**
    Currently Professor of Applied Physics, and was formerly
    Associate Dean of the Graduate Division at Stanford
    University.

12. **Dr. Albert D. Wheelon**
    Currently Executive vice president, Hughes Aircraft
    Company. Holds a Doctorate in Physics from Massachusetts
    Institute of Technology.

13. **Brig. General Charles Yeager USAF (Retired)**
    Former experimental test pilot. In 1985 appointed as a
    member of the National Commission on Space. He was the
    first person to penetrate the sound barrier and the first to fly
    at a speed of more than 1,600 miles per hour.

14. **Dr. Alton G. Keel, Jr., Executive Director**
    Detailed from his position in the Executive Office of the
    President, Office of Management and Budget. Holds a
    Doctorate in Engineering Physics from the University of
    Virginia.

GORE'S ORGANIZATIONAL INNOVATION FOR LEVERAGING HUMAN CAPITAL

Dr. R. RAY GEHANI

Institute for Innovation and Technology Leadership (IITL)
Akron, Ohio

Abstract

Wilbert L. Gore innovated a unique "unmanagement" way of managing his polymer technology-driven enterprise. His "lattice organization" is based on small plant facilities with less than 200 employees. The small size facilitates face-to-face communication with no hierarchy and few rules. W.L. Gore & Associates has steadily grown in size innovating new products and markets. These are based on the associates' creativity, mutual trust, and innovation. This case presents the advantages and limitations of such 'structure-less' organization design with amorphous culture.

Caveat:

In March 1999 *The Workforce* magazine gave its annual *Optimas Award for Innovation* to W.L. Gore & Associates. The manufacturer of Gore-Tex and other high-performance polymeric materials was commended for its unique human resource management. The company's HR department played a strategic role in the company's growth and transformation.

Gore & Associates was founded by an ex-Du Pont employee Wilbert L. Gore. From the start he organized his company in a unique way based on his vision of 'a lattice organization.' Bill Gore became interested in Douglas McGregor's classic, *The Human Side of Enterprise* that promoted Theory Y and empowerment of people. By keeping small plant facilities with less than 200 associates, it relies on person-to-person communication. It has associates and not employees, has sponsors and mentors but no bosses, and it uses self-commitments instead of sales or production quotas. The company encourages associates to be creative. The Associates have profit sharing, Associate Stock Option Plan (ASOP), and the compensation is decided by committees.

THE EARLY YEARS OF AN ENTREPRENEUR

Bill Gore started his career as a research chemist at Du Pont. He worked on a task force developing applications for poly-tetra-fluoro-ethylene (PTFE) commonly known by its stick-free brand name Teflon. He was so committed to his work, that he often did some experimental tinkering at night in his basement at home. On one such occasion, he discovered that PTFE could be processed to coat electrical cable wires for insulation. Bill took his innovative idea to Du Pont managers. Du Pont considered its business primarily bulk polymers, and was not interested in developing Gore's low-volume product application. In 1958, Bill Gore and his wife Vieve, started W.L. Gore & Associates in Newark, Delaware, not far from Wilmington, Delaware headquarters of Du Pont.

Technology-based Entrepreneurship

Wilbert L. Gore was born in 1912 near Boise in Meridian, Idaho. As a child he enjoyed hiking in Wasatch Mountain Range in Utah. In a church camp there he met his future wife *Genevieve "Vieve"* and married her in 1935 for a lifelong partnership. In 1933, Wilbert Gore completed a Bachelor of Science degree in chemical engineering from the University of Utah. From the same university he earned Master of Science degree in physical chemistry in 1935. In 1936 Gore started working at *American Smelting and Refining*, moved to *Remington Arms Company* in 1941, and to *E.I. du Pont* in 1945. There Gore became research supervisor and head of operations research, doing research on developing applications for poly-tetra-fluoro-ethylene (PTFE, or *Teflon*).

DEVELOPING TEFLON AT DU PONT

Teflon is one of the most familiar and versatile of American chemical products. It was discovered accidentally at **Du Pont**. Yet, each step, along the way to its final discovery, drew heavily on the skills of researchers trained to nurture scientific discoveries to commercial success. Teflon was developed as a byproduct of **Du Pont**'s interest in chloro-fluoro-carbon (CFC) refrigerants. In these compounds some of hydrogen in the hydrocarbon are replaced with fluorine or chlorine.

The CFCs were first brought to the attention of Du Pont's researchers by the **Frigidaire division of General Motors**. In the early 1930s **A. L. Henne and Thomson Midgley**, research chemists at General Motors's Frigidaire refrigeration equipment division, brought samples of Freon 11 and Freon 12 CFC refrigerants to Jackson Laboratory of Du Pont's Chamber Works in Deepwater, New Jersey. Freons were developed to replace and improve on traditionally used refrigerants such as ammonia, propane, or sulfur oxide. These older refrigerants were less efficient, more toxic, or dangerously explosive for domestic use. GM and Du Pont launched a joint venture, **Kinetic Chemicals** to research and develop Freons. Together they developed and tested a wide series of chloro-fluoro-carbons (CFCs). The commercially most viable CFCs, such as Freon 114, or tetra-fluoro-dichloro-ethane ($CF_2.Cl.CF_2.Cl$), were scaled up. Kinetic was contractually committed to supply its entire production output of Freon 114 to Frigidaire/GM. Du Pont, therefore started a project to develop an alternate refrigerant to sell to independent customers and assigned the 27-year-old **Dr. Roy J. Plunkett** to this project.

Plunkett was hired in 1936 by Du Pont after he earned his doctorate at Ohio State University. He reacted tetra-fluoro-ethylene (TFE) a gas at room temperature, with hydrochloric acid to synthesize a new CFC refrigerant. Plunkett and **assistant Jack Rebok** made 100 pounds of TFE and stored it in pressure vessel canisters. These were cooled with dry ice to prevent explosion. The researchers connected the pressure vessel to reaction vessel, to release some TFE into a heated chamber where hydrochloric acid was sprayed. On April 6, 1938, when they opened the valve nothing come out. They fiddled with the valve but found nothing wrong with the valve, so they feared that the TFE gas had leaked out. When they weighed the pressure vessel, the weight seemed normal.

In frustration, Plunkett disconnected the valve, and turned the pressure canister upside down. When they shook it, white waxy powder sticking to the walls of the canister fell out. Even though previous attempts to polymerize fluorinated or chlorinated ethylene had failed, Plunkett suspected polymerization and wrote in his notebook, "A white solid material was obtained, which was supposed to be a polymerized product."

After two days of more tests, Plunkett wrote, "It is thermoplastic, melts at a temperature approaching red heat, and boils away. It burns without residue; the decompositive products etch glass." The material was insoluble in a variety of solvents including cold and hot water, acetone, Freon 113, ether, petroleum ether, alcohol, pyridine, toluene, ethyl acetate, glacial acetic acid, nitrobenzene, isoanyl alcohol, ortho-dichloro-benzene. Even concentrated sulfuric acid, sodium hydroxide, and concentrated nitric acid did not dissolve it. A soldering iron or an electric arc did not melt or char it. It did not swell or rot with moisture. Prolonged exposure to sunlight did not degrade it. It was even impervious to mold and fungus. The accidental material had amazing resistance.

Plunkett duplicated the accidental conditions in the canister to produce polymerized tetra-fluoro-ethylene (PTFE). On July 1, 1939 a patent was applied for and assigned to Kinetic Chemicals. In 1941 the patent was granted. After the patent application, Plunkett (an expert on freon chemistry) handed over the project to others concerned with polymer chemistry and process development.

During the World War II Du Pont was encouraged to produce whatever PTFE they could produce as gaskets and seals for Manhattan Project. To separate rarer isotope U-235 from more plentiful but inert U-238 using gaseous diffusion, Du Pont was asked to design a separation equipment that withstood highly corrosive uranium hexa-fluoride gas. The Manhattan project consumed about 2/3rd of Du Pont's PTFE production, and the rest was used by other military applications, such as in nose cones, airplane engines. PTFE was the best material to wrap copper wires in the radar systems of army night bombers. At a cost of $100 per pound, a 0.002-inch thick tape was painstakingly shaved from a solid block of PTFE.

In 1944 Du Pont registered the trademark Teflon. After the war, Du Pont decided to develop the civilian industrial applications of Teflon as specialized polymeric materials with premium prices. The company's standard marketing strategy was to go after markets with bulk use.

GENESIS OF TECHNOLOGICAL ENTREPRENEURSHIP

Bill Gore noted the growth of transistors, semiconductors, and computers and believed that PTFE had the insulating characteristics ideal for insulating the computer ribbon cable. He unsuccessfully tried many alternate ways to coat ribbon cables with Du Pont's PTFE.

One day, in Gore's basement laboratory at home, son Bob, then a chemical engineering student, suggested using PTFE sealant tape produced by 3M to coat computer ribbon cables. Father Bill Gore told son Bob that everybody knew that PTFE couldn't stick to itself. Son Bob went to sleep, but father Bill stayed on to validate his own statement. At 4 am father Bill excitedly woke his son Bob and told him that what everybody negated had worked. Next night father Bill and son Bob successfully coated ribbon cable with PTFE in their basement laboratory.

For the next four months Bill Gore tried unsuccessfully to convince decision makers at Du Pont to develop and produce a new product based on PTFE-coated ribbon cable. It soon became clear that Du Pont decision-makers believed their business was limited to producing bulk polymers and resins, and not low-volume special applications. Bill Gore knew how Du Pont decided. It was hard to walk away from his job after 17 years at Du Pont.

A NEW GORE BUSINESS IS BORN

Bill Gore talked to wife Vieve about started own business around PTFE insulated wires and cables. On their 23rd anniversary on January 1, 1958, Gores with 5 children launched W.L. Gore & Associates with their first facility in the basement of their home. They started working soon after having their anniversary dinner. Bill Gore sacrificed his good steady salary after 17 years of service at Du Pont, and instead mortgaged their house and took $4,000 from their savings to finance their business for the first 2 years. First few years were financially rough. To employees instead of salaries Gores provided room and board in their home. The number of boarders rose to eleven at one time.

TURNAROUND

One day the water department of the city of Denver called Gore & Associates to ask product manager some technical questions. Vieve informed that he was out. Then the inquirer wanted to speak to sales manager, or president, and Vieve admitted that they were out too. The inquirer was surprised, but Gore & Associates tactfully obtained an order for $100,000. This provided the much-needed financial strength for the young company to continue and be profitable.

In 1960, W.L. Gore & Associates moved into its first plant in Newark, Delaware, the company's headquarters.

Gore & Associates developed many new products based on applications of PTFE, including Gore-Tex, all weather outdoor jackets.

Bill Gore died in 1986 while backpacking in the Wind River Mountains of Wyoming. At that time he was the chairman, son Bob was president, and wife Vieve was secretary-treasurer, the only other officer of the company. Bill Gore did not want the titles, but by law and their articles of incorporation they were expected to have these three officers.

FINANCIAL AND STRATEGIC PERFORMANCE

Gore & Associates was a privately held corporation. Most financial information was held confidential. In early years, the Gore family and the veteran associates held about 80% of the company's stock, 10% was held by the current associates, and others held the balance 10%.

According to strategic measures, in the first 20 years sales of Gore & Associates grew steadily by over 18% annually (discounted for inflation).

Year	1969	1982	1983	1985	1987	1988	1989
Sales, ($Mil.)	6	125	160	250	400	426	600

Year	1991	1992	1993	1994	1995	1996	1997	1999
Sales, ($Mil.)	660	700	804	828	958	1064	1160	1,400

By 1999 Gore & Associates had approximately 6,500 associates working in 45 locations around the world (Anfuso, 1999: 48). The company developed, produced, and marketed PTFE applications in four areas: electronic products, fabrics, industrial products, and medical products. Estimated worldwide sales were approximately $1.4 billion in 1999. In 1997, the experts estimated the company to cross $2 billion revenue mark in 2001.

Forbes magazine estimates the operating profits for the largest privately held companies in the U.S. According to the magazine, the operating profits for Gore & Associates increased from $120 million in 1993, to $140 million in 1994, $192 million in 1995, $213 million in 1996, and $230 million in 1997.

THE LATTICE ORGANIZATION:

INNOVATING ORGANIZATION CONFIGURATION

Bill Gore was not just an ordinary technology-based entrepreneur looking to make big wealth for him. He was also a visionary. Gore had thought a lot about what made a workplace either great to work or too awful to go to. He had a radical vision of developing an organization where "Associates" (never called employees) like to work and contribute their most, without being overwhelmed by unnecessary rules and oppressive hierarchy that added little value. He called this "the lattice organization." This organization is based on Theory Y and collaborative workplace, rather than Theory-X hierarchy run by autocrats.

W.L. Gore & Associates became a company without hierarchical titles and conventional structures. Only the titles of president and secretary-treasurer were used because of legal and regulatory requirements of the laws of incorporation.

Trying to implement this radically different organization configuration was not easy or smooth. No bosses, hierarchies, or rules pushed decisions through the organization. Without pre-determined channels of communication, associates have to communicate with each other directly. With no titles, associates are not locked into pre-determined tasks. They are, therefore, free to take new challenges and commitments.

GUIDING GORE PRINCIPLES

Gore & Associates had few rules, no corporate-wide mission or code of ethics statement. One underlying mission of Bill Gore was "to make money and have fun." Bill Gore's "unmanagement" style was guided by his experiences in teams in Du Pont. Bill Gore, however, did not prohibit when a few business units developed their mission statements. One Associate believed that the company was driven by two underlying philosophies:

A.   Company's four basic governing principles cover the ethics required of all the associates and the company, and

B.   Company will not support or tolerate any illegal practices.

CORE GORE VALUES

All Associates had to agree on four governing principles for the Lattice Organization to be successful. These principles are:

1.   Fairness. Sincerely try to be fair with each other, with suppliers, customers, and other persons with whom they transact or come in contact.

2.   Life-long Learning and Growth. Allow, help, and encourage other associates to grow in knowledge, skill, scope, responsibility, and a range of activities.

3.   Self-Commitment. Make own commitments, and keep them.

4.   Consultation. Consult with other Associates before taking actions that might be "below the waterline," and cause serious damage to the enterprise and survival or growth of many Associates. Bill Gore believed that certain issues "above the waterline" have marginal effect on survival or growth of organization. Building a new plant is a "below waterline issue" demanding consultation and agreement of other Associates. Launching another product in an existing product line is "above the waterline" issue, which can be executed without extensive discussions.

Some Associates believed that there was a fifth principle: maintain ambiguity to remain flexible, and capture reality. When some Associates try to introduce two-dimensional structure, and freeze it on paper, other associates reintroduce ambiguity. They sincerely believed that when an environment, a community, or a culture is reduced to a definition – it acquires fewer dimensions than what it is in reality.

RECRUITING NEW ASSOCIATES

In the 1970s, new employees, to their great surprise and frustration, were given an office and a desk, and often told to look around and find something useful to do. After weeks they started doing something. Over years they can change their jobs from one functional area to another, and be good at cross-functional integration.

By early 1990s, the new employee orientation was more structured. New Associates spent a few weeks through different steps in Gore's production process before settling down for the assignment they were hired for. Thus, the employee hired for sales and advertising may learn how the Gore-Tex fabric is laminated, customer complaints are answered, and capital investment selection. They were often instructed to examine new opportunities and examine their commitments.

Recruiting at Gore is taken very seriously, and treated as "below waterline" issue. No one gets hired until a company Associate agrees to "sponsor" the person, including finding work for the Associate. Recruiting is intimately driven by the four core Gore values. Interviewing process involves numerous Associates. For example, for recruiting an HR generalist position at plant level, the plant-level leadership team and HR specialists at corporate level who know the needed competencies were involved (Anfuso, 1999).

Interview questions explore not only technical skills but also other skills critical to the success in Gore's amorphous culture. These include questions regarding team skills, communication skills, and problem-solving skills. Some examples are given below (Anfuso, 1999).

"Give me an example of a time when you had a conflict with a team member,"

"Tell me how you solved a problem that was impeding a project."

After a potential candidate is identified, recruiters conduct many reference checks. Sometimes ten references are contacted, including the potential candidate's peers, superiors, and subordinates. They make sure that a candidate has the right stuff that fits well with Gore's amorphous culture (Martin, 1998). They inquire not only about the candidate's title, time, and grade but also about the traits and the fit with the company's needs. Continuous learning is a critical expectation of all associates (Core Gore Value #2).

SELF-SELECTED NICHES AND COMMITMENTS

Gore Associates, after they are hired, are not assigned jobs but expected to discover their own niches. When Associates join, they are advised to go to different areas, and see how they can help. Then the

Associate has to carve out a niche for himself or herself. This is very different from other enterprises, from where the Gore associates may come. In their previous jobs, Associates usually had a rigid title, were told what was expected of them, and what specific position they were working in. Not everyone can work well under the ambiguity at Gore & Associates.

Unlike at other large organizations, Associates at Gore can choose to do research even if they do not have Ph.D. They are not held back by lack of credentials. Instead at Gore, new Associates are told that they are what they do. If they do something good, Gore will pay them more. Associates are not boxed by their credentials. They can set their own course. They can do technical work as well as marketing work, as long as it makes a contribution to the business and the company.

Gore Associates are not assigned narrowly defined jobs and titles with limited task responsibilities (Core Gore Value #3). Instead they have general expectations within functional areas (Anfuso, 1999: 52). This is because, Bill Gore believed that people take greater responsibility for what they have volunteered for and committed to rather than to something that they are told to do.

When a new Gore Associate is hired, s/he has or is assigned a sponsor. The sponsor is an Associate who made a commitment to help the new Associate to get to "the quick win." The sponsor helps the new Associate grasp the basic understanding of her/his commitments, and what it will take to be successful in those self-commitments (Anfuso, 1999: 52). Over time an Associate and the sponsor may decide to change the commitment, as well as their mutual relationship. The sponsors collect feedback and information from peers and leaders of the new Associate. This is shared with the new Associates and the relevant compensation committees.

NEED SOLUTIONS, NOT MANAGERS' TITLES PLEASE

In the Lattice Organization, Associates do not have authoritarian titles or formal chains of command. When Gore Associates meet outsiders, the outsiders are perplexed with their lack of titles. So, Gore Associates can call themselves anything that the outsiders would like. Associates are free to print whatever they want on their business cards. One Associate printed her title in the business card as Supreme Commander. Bill Gore often shared this story with others.

Some Associates agree with the futility of hierarchical titles for coordinating work in an organization. They prefer to go to fellow

Associates who have solutions for their problems, rather than good-for-nothing but impressive titles. Associates develop trust and reliance on other associates for guidance or technical information. Theirs is not a formal transactional protocol but a trust-building informal relationship. This eliminates a lot of unproductive pretense, and much more focus on getting the job done.

NATURAL LEADERSHIP DEFINED BY FOLLOWERSHIP NOT RANK

At Gore, the Associates who have answers for other associates gain followership, and emerge as natural leaders. Associates with an innovative idea for a significant value-adding project share it with other Associates who decide whether to join him/her or not. The originating leader of the project idea may identify certain project objectives, but the followers who join can influence and help redefine these objectives. Natural leaders earn commitment from followers, rather than give them orders. Bill Gore believed that all commitments are self-commitments offered by associates. Authoritarian bosses can only impose orders, not commitments. The difference in the two approaches is in the enormous response from an Associate for the former. In a survey, about half of the Gore associates admitted that they considered themselves to be a leader in their plant (Levering & Moskowitz, 1993).

COMPENSATION BY SPONSORS AND COMMITTEES

If there is no hierarchy, no bosses, no formal chain of command, then how is the performance of Gore Associates evaluated? Bill Gore innovated a system of evaluating the performance of associates by sponsorship system. According to Bill Gore, a sponsor is knowledgeable about the activities, accomplishments, ambitions, progress, and personal problems of the Associates s/he sponsors. Associates saw their sponsors not as bosses, but as coaches or mentors, who helped them succeed. Sponsors thus kept track of an Associate's activities, and acted as his/her advocates in discussions of compensation.

Compensation of associates is based on their contributions, and not the number of hours they spent working. Yet, many Gore Associates put in much more than an 8-hour shift. But the extra hour or two a day Associates put in, most say is not by force from the top, but by their choice. Associates felt that every little contribution they made impact on their stocks. Other Associates who put in a regular 8 hour per day did not feel that they were penalized for doing so.

Gore Associates also had the freedom of a flexible benefits program. According to the national survey of compensation by Hewitt Associates Gore ranked 23% higher than comparable companies (Levering & Moskowitz, 1993).

In 1999 there were 15 compensation committees for the different functional areas, such as engineering, manufacturing, and HR. The committees include leaders who understand the technical excellence and the value an Associate adds in that functional area. HR generalists at the plant level (often members of the plant-level committees), with specialists at corporate level facilitate the compensation process to be fair.

The compensation committees compile the feedback and information they get on each Associate in a function. Sponsors may check with customers to find more about an Associate's contributions. The Associates in a functional area are then ranked based on not only their personal skills but also on the Associates' contributions to the success of their business. Using guidelines based on external salary data, the Associates are compensated so that they are internally fair and externally competitive. W.L. Gore & Associates benchmarks its compensation and benefits with leading companies such as Du Pont, 3M, IBM, and Hewlett-Packard. Associates are paid fairly based on the success of the business (Core Gore Value #1). Compensation committees do consider the possibility that an Associate may make significant contribution to a business that was not so successful. For example, an Associate's leadership skill and willingness to help others develop to their fullest potential are also considered.

Associates' profit sharing component has gradually become more formalized and is based on Economic Value Adding (EVA). Earlier the profit sharing used to be spontaneous, and based on creative work of an Associate. Associates, therefore, did not worry about their due profit share. By using EVA, the associates know the EVA created and calculated at the end of each month. When a certain EVA target is met then Associates can expect to get profit share. Associates know what they need to do.

ASSOCIATE OWNERSHIP

Gore is big on ownership by Associates. Part of Associates' compensation is with stock ownership and profit sharing. Gore Associate Stock-Ownership Plan (ASOP) has helped Associates own approximately 25% of their privately held company. (The rest of W.L. Gore & Associates is owned by the Gore family). Many Gore Associates may earn more in the ASOP than in their W2 income forms, accumulating enough for retirement. One machinist who worked in Gore for 25 years could retire as a millionaire.

SMALL PLANT SIZE

Gore & Associates is organized into small plants. One Monday morning in 1965, Bill Gore was taking his usual walk through a fast growing plant facility on Paper Mill Road in Newark, Delaware. He realized that he did not know all the associates. The team had grown too large. Gore developed a "get big by staying small" policy so that all the plants in his Lattice Organization will have a size smaller than 150-200 associates. Gore believed that in a plant with less than 200 associates, everyone could know everyone else directly, and work with one another face-to-face. This helps develop a close-knit workplace. In plants larger than 200 associates, an impersonal bureaucracy emerges inevitably with rules that do not add true value.

By 1991, Gore Associates had 5,300 associates distributed in 44 plants worldwide. In Flagstaff, Arizona facility four plants were clustered on the same site. In the United States 27 plants were located. The rest 17 overseas plants were located in Germany, France, Scotland, Japan, and India. Approximately 6,500 associates were working in 44 Gore plants in 1997.

INNOVATIVE OUTCOMES

Gore's visionary Lattice Organization with freedom has gotten the innovative jobs done again and again over the years. Gore associates believe that their freedom has helped them identify and develop a wide range of innovative applications for the PTFE material. In 1969, Bill Gore's son Bob Gore innovated stretching of PTFE into a unique textile fabric – as the next generation of fabric to replace the rubber raincoats of the Nineteenth Century. This was patented as Gore-Tex™. Gore-Tex fabric has small pores that keep the raindrops out. The pores are, however, big enough for perspiration to evaporate out. Gore-Tex earned a great reputation for outdoor clothing using this material.

Gore also developed applications of PTFE in a wide variety of other applications. This included use in space suits, air and water filters. Many medical applications of PTFE were developed as artificial ligaments and arteries. Gore & Associates made hundreds of such products, and received more than 400 patents, averaging more than 10 patents a year over its young life (Levering & Moskowitz, 1993).

RESEARCH, DEVELOPMENT AND
PROPRIETRARY KNOW-HOW

Like the rest of unstructured organization at Gore & Associates, the research and development was also highly unstructured. Bill Gore encouraged all Associates to draw on their creative potential. Anyone could ask for some raw PTFE, referred as silly worm, to experiment and invent. Many inventions were held as trade secrets or proprietary know-how, though the company had applied for and was awarded an impressive number of patents.

The research and development at Gore uses a lot of creativity and intuition. Gore associates are encouraged to generate creative ideas, experiment, and develop it to profitable commercialization. In 1985, Bill Gore asserted, "The creativity, the number of patent applications, and innovative products (at Gore & Associates) is triple" that of Du Pont. Education and ranks of associates did not hinder the invention and innovation process. An associate with an elementary education was encouraged to design and develop wire-wrapping machine.

Bill and Bob Gore often became the role models for other associates. In 1969 the wire and cable division started facing increasing competition. Bill Gore thought of straightening out and unfolding the PTFE molecules to introduce air into its molecular structure. This would increase volume per pound, reduce fabricating costs, and improve profit margin. Bill and Bob Gore systematically heated PTFE rods at different temperatures, and stretched them slowly. The rods always broke no matter how gradually they stretched. One late night, after many failures, son Bob Gore yanked violently at the rod he was holding. To his great surprise, it did not break. Next morning, son Bob Gore dramatically re-enacted his frustration-amazement incident to his father Bill Gore. The ability to orient the PTFE molecules radically changed the wire and cable products.

PTFE stretching also led to the development of highly successful Gore-Tex™ products, which later became the largest Gore division (See Exhibit –1). In the summer of 1970, Bill and Vieve Gore hand-sew a tent from patches of Gore-Tex, and decided to field-test it on their annual camping trip to the Wind River Mountains in Wyoming. They had hailstorm on the first night out. In the top of the tent the hail tore holes, but the bottom of the tent filled up like a water tub. The Gore-Tex tent was waterproof but needed to be stronger against hail.

While skiing in Colorado, Bill Gore showed a section of Gore-Tex to friend Dr. Ben Eiseman of the Denver General Hospital. Dr. Eiseman offered to try it in a vascular graft on a pig. Two weeks later Ben informed Bill that the graft worked. Bill asked him to contact Pete Cooper in Flagstaff plant to figure out what to do next. Thus Gore-Tex vascular graft was commercialized, and became the second largest Gore division.

GORE'S INTELLECTUAL PROPERTY

Gore's high success in high-performance Gore-Tex™ fabrics often attracted imitation from unauthorized users of its patented technology. Gore challenged these violators in the court. In 1993 the basic patent for manufacturing Gore-Tex™ fabric expired. This did increase the competition with competing waterproof fabric laminates. In the meantime, however, Gore has acquired a series of other derivative patents for Gore-Tex graft patches, vascular graft, Gore-Tex industrial sealants and filtration materials. This helps protect Gore in these niche markets.

PRODUCT DIVISIONS

As Gore & Associates grew, its structure was organized in multiple product groups. These included, electronics, waterproofing fabrics, fibers, medical, industrial seals, coatings, filtration, and microfiltration (Shipper and Manz, 1994).

The electronic products division produced highly reliable insulated cables and wires for high-performance applications in computers, telecommunications, defense, and aerospace. In these demanding applications, the conventional wires and cables were not reliable enough. Gore wires and cables were also used in the moon vehicle that scooped up moon rocks. In the space shuttle Columbia the Gore wire and cables withstood the wide thermal fluctuations from high temperatures in ignition and reentry to cryogenic temperatures in space. Microwave technology was made feasible by the complementary capability of Gore's microwave coaxial assemblies.

In fast computers the Gore cables transmitted electrical signals at speeds of about 90% of the speed of light. The physical characteristics of the highly reliable Gore-Tex™ products were applied to electronic components in electronic switching for telephony, industrial and scientific instrumentation, defense systems, microwave communications, and industrial robots.

Gore-Tex fibers and fabrics were impervious to sunlight, heat, cold, and many chemicals. It was strong and resistant to abrasion. Gore-Tex waterproof, windproof, and yet breathable fabric emerged as essential gear for mountaineers and adventurous hikers. The PTFE membrane blocked rainwater and wind from entering but allowed sweat vapors to escape. Lightweight Gore-Tex™ fabric shell outperformed and replaced a poplin jacket and a rain suit. Large number of sailors, skiers, runners, hunters, fishermen, bicyclists, and other outdoor adventurers have become regular users of Gore-Tex™ fabric. Gore-Tex liners helped waterproof boots and gloves, for recreation or work under severe conditions. Military personnel used Gore-Tex™ in pants, gloves, boots, headgear, parkas, and wet suits as standard requirement.

A flexible joint sealant cord of porous PTFE was developed and marketed for application as a sealing gasket in complex shapes, extreme temperatures and pressures, and corrosive chemicals. Steam valves with Gore-Tex valve stempacking have long life without replacement.

A patented Fluoroshield protective coating process was developed to apply and coat layers of PTFE to steel castings and other metal articles for applications as vessels for processing corrosive chemicals.

In Industrial filtration, Gore-Tex filter bags economically removed or recovered solids from gases and liquids. These helped become Coal-burning plants become smoke-free and less polluting.

In medical applications, the Gore-Tex™ expanded PTFE products combated cardiovascular disease. Gore-Tex™ artificial arteries replace seriously damaged or plugged arteries blocking smooth flow of blood. The patient's tissue grows into the open porous spaces of grafts of Gore-Tex arteries and patches. The Gore grafts are therefore not rejected by the receiving body. Gore-Tex™ grafts in many sizes improve circulation and save limbs from amputation. In newborn babies tiny grafts relieve pulmonary problems. People with kidney-related troubles also use Gore-Tex products. New Gore-Tex™ cardiovascular patch membranes for surgical reinforcement were developed to repair holes and aneurysms.

Gore-Tex™ microfiltration products were developed for use in medical devices, pharmaceutical production and chemical processing. Gore-Tex membranes helped sterilization by removing microorganisms and bacteria from air or liquid.

In 1994, a no-stick dental floss, called Glide was introduced.

CUSTOMIZE MARKETING

Gore tried to develop the best-valued products for customized application needs of major customers.

Usually first a product specialist leader becomes a product champion, passionately supporting a technology. The product champion then markets the products to sales representatives who make self-commitments about the future sales. The sales representatives do not have sales quotas or bosses telling them what to do. Together, as a team they agree to pursue a new market. The sales representatives do not rely on commissions but on salaries and profit sharing under Associate Stock Option Plan (ASOP).

As the product concept evolves, the product champion recruits more team members. The teams grow and splinter into multiple teams and manufacturing cells. Each cell has a leader that evolves from within based on a consensus and discussion, not a vote.

Word-of-mouth and cooperative advertising play important roles in implementing Gore's marketing strategy.

Gore-Tex™ fabric products were promoted by cooperative advertising with a number of clothing manufacturers and distributors. Gore pursued cooperative advertising strategy with the hope that satisfaction with one product (say in parks) will have spillover effect on purchasing of other related products (say gloves or boots) in future. Gore's cooperative arrangements include Lands' End, Timberland, Apparel Technologies, Austin Reed, Woolrich, North Face, Grandoe, and Michelle Jaffe. Gore-Tex™ was becoming the preferred lining material in high performance yet stylish gloves.

Gore believes that informal advertising in technical markets relies heavily on the reputation of the company and its brand. The sale to an industrial customer was often made based on Gore's reputation reaching them before the sales representatives called. If a company or brand did not have a good reputation, its products were not even considered by industrial users.

Gore had successfully achieved market leadership in a number of areas, including weatherproof outdoor clothing, vascular grafts and others.

KNOWLEDGE SHARING AND MANAGEMENT

The success of Gore & Associates in high performance materials markets depends on its ability to finely target its sophisticated polymeric products to the specialized needs of its key customers. Success in aerospace business, for example, depends on being able to get into and out of markets quickly. This demands close links among marketing, product development, and production employees in its value-adding chain (Anthes, 1998). The company achieves this by using a knowledge management system based on Lotus Notes, Notes databases of product and customer application data, and an intranet. This was developed and operationalized in 1997. Within one year it was in use by 600 Associate members in 30 teams (Anthes, 1998).

Gore's Chief Information Officer David Clarke shared,

"We have done a good job of connecting a worldwide field sales force with our product development teams. We are solving customer problems faster, and that translates directly into higher sales. (For example) ...a field engineer (testing a new material in aerospace business) may be taking notes on a laptop while with a customer, and that shows up in our database within hours of flying the field trial " (Anthes, 1998).

Previously it took days or weeks for the field test results of a new material to be typed in a paper report and circulated among different developers. The new knowledge management system has greatly speeded communications between teams and their customers scattered around the world. In late 1997 the information system organization at Gore & Associates made a subtle but important change by calling itself the communication and collaboration team. The IS did not think enterprise planning system as a big transaction engine attached to a database, but as a communication system.

W. L. Gore & Associates was building a communication and collaboration system for production planning. This system uses a commercial enterprise resource planning package, Notes, and intranet, and videoconferencing. It brings together material and finished goods inventory. The product-related, customer-related, and manufacturing-related data from multiple sites was integrated and presented as a "shared model" for the use of production planning teams (Anthes, 1998). The goal was to develop a shared space for the production team. Instead of each associate making own decisions based on multiple reports and screen printouts, all the team members have the same picture of production capacity (Anthes, 1998).

Gore & Associates used knowledge management for communications and collaboration in conjunction with its amorphous culture and lattice organization.

NOT EASY-TO-MIMIC BUSINESS MODEL

The Gore Lattice Organization model is not easy to imitate. Organizations with long-held hierarchical organizational structures are not likely to be successful in quickly adopting Gore's Lattice Organization. The transfer is likely to be much easier in newly forming companies.

One challenge includes difficulty to transfer this lattice organization design to foreign countries, particularly in cultures with high power distance between bosses and subordinates. This business model also depends on the proactive self-commitment by associates. Some cultures do not encourage such individualistic commitment.

FRUSTRATING FLEXIBILITY

As stated earlier, not all individuals can work well in the Lattice Organization. Old-time Gore Associates believe that it takes higher stamina to succeed at Gore & Associates. Associates have to be self-starters, and take lot of initiative to get projects started and finish these successfully. It is not easy to get results. Rules and regulations do not help at Gore.

Many of Gore's core values and guiding principles sound great, but are not so easy to use in practice (Giovale, 1995: 37).

Self-commitment is a key core value. Self-commitment makes it easier for an Associate to see himself or herself as the source of results and owner of outcomes (instead of as a passive victim or recipient of others' actions). This requires an Associate to identify opportunities that match their skills. The Associates must gain support from other Associates for their commitments to tasks and projects that advance the business's success in a significant way. This is a proactive process requiring inputs, support, and buy-in from other Associates. Most young persons are not used to making such self-commitments. They are used to following others, or do as their parents or teachers instruct them to do (Giovale, 1995: 37).

Since each Gore Associate is expected to make self-commitment, it is hard for anyone to use power to command others to participate. Instead each Associate must convince other Associates that their participation is worthy of their energy and time. Without any authority, personal power to solicit others' followership and participation depends on how well an Associate can foster confidence in his/her initiative. This gives birth to natural leaders who make self-commitments and take initiatives to help the business succeed and the corporation gain competitive advantage (Giovale, 1995: 37).

BILL GORE'S SPIRIT CONTINUES

In 1986, Bill Gore passed away. But by then he had laid a firm foundation, so that his spirit survives him at Gore & Associates. Many old-timer Gore Associates regularly share legends of how Bill Gore trusted associates. Bill Gore put so much trust in people that he was confident that they would learn and grow from their mistakes if they persisted. Gore often said, "…maybe it's not a mistake…maybe it's an invention."

Gore's Chief financial officer (CFO) Shanti Mehta, who joined Gore & Associates in 1970, shared with Robert Levering and Milton Moskowitz, authors of *The 100 Best Companies to Work for in America*, that Bill Gore never called her into his office.

"He always came to my desk, sat on my desk, and talked to me as if he had all the time in the world. He was a real spring from which love flowed throughout the organization. And the culture was nourished that way. After his death, the responsibility of doing this has fallen… on the shoulders of all of us…and it is important we do that."

Shanti has started mimicking Bill Gore by going to associates' desks and chatting with them. He shared that when he did that four or five times, his "adrenaline just started flowing and I was a new man." He saw maintaining the Lattice Organization as his most strategic mission, keeping the plants small and continue this kind of relationship.

During the 1980s Gore & Associates had grown at an impressive 20% a year. In 1990, Gore & Associates had $600 million in sales, with 40 plant facilities worldwide, and more than 5,000 employees. Gore's plants in the U.S. were clustered around Newark, Delaware, and Flagstaff, Arizona, but have employment facilities in Maryland and Texas as well (Levering & Moskowitz, 1993).

In 1991, the process of acclimatization for new Associates was slightly more structured than before. They worked through the different stages in their business for a few weeks, irrespective of the position for which they were hired. They may be exposed to production, finance and investment, selling and marketing. Then they settle into a position of their own.

From time to time, different markets have dwindled for one Gore division or the other. In the mid-1980s and 1989 falling consumer interest in high-end jogging and athletic suits affected Gore's fabric division. By 1995, the division was once again the fastest growing division.

In the early 1990s, when the personal computers gained popularity at the expense of the mainframe computers, Gore's electronics division suffered. By 1995 the electronics division recovered by developing many electronic products for the medical industry. Gore's medical products division anticipated an increasing need for health care because of the ageing population in the United States and other industrialized nations.

SELF REVIEW QUESTIONS

The above discussion raises a number of interesting managerial issues.

1. Gore's Lattice Organization and "unmanagement" style is a unique way to manage highly motivated technical professionals. What preparatory work is needed to transfer this vision to other technology-driven organizations?

2. What will Gore Associates do if they realize that they have hired a number of unmotivated Associates?

3. What happens when Gore Associates get burn out?

4. How can Gore Associates protect themselves from a Gore family member trying to sell the company to the highest bidder?

5. Discuss advantages and disadvantages of diversifying to non-PTFE-related products and businesses.

6. Give your short-term and long-term recommendations for W.L. Gore & Associates to sustain more than 20% annual growth in the 21st Century.

Exhibit – 1

SELECTED GORE FABRICS

Brand name	Target Application(s)	Characteristics
Gore-Tex™	Outdoor weather protection From wind, rain and snow	Waterproof, Windproof Very breathable
Immersion™	Fishing and paddle sports Technology	Waterproof, Windproof, Very breathable
Ocean ™	Coastal and Offshore sailing Technology	Waterproof, Windproof Very breathable
Windstopper™	Windy and Cold	No Water resistance, Windproof, Very Breathable
Gore Dryfloat™	Windy, Cold	Water resistant, Light precipitation Windproof, Extremely breathable
Activent™	Windy, Cold/cool,	Water resistant, Light/precipitation Windproof, Extremely breathable

Source: Adapted from company documents and web-page
(www.gorefabrics.com)